ROOTED

THE AMERICAN LEGACY OF LAND THEFT AND THE MODERN MOVEMENT FOR BLACK LAND OWNERSHIP

BREA BAKER

ONE WORLD
NEW YORK

Hardback ISBN 978-0-593-44737-6
Ebook ISBN 978-0-593-44738-3

Printed in the United States of America on acid-free paper

oneworldlit.com

randomhousebooks.com

2 4 6 8 9 7 5 3 1

FIRST EDITION

Book design by Barbara M. Bachman

For Alfred and Jenail,
whose love for land birthed my own.

For my son.
May you always know and love the Land.

"The way to right wrongs is to
turn the light of truth upon them."
—IDA BELL WELLS-BARNETT

"Another world is not only possible, she is on her way.
On a quiet day, I can hear her breathing."
—ARUNDHATI ROY

"The South has something to say."
—ANDRÉ 3000

ROOTED FAMILY TREE

BAKER FAMILY

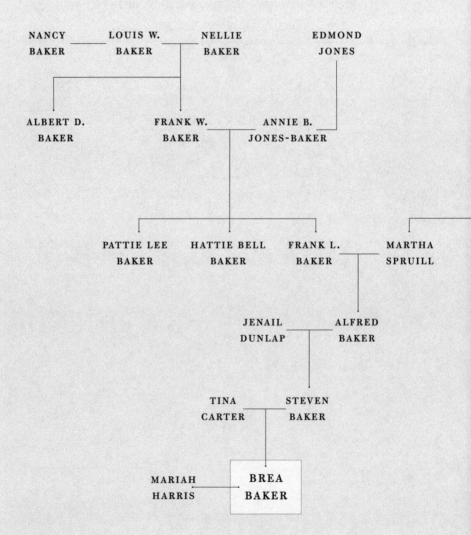

NANCY BAKER — LOUIS W. BAKER — NELLIE BAKER   EDMOND JONES

ALBERT D. BAKER   FRANK W. BAKER — ANNIE B. JONES-BAKER

PATTIE LEE BAKER   HATTIE BELL BAKER   FRANK L. BAKER   MARTHA SPRUILL

JENAIL DUNLAP — ALFRED BAKER

TINA CARTER — STEVEN BAKER

MARIAH HARRIS — BREA BAKER

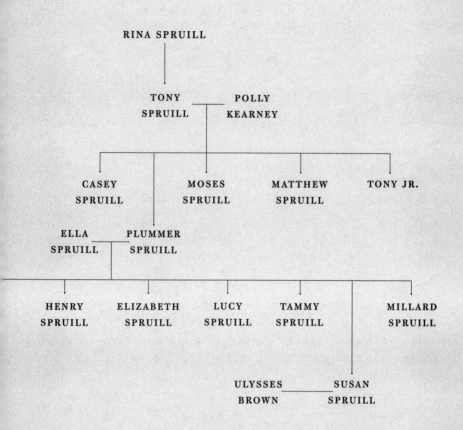

ROOTED FAMILY TREE

CARTER FAMILY

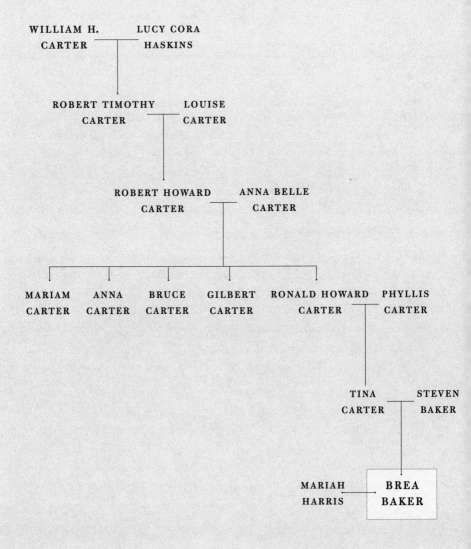

WILLIAM H. CARTER — LUCY CORA HASKINS

ROBERT TIMOTHY CARTER — LOUISE CARTER

ROBERT HOWARD CARTER — ANNA BELLE CARTER

MARIAM CARTER   ANNA CARTER   BRUCE CARTER   GILBERT CARTER   RONALD HOWARD CARTER — PHYLLIS CARTER

TINA CARTER — STEVEN BAKER

MARIAH HARRIS — BREA BAKER

CONTENTS

PART ONE: THE HEIST

PART TWO: THE PHOENIXES

PART THREE: THE HEIST REVISITED

PART FOUR: THE OUTCOME

PART FIVE: THE TAKEBACK

INTRODUCTION

WITNESSING

I am reconstructing a world where Black people thrive and relish in the "fruit of our labor," as Rev. Garrison Frazier told Union general William Tecumseh Sherman in 1865. My grandfather envisioned an America where Black people are surrounded by love and sustained by the land. On August 14, 2021 (nearly a decade after he bought his land), this dream was manifested when I married the love of my life on Bakers' Acres, a family plot of land. Our guests lovingly probed the significance of the location, and in our ceremony we addressed it head-on. This land was hard-fought-for by generations of Black people like my grandfather who knew that Black land ownership was essential to true freedom. But before them, and long before colonization, this land was home to the Lumbee people for at least 14,000 years. According to tribal history, the Lumbee Tribe is the largest tribe in North Carolina and the largest tribe east of the Mississippi River. A Native American elder of the Ojibwe Tribe, Mary Lyons, once said, "When we talk about land, land is part of who we are. It's a mixture of our blood, our past, our current, and our future." What better symbol of love, legacy, and loyalty is there?

My wife, Mariah, and I now live in Atlanta, on one acre of land. Each morning, Mariah and I wake up and go about our morning routine. Let the

Mariah and me on Bakers' Acres (AOJO PHOTOGRAPHY).

dog out, use the bathroom, check on the chickens. As I write this, we have two roosters and nine hens. There's Hootie, who looks a lot like an owl, and Angelica, named after the bossy little girl from *Rugrats.* Then there's Logan, after our cousin whose nickname is "Chicken." We got Little Brother's name from the movie *Mulan,* and Reptar's name also comes from *Rugrats.* My sister Brooke named Henrietta, and my sister Blair named one Zen after our nephew and godson. My father said we needed a Disco and a Chicken George, so those two names quickly followed. April, like Tejano singer Selena Quintanilla-Pérez's childhood hen. And, lastly, Ruby the Rhode Island Red.

When we first got them, all eleven chickens lived in a cardboard home within our garage until they were big enough to move into the chicken coop we built for them. Soon, my morning routine will require a walk into our backyard to gather eggs and ensure no chickens were harmed in the night. Each morning as I feed them and replenish their water, I have to remind myself that we built this life and this coop ourselves.

My wife and father-in-law studied other coops and raised-bed configurations before drawing up the blueprints for our own. During the week, they traded messages planning for the purchases and work ahead, and during the weekend, we executed. Between writing sessions, I was grateful to be their dutiful apprentice taking on whatever tasks they delegated to me. That position gave me the chance to watch them at work, one the miniature version of the other. Watching them cut planks of wood on the table saw before screwing them together in new formations, I was struck by how easily the work flowed.

I wasn't only their sous-builder; Mariah and Tony Harris also called me their historian, because I was always snapping photos of them in action. "For posterity," I'd say. Really I wanted—needed—to remember the wonder I had. In my wildest dreams, I never imagined I'd take on projects like this. Building a chicken coop most certainly felt like a job for actual architects. Surely we could buy one that came in large parts and only needed light assembly. But Mariah and Tony had different plans. Plans of raised gardening beds full of vegetables and fruits like arugula, tomatoes, asparagus, rhubarb, peppers, spinach, broccoli, and cauliflower. A peach tree and berry bushes lining the beds, all pushed back deep into our acre plot of land. A wooden chicken coop to keep our hens warm, a walled-in chicken run for them to roam free of hawks flying overhead, and a large barrel to collect fresh rainwater.

Their confidence was infectious. Working at their side, I never doubted that we could do hard things. My mother reminded me how far I've come. "I can't believe you've got Brea touching chickens," she said to Mariah. "Well, they're cute right now, Mama," I retorted. "Let's see how much I'm around them when they're big and ugly." We all laughed at the truth.

Prior to Mariah, I was not a very "outdoorsy" person. I enjoyed Bakers' Acres in small doses, always returning to my urban or suburban life after the brief reprieve. I'd never let myself imagine what it could look and feel like to grow my own food, raise my own chickens, and generally be hands-on with the planet around me. Mariah, on the other hand, had a childhood full of fresh produce, fishing trips, and other reminders that the natural world has an abundance to offer.

It is through my wife, Mariah, that I learned to stop over-intellectualizing my love of Black-owned land. "You can't love the land through proximity," she once told me. "You have to put your own hands in the dirt." Initially I was low-key offended. Was she insinuating that my love wasn't as real as hers? No, she was inviting me into a deeper relationship that wasn't exclusively predicated on the past. Ancestors, former deeds, what was. How about what *is*? We have the chance now, she reminded me, to be land stewards and to share that love with our children, who will only know ownership.

It's been somewhat ironic to truly fall in love with land through my wife, considering I had access to land long before she and I ever met. I was born and raised up north, but both of my parents made it a point to ensure we had regular visits to North Carolina. My first visit to our land came when I was still forming in my mother's womb.

At the time, and for most of my life, our extended Baker-Spruill family held just over one hundred acres of land collectively. I can only remember some of the trips we took to our family land, so I asked my father how frequently he remembers bringing us down south. "All the time," he responds quickly before adding "at least two or three times a year" for specificity. "What were we traveling for when Thanksgiving was still celebrated in New Jersey?" I asked him. My father thought for a moment before shrugging and replying, "Just because." Like his father, Alfred, my dad took any chance he got to pack up his wife and car and take the drive down. My mother had just made it out of her first trimester with me when she and my father found out about a death in the Baker family. A funeral was surely cause to be in community with loved ones. To North Carolina they went.

My parents had been married for a few years by this point, but my mom was still meeting cousins and aunts. (My father had sixteen aunts and uncles and literally hundreds of cousins.) When my Aunt Sue called out for someone to help her cook the chicken, my mother quickly volunteered! She may not have been a country girl but she knew how to fry some chicken. This was the perfect chance to get closer to her in-laws! Grateful for the help, Aunt Sue told my mother to wait right there in the front yard for Uncle Plummer. Before my mother could ask why she wasn't being led inside to the kitchen, Uncle Plummer emerged in denim overalls. With little fanfare, he wrung the chicken's neck and went about his business. My mother stood there mouth agape as the chicken ran around the yard without its head.

First frantically, then slowly before coming to a stop that signaled its death. My mother didn't help cook the chicken that night. She didn't even eat it when someone else stepped in for her to skin and clean it. Instead, she had my father drive her to Golden Corral for a meal with a little less intimacy.

Most of my visits down south have been for funerals. Distant family for whom attending the funeral is how we show up for the living. Close loved ones whose losses remain with us to this day. When not returning family members "home" to the ground, more often than not our visits revolved around family reunions and church conventions that doubled as family reunions. On lakefront shores, a horde of Black bodies wearing baggy shirts with large trees printed on the front. Printed zines recapping our genealogical history and documenting the many branches of the Baker and Spruill lines. An uncle on the grill. A parent juggling a sleeping child and a plate of food. Older kids leading younger ones on adventures. Elders sucking their teeth at the short shorts and crop tops. A few cousins put poles in the lake.

Throughout my childhood, I was surrounded by vivid scenes of Black people enjoying themselves on land. But because those trips always ended eventually, I never accepted it as my way of life or norm. What did become ingrained in my psyche was a love of communion. The sound of roaring laughter and cards smacked onto tables during spades games. The smell of freshly butchered meat and salty sweat from working just hard enough. The feel of wrinkled hands caressing smooth babies incredulously; proof of a continuing lineage.

I asked my father what stood out about our trips down south. Ten-hour drives with several kids is no easy feat. I wanted to know what made the trips so worth it for him. "I loved seeing you all with Grandpa," he said to me. "He loved the trips just as much as you all did and he took you everywhere with him." Though I can't recall, my dad reminded me that my grandfather took all of his grandchildren fishing for the first time. Only one of us caught anything at the small pond where he lined us up that day, but catching fish wasn't the objective at all. He wanted us to love the land as much as he did.

There were so many times as I researched and wrote this manuscript that I wished my grandfather was still alive. That I could share my discoveries with him to change his perspective on a few points, and have him change mine as well. That he could watch Mariah and me swap seeds with Auntie Karen and take the five-hour drive to Georgia and meet Hootie, Logan, Little Brother, Reptar, Henrietta, Zen, Disco, Chicken George, April, and Ruby. Even though I still don't want to bait my own hook or exert myself too much, his granddaughter loves the land.

I wonder if my grandfather would even take any of the credit for himself, or if he'd thank God for sending me a wife who'd steer me back to myself. I'd like to think it would be a bit of both but the truth is that I don't know who I'd be without Mariah and her family. Their active and ongoing love for land—hunting, fishing, growing—reignited my desire for a birthright I'd given up on. Having access to land, I'd grown complacent, not realizing how much it had taken to acquire let alone keep it. My wife's paternal grandmother, whom we lovingly call Mama, once told me, "All my kids love the land 'cause we never owned any." I wonder what my grandfather would say about that. If he'd agree that even when referring to land, absence makes the heart grow fonder and ache deeper. If displaced Black people are more attuned to what's been taken from them, no wonder so many Black Americans are craving a sense of self through homeland. Why without one, we will always be like lost wanderers following a north star to freedom. Where and when do we get to lay down our baggage and make ourselves at home? To enjoy the fruits of our labor?

On Juneteenth weekend in 2022, Tony and I set out for a road trip from Georgia to West Virginia, where a wedding and family reunion was to be held. When driving on the I-85N from Georgia through South and then North Carolina, the highway was littered with deer carcasses. The bodies were either maimed by vehicles or bloated and left for dead.

I lost count of the carcasses by the time we crossed over the border into West Virginia. I couldn't help but think two things: *poor deer* and *wasted venison.* Clearly I-85N and similar expressways ran through what used to be safe havens for these animals. My father-in-law coached me on what to do if a deer ever darted out in front of my car. *Brace for impact.* What are the chances of the deer making it? *Depends on how fast you're going and how big it is. Hopefully it's not a doe or children, and it will be injured but alive. Otherwise . . .* What of the body left behind? Could a hunter at least make use of the lost life? *Of course not. Man-made vehicles mangle the ani-*

mals unlucky enough to come into contact with them. No one except vultures benefits from the roadkill.

Sometimes those vultures fly overhead before swooping in on a body to pick apart. They peck away—alongside the maggots—finding nourishment in another's demise. Other vultures stand on two legs, but they feast on death just the same. These vultures call themselves "private developers," and they wait for a Black family to become just vulnerable enough before they swoop in. When they do, those vultures take land and legacy, leaving pavement and cookie-cutter buildings in their wake. By the time the dust settles, those vultures are long gone and on the hunt for their next carcass. The rest of us are left with no choice but to drive down the six-lane interstate highways lined by pine trees and dead animals, wondering what was there before.

I didn't always wonder about *before*. Rural countrysides before turnpikes. Cities before skyscrapers. North Carolina before plantations. America before colonization. That world felt so far away and impossible to return to. Until I began seriously considering what reparations and sustainability would look like in practice. To reconstruct this nation the way we should have done after the Civil War. To dream without wildest imaginations about what reclamation would look like for Black and Indigenous people—and thus, the rest of the country.

My paternal grandfather, Alfred Baker, was born in North Carolina and fled to the North as a young teen, as many in his generation did. Throughout his time in New Jersey, my grandfather maintained a connection to the South through the parcels of land he and his siblings owned there. It was this connection that eventually inspired him to return. Grandpa fantasized about loamy grounds, home to critters, creatures, and us. Land that would welcome us for holidays, family reunions, and everything in between. A place to call our own.

After retiring from a decades-long career as a working-class engineer, he moved back to North Carolina just as I was making my way through high school. The small mobile home he and my grandmother lived in, which welcomed us for many holidays, was but a "temporary dwelling," my grandfather was sure to remind us, a carryover until his true vision could be fully realized. He dreamt of a home rooted to the ground for our entire extended family. Oftentimes as we gathered around the living room table, he'd whip out blueprints and maps to marvel at his big, big plans.

At the time, I didn't fully appreciate those plans. I grew up in Long Island, the outskirts of the greatest city in the world, and like any New Yorker, I have always taken pride in being a city-ish girl. New York can make one feel as though the world revolves around those cement streets.

Each summer that my dad drove us down south for the family reunion, I felt a disruption of sorts. I loved my family and the cultural aspects of having Southern roots—like fried chitterlings dipped in apple cider vinegar, and getting to use wide swaths of land as a jungle gym—but I had no desire to be away from my TV, cell service, and Gameboy. My father would come find me, tucked away in my grandparents' home, and tell me to come outside, to enjoy our land, that it was rare and I had a right to connect to it. He would always remind me that we owned the land, emphasizing that all the soil and grass and trees were ours.

The older I got, the more stifled I felt in big cities. As I began to travel more and marvel at the beauty of the world beyond America's borders, the more I wondered what this land—America, and more specifically the U.S. South—had looked and felt like before colonization. I avoided the obvious answer: I visited a slice of natural haven every time I traveled down south.

My paternal grandparents, Alfred and Jenail, at my parents' wedding.

I knew intimately that there was more to this country than the skyscrapers, polluted air, and confinements that dominate the coasts. I knew I did not have to travel abroad or far for awe-inspiring nature.

By 2012, Grandpa had succeeded in buying about eighty-six acres of land covered in thin, towering pine trees, roaming white-tailed deer, and two sprawling freshwater lakes fed by a winding brook—the perfect venue for a hunter with a fire in his belly and a dream to construct a haven for his family. Less than a decade later, between 2016 and 2018, my grandparents built their dream home. A beautiful blue house was built on the newly dubbed "Bakers' Acres," offering space for leisure and sustenance for any of his children or grandchildren who chose to make North Carolina home again. Over time, it became harder to deny how special it was to be from a family with access to land.

Sometime during college, I stopped acting too good for the South and began immersing myself in my grandfather's dreams. Soon, I was actively calling to check in on his progress with building a home and moving back to North Carolina for good. He had sold me on the vision of rural land ownership, and his optimism about the land was infectious. As the dream grew closer and closer to becoming a reality, my interest continued to swell and the questions grew to be not only about the future plans, but also the past that made his dream such a fervent one.

In my senior year of college, around 2015, I began digging deeper into my family history. Through this research, I discovered that one branch of my ancestral line was likely enslaved on a plantation owned by George Evans Spruill, a prominent lawyer and state's attorney in the early 1800s. The land on which my family was enslaved was located not too far from the land my grandfather had been fighting so hard to reclaim. It all began to click.

This land, originally belonging to the Haliwa-Saponi and Lumbee tribes, had been tended by my ancestors. Growing up in the shadows of the broken promise of forty acres and a mule, my grandfather used his righteous rage to make his own freedom a reality, no matter the cost.

Through Grandpa, I learned about the lumber, tobacco, and soybean industries that dominate North Carolinian agriculture. He began to share more with me about his love for hunting and self-subsistence. The idea that the land we live on could provide for all of our needs had never occurred to me. I was learning a lot about how humans have always provided for ourselves, and how much better it is for our bodies, as well as the planet, for us to reconnect with this mindset. Yet we rarely have the opportunity to cultivate a real relationship with the land we depend on so much for our survival.

Many city—and even suburban—residents aren't fully aware of just how much we depend on the planet around us. When I looked to my left and right, people were dying—loved ones, acquaintances, co-workers, and friends at school were dying from cancer, heart disease, and body-breaking work. Or they were funneled toward a slow death via chronic illness. Twenty-seven-year-old Erica Garner died after a heart attack following the murder of her father by NYPD officer Daniel Pantaleo. Children in cities like Newark and Flint are still exposed to poisonous water and toxic air. The rest of us urban dwellers are only relatively better off, having normalized a culture where we can't pronounce the ingredients in the foods we eat.

As I saw the impact of gentrification and food apartheid (as coined by activist and farmer Karen Washington) in my beloved city, I questioned aloud where all of us pushed-out people were expected to go. My grandfather suggested the South had more than enough space to welcome us back. All of us. Not just Black people, but also Indigenous people who first called the South—and all of the Americas—"home." Capitalism leads us to believe that everything is scarce, but the first Americans operated off of an abundance mindset, understanding that the Land and Her renewable resources could more than sustain us if we didn't let our greed dictate Her pace.

This isn't to minimize the very real and current presence of gentrification across Southern cities, but to allude to a birthright of all Black people. I am not suggesting we all need to trade in our MetroCards for tractors or our cocktails for sweet tea; rather I'm asking: What does it mean to reclaim that tainted history and desecrated land, land rightfully associated with trauma; what does it mean for such land to become not only a home but also a vehicle for equity?

As I write this, less than 1 percent of rural land in the United States is owned by Black people, despite the centuries of grueling labor our ancestors put into said land. This, combined with historic redlining and employment discrimination, has boxed Black people out of sovereignty and autonomy for far too long.

It is no small feat to go up against large institutions, both private and public, that make the process of land ownership near-impossible for Black people, but my grandfather could not be deterred. He would not wait for the federal government to do right by us and distribute land to the descendants of this land's forced laborers. He understood what had taken me time to discover: This country has always been happy to have Black people working the land but never owning it. The relationship between labor and ownership, then, is an intentionally severed one. We cannot discuss homelessness, racial wealth gaps, or chronic poverty in Black communities without putting white America's calculated raids of Black land under a magnifying glass. Many white institutions and the generational wealth our society marvels at today are the direct products of the investments in enslaving people and looting land.

Following emancipation, everyone knew that the most regenerative way for Black people to build political power and wealth was through ownership, and thus the project of white supremacy unleashed vicious and successful attempts at land theft. It went against the racial hierarchy in this country for Black people to live autonomously and exist in positions of power over others as farm owners and employers. I now know it was no coincidence that I have this fire within me, and that I felt such a sense of urgency to dismantle systems of oppression.

In a 1984 interview with Julius Lester, James Baldwin said: ". . . I have never seen myself as a spokesman. I am a witness. In the church in which I was raised you were supposed to bear witness to the truth . . . A spokesman assumes that he is speaking for others. I never assumed that."

I am my grandfather's witness. I hope to be one of many witnesses, amplifying the voices of Black Southerners like my grandfather. My elder-turned-ancestor had a story within him, one he worked feverishly to unearth and document for our family. Therefore, with this book, I let him speak *through* me.

After his passing, I became deeply invested in understanding his life's work of land ownership. How is it that my father's family was able to achieve ownership while my mother's family did not? Both were working-class, both had known ties to the land. Was my paternal grandfather an anomaly or merely one of the last few standing—or both?

How difficult is it for a Black person in the twenty-first century to achieve generational wealth through land ownership? What happened in past generations to make people like my grandfather so rare? Who is behind the past and present theft of Black land, and who are the activists—like my grandfather—keeping alive the fight for autonomy through ownership? Currently, Black people are being pushed off of their land as gentrification continues to envelop major cities. Is there anywhere for Black people to call home in this country? To control the fruit of our labor? To be more than our output? If we ask history, we may feel dismayed, considering how high the cards are stacked against us.

This country has gone to hell (though perhaps not back) in order to keep Black people from building economic stability and achieving safety. How much further will we have to go before we make a U-turn and choose another way? This book will do what Mariame Kaba reminds us to do: It will leave you radicalized, rather than despaired. The road may be long and winding, but it is not impossible to traverse. People like my grandfather are proof of that, and this book will be a reflection of his legacy—one we must keep alive.

My dad would tell me about childhood visits to county officers to look at records, as well as his visits to loved ones to gather family history. "People would give him photos and he'd get them blown up," my dad told me, reminiscing on his father. "He didn't just archive information, he offered information. He believed it all was valuable and I remember him asking sometimes 'can you make three copies of that' so that he could share it all." That is my hope with this book: to distill what I've learned and plant those seeds in each of you.

This book is an ode to those Black folks who never gave up on the South; we are meeting them where they are. The research and anecdotes compiled here sometimes rely on oral history and informal records. In turning these pages, you will know the names and stories of the Black farmers who chose to make a home in the belly of the beast rather than flee. In their honor, we build upon, rather than settle for, their legacy.

Let's start at the genesis.

PART ONE

——

THE HEIST

Our land is everything to us . . .
We remember that our grandfathers
paid for it—with their life.

—JOHN WOODENLEGS, EDUCATOR
AND FORMER TRIBAL PRESIDENT OF
THE NORTHERN CHEYENNE

IN THE BEGINNING

When I close my eyes, I imagine a world where Black
people are joyful and the Earth is safer and thriving.

—LEAH THOMAS

Mother Earth is not a resource, she is an heirloom.

—DAVID IPINA, YUROK TRIBE

In the beginning, there was the Land and the Land was no one's because
the Land was everyone's—an extension of us. The Land was living—taking
as much as She gave. She spoke to us and we helped to cherish and cultivate Her. She listened, held, and fed us. And when other living things
died, the Land took them in. She let the dead help us keep on living and
learning, evolving and teaching.

In the beginning, "generational wealth" was the planet and all that She
bears. Surplus was an opportunity to lead a happier, healthier life. Everyone had access to the same air, water, and right to housing. That is not to
say that certain tribes and communities didn't succumb to greed but that
capitalism was not the normative social order. Before outsiders tried to
outsmart the Land, whose wisdom and memory reached further back than
theirs, the people learned from and tended the Land, in a loving exchange.

In the beginning, the Americas were just as populated as any other
continent. However, the people were far less extractive in their relationship to the land. The first Europeans to cross the Atlantic did not find
wilderness. Rather, the eastern coastline of what we now call the United
States of America was lined with Indigenous-designed irrigation systems
rivaling Venice and terraced fields à la Vietnam, though home to different

seeds. Pastures fed herds of bison, which in turn fed the tribes who sustainably hunted them. The coasts of North Carolina made for great fishing, and the (then) forested barrier islands, now known as the Outer Banks, sustained a biodiversity we can only imagine now. Roanoke-Hatteras Algonquin, Chowanog, and Poteskeet peoples filled their bellies with oysters, flounder, and trout, and their communities retained a strong sense of interdependence. Everything and everyone existed in a finely tuned balance, taking as much as they gave.

Scientists in the United Kingdom have studied the impact that European "arrival" to the Americas had on our planet, and it is painfully clear that Earth mourned and suffered the loss viscerally. An estimated 56 million Indigenous people were killed across the Americas—either by these new viruses or the violence committed by those who transported them. Ninety percent of the population that tilled and nourished the land died; and the land did more than rewild. Stone pyramids and temples lay hidden under layers of vegetation. Trees and brush took over. Approximately 55.8 million hectares of land—about one-third of Russia's landmass—overtook itself and reforested.

The last time Earth went through a period of cooling—in contrast to the global warming we're currently experiencing—was in the sixteenth and seventeenth centuries, when the decimation of Indigenous populations led to a drastic drop in CO_2 levels. It ultimately sent the planet deeper into the Little Ice Age, where northern harbors closed their ports and famines traveled from continent to continent.

When those boats disappeared into the hazy horizon, the Land and Her stewards were already forever changed.

———

The modern concept of private property went against everything Black and Indigenous people knew about life. As Matthew Desmond wrote in his essay on capitalism for *The 1619 Project: A New Origin Story*, "[Private property] is what enables a private landowner to fence off natural resources and forests and rivers, assets that originally belonged to no one and were stewarded by the surrounding community, transforming common goods into commodities controlled by a single person or business entity." Land in the Americas had become politicized since the arrival of the first European colonists in the fifteenth century, and that only snowballed into the eighteenth and nineteenth centuries.

Settler colonialism, the violent replacement of Indigenous peoples by (often European) outsiders, created deep inequity as land became a chess piece for the powerful. Access to land meant so much more than purely where you laid your head or where you kept your things. In *I've Been Here All the While,* Dr. Alaina E. Roberts writes, "Native peoples have long established their connection to the lands they occupied . . . through medicinal, food, and spiritual traditions that utilize plants and animals indigenous to the area . . . Removal meant that [Indigenous people] were not only physically uprooted but also spiritually uprooted." And when it came to Black people, Desmond continues reminding us that "slavery, then, required 'the magic of property.'"

The more land Europeans could push Indigenous people off of, the more demand for forced labor to produce ecologically unsustainable, yet highly lucrative, amounts of cotton, tobacco, rice, and sugarcane.

Men with alabaster skin and bleached worldviews wanted a monopoly on life itself. They literally and figuratively lassoed their surroundings into submission. They did not realize that their existence depended on the health of the entire ecosystem, nor did they understand what Black and Indigenous peoples, no matter which continent we've called home, inherently understood—that one's relationship with the land should be familial, spiritual. Marilyn Berry Morrison, of the Roanoke-Hatteras Tribe, in an interview with the *Island Free Press,* offered, "Long before conservation efforts were ever dreamed of—or needed—stewardship was simply an innate part of everyday life . . . We lived with nature, and everything that we had came from nature . . . and we were appreciative of that."

Freedom for both enslaved African people and dispossessed Native Americans relied on alliances against the imperialism that had already transformed the African and American continents. Freedom was community in the face of violent individualism, which makes it no surprise that some of the first acts toward Black liberation were *marronage*—the art of stealing oneself and building community with other self-liberators—rather than more individualized approaches to getting free. To put it plainly, maroons are escaped Black people, and their descendants, who fled plantations and established new communities just under the noses of their former enslavers. Oftentimes, maroons found refuge with nearby Indigenous tribes and forged a new society together, one that resisted capitalism, white supremacy, anti-Blackness, and anti-Indigeneity. Which is to say that their societies didn't let the lust for profit get in the way of prioritizing connection: to one another, to the living things all around us, and to the land.

Dr. Neil Roberts, professor and author of *Freedom as Marronage,* explored the sociological, political, and economic structures underpinning marronage, which he defines in his introduction as "a group of persons isolating themselves from a surrounding society in order to create a fully autonomous community." He goes on to remind readers that marronage existed across the Americas, in Haiti, Jamaica, the Dominican Republic, Suriname, Venezuela, Cuba, Colombia, and Mexico. In Brazil, where more than 50 percent of the nation's population is Black, *quilombo* is the word used to describe rural communities of Black escapees, and over three thousand of them exist to this day. Clébio Ferreira, who founded Quilombaque, a quilombo in the Perus neighborhood of São Paulo, explained why he invests in modern-day marronage: "When we build a quilombo, we are coming together to build a new world."

Despite being continents away, these maroon, cimarrón, and quilombo societies were structured very similarly: always situated in rural areas, defended through guerilla warfare, spiritually grounded, and noticeably equitable. Before the existence of modern technologies, without ways of knowing and replicating what was transpiring thousands of miles away, maroon communities across the Americas tapped into a common ancestral feeling and let that be their North Star.

Maroon communities were not formed haphazardly, and their intentionality can and should be a beacon for those committing to justice in the twenty-first century and beyond. According to Dr. Neil Roberts, "Marronage is a multidimensional, constant act of flight that involves what I ascertain to be four interrelated pillars: distance, movement, property, and purpose," with movement being the central principle. Movement, defined as autonomy and control over one's motion, is an obvious component of freedom for a group of people previously transported against their will to work for others. What made distance, property, and purpose critical is that autonomy and access to land were so interconnected. As Dr. Neil Roberts describes, "Land is a space of cultivation. It is where one can work and rest."

Land that was difficult to reach yet bountiful enough to subsist off of became prime "real estate" for these refugees. One of the more celebrated historic examples is the Florida maroons who built deep alliances with Seminole peoples. Louisiana's cypress swamps were a refuge to maroons who wanted to remain hidden from the French waterfront estates. Thousands inhabited the Virginia and North Carolina marshlands, as documented by Harriet Beecher Stowe in her novel *Dred: A Tale of the Great Dismal Swamp.*

"The Africans who were left there became water people, people who lived by fishing and tides, but also people who understood water to be the most feasible path to escape." Dr. Imani Perry was describing the Gullah Geechee, her people of Georgia, but her words also apply to the maroons of the Great Dismal Swamp of Virginia and North Carolina. In both of these cases, water, the initial vehicle for expanding and sustaining slavery, was appropriated for a higher calling. The water and harsh conditions made it difficult for armed men to root them out, and many maroons lived long and clandestine lives just out of the wealthy slavers' reach. A century or so later, in the nineteenth century, these same waterways would become part of the Underground Railroad.

"The ancestors did not simply reject colonial rule and enslavement. They opposed Western civilization in its entirety, which included capitalism." These are the reflections of Chief Michael Grizzle of the Trelawny Town Flagstaff Maroon Council in regard to marronage in Jamaica, but they ring true for maroon communities in the United States as well. Maroons knew that alone, they could easily be picked off. But together, united and moving as one, maroons posed a real threat—the chance to chart a new path forward on this land. The Gullah people of the Lowcountry, to this day, have maintained a unique cultural identity within the larger African American community, mostly thanks to the marronage they engaged in.

The most famous maroon community in the present day may be the Black Seminoles of Florida. Black Seminole communities feature rice fields, roofed homes, and a vibrant culture of music and storytelling.

Matriarchal social structures replace the normative European patriarchal mindset, and egalitarianism undergirds all decision-making. Several generations were born in the swampy brush that allowed these free people to live covertly. The fierceness of Seminole guerilla warfare struck so much fear in the hearts of European colonizers that rather than re-enslaving Black Seminoles on plantations where they could organize other enslaved Black people, they were exiled to modern-day Oklahoma. This was a rare scenario, though, as most Black Seminoles thrived undetected along the Florida coastline, reclaiming the land for themselves.

Dr. Neil Roberts tells us about the historic inevitability of marronage when we consider the role of "peasants" across history. "From the earliest phases of the revolution, peasants associated land with freedom. They deplored the forced tilling of land as slaves . . . Peasant revolutionaries argued that civil orders were strengthened where shared access to land was realized." It's no wonder then that the word for these first freedom fighters is derived from the French word *marron,* which translates roughly to "fugitive" or "runaway." In the colonized Americas, freedom needed to be assembled out of sight, yet defended at any cost. As C. L. R. James reminds us in *The Black Jacobins,* "The slaves had revolted because they wanted to be free."

———

The creation and expansion of the United States as a world power depended on the speed at which the federal government could secure more land and enslave more people. Dr. Alaina E. Roberts lays this out plainly in her book: "Native land served as the literal foundation of negotiations over slavery and states' rights." Rather than treasuring the renewable wonders of this planet, white men and capitalists began a centuries-long process of hoarding land and extracting as much as possible from it. Inextricably linked to that aim was the demand for people from whom to extract labor, birthing the racial capitalism that is so pervasive to this day.

Land-grabbers needed slavery to tend to their empires, and the industry that developed to support those empires needed land to sustain it. Landless, poor white people were given ample opportunity to grow their landholdings so long as they continued to enforce the racial hierarchy. During the Revolutionary War, Indigenous people knew that between the

British and the American colonists, they were choosing between two evils. Two factions with the same bloodthirsty look in their eyes. Yet, having seen the greed of the colonists up close, many tribes took their chances siding with the British, who had been relatively limiting expansion efforts. Defeat would surely mean further genocide, removal, and theft, so what did they have to lose?

Some enslaved Black people made the same choice when they escaped plantations and fled to British lines. The British, desperate to crush their colonialist offspring, issued a call extending the promise of freedom to any enslaved people who joined their ranks. This was a recruitment strategy and nothing more, as Britain felt no sense of responsibility to the millions of enslaved people being transported across the global British empire. The strategy worked to an extent; more than eight hundred Black men accepted the call, taking their chances while knowing that the colonialists' only allegiance was to their profits.

Both Black and Indigenous people soon found out how right they were in 1776 when the Declaration of Independence was signed, and in 1781 when the new U.S. government was cemented following the British surrender at Yorktown. In those moments it was clear that the liberatory language of the American Revolution extended only to white men.

Black and Indigenous people looked west for respite. They weren't the only ones. Having beaten the British Empire at their own game, white Americans jumped at the chance to exert their brawn over Indigenous and Black people to further their mission. They called it Manifest Destiny and used God's name to justify what they'd done. The agrarian society they'd built was turning this former colony into the richest country in the world. White supremacy was given free rein following independence, and the West certainly became a dangerous place to be, the colonial "savages" taking any and every living thing they could as prisoner.

Territories to the north and Mexico to the south had historically been the unwritten path to freedom for those escaping enslavement. That soon changed, as border states like Missouri, Florida, and Texas entered the Union as slave states. As Dr. Anna-Lisa Cox reiterates in her book *The Bone and Sinew of the Land,* "Slavery's advocates would go to amazing lengths." They seemed to be now saying, *Give me dominion or give me death.* Time would soon test their commitment to this way of being. Anyone standing in the way of those endeavors would be moved by force, in accordance with whatever whim served whiteness in that moment.

In *Black Indians,* William Loren Katz writes, "For white U.S. citizens in the eastern states, problems . . . were solved in a single dramatic stroke by the Indian Removal Act of 1830. It provided for the mass deportation of the Five Nations from their huge, fertile homelands in the southeast." Each time gold or oil was found in land not yet claimed by white Americans, there was a new excuse to inch the frontier further back until it was decided there was no need to wait any further. In what we now refer to as the Trail of Tears, an estimated 60,000 Indigenous people and thousands of the Black people enslaved by them were violently forced west to make space for white ambition. By the early 1800s, the Native population had been decimated, dropping from almost 20 million people pre-colonization to approximately 600,000. While much attention is given to the Five Nations—the Cherokee, Chickasaw, Choctaw, Muskogee (Creek), and Seminole tribes—there are over five hundred distinct tribes that called this land home and resisted white encroachment.

The Seminoles of Florida saw the writing on the wall and fought removal tooth and nail, choosing to defend their sovereignty alongside their Black Seminole comrades, leading to all-out wars with the U.S. military. Many were captured and killed, yet a significant number of Seminoles eluded the military and continued to live in maroon settlements.

The extent of the pain endured during and after deportation cannot be overstated. The Choctaws, originally known to themselves and others as the Chahta peoples, were the first to be displaced after negotiating for new property in the West, along with transportation and relocation support. The inept federal government agreed, then later reneged on that promise, leading to a brutal journey with little food, medicine, or water. The Muscogee (Creek) people followed several years later, finding a similar fate. The Chickasaw Nation was untrusting of white Americans' promise to handle their landholdings and transport their community members—so the Chickasaw handled their relocation themselves. Their path, though still inherently violent, was a lot smoother than those of other tribes in part due to this arm's-length approach to the federal government.

Outside of the Seminoles, the Cherokee Nation held out the longest, sparking the fury of then-president Martin Van Buren. He ordered soldiers to remove them from their land by any means necessary. In service of this country, seven thousand white men marched into Indigenous communities and held people at gunpoint while raiding their homes and businesses. As Katz describes, "Homes were burned, livestock, tools, printing presses, and personal possessions seized and destroyed." These armed, white militiamen held the Cherokee people in makeshift internment camps before marching tens of thousands—through long and dangerous, disease-filled terrain or on riverboats—to the newly dubbed "Indian Territory."

Four of the Five Tribes, including the Cherokee Nation led by Chief John Ross, brought with them their enslaved Black people. There was an explicit expectation that Black enslaved people would carry the strenuous loads. They carted wagons, carried supplies, and led the taxing work of starting anew on more stolen land. Somewhere between 8,000 and upward of 12,000 Indigenous and Black people never made it to the other side; they were effectively assassinated.

Many are surprised to hear that Black people were also casualties of this forced removal, or that Black people were enslaved by Native tribes at all. The truth is messy. Disunity was incentivized by white settlers who feared what would be possible if those they'd subjugated rose up as one. Indigenous nations were coaxed into enslaving Black people and engaging in more capitalist practices. Many large tribes became dependent on the lifestyles made possible through chattel slavery, and Black people were again the collateral damage. In an interview with *Smithsonian Magazine,* Paul Chaat Smith, museum curator and member of the Comanche Nation, noted that "the Five Civilized Tribes were deeply committed to slavery . . . immediately reestablish[ing] slavery when they arrived in Indian Territory." But America is expansive and the Five Tribes were not the only Indigenous nations on this soil. Hundreds of others had no connections to American slavery and were only just coming into contact with Europeans as westward expansion continued unabashedly.

In 2002, the U.S. Department of Agriculture released a report that acknowledged: "Historically, of course, American Indians had access to practically all the land in the present-day United States. White settlers and the Federal Government subsequently dispossessed them of most of the land. Between the Allotment Act of 1887 and the Indian Reorganization Act of 1934, American Indians lost an additional 90 million acres."

How was the Land treated after this series of heists? By whom is She now held? The Land remembers and becomes less willing to shoulder the pain of man's actions. We have only just begun to collectively scratch the surface on the scale of environmental and economic destruction unleashed by colonialism.

CLAIMS TO LAND

===

**Everything that you fought for was not for yourself.
It was for those that come after.**

—CHADWICK BOSEMAN

When Black people were first kidnapped and brought to this land, the relationship was contentious. For some, the land was a shrieking baby not of their own womb, yet forced into their bosom to be suckled six days a week. The burden of tending this land at the expense of themselves felt like torture. Though the Land was not the abuser, like a crying baby, Her needs superseded those of the Black people forced upon Her.

Leah Penniman detailed this ancestral conversation between Black people and land in her book *Farming While Black:*

> Our great great grandmothers in Dahomey, West Africa, witnessed the kidnapping and disappearance of members of their community and experienced a rising unease about their own safety. As insurance for an uncertain future, they began the practice of braiding rice, okra, and millet seeds into their hair. While there were no "report backs" from the other side of the Trans-Atlantic slave trade and rumors abounded that white people were capturing Africans to eat us, they still had the audacity of hope to imagine a future on soil.

As Black people continued to be both brought *to* and born *in* the Americas, many saw past the cruelty of man and came to love the land here in the Americas as much as they had loved the land of the African continent. Many of the survivors of the Middle Passage had the foresight to braid seeds into their hair, to assure that sustenance could be created—planted—wherever they were being taken to. Without any awareness of what the future would hold, they had the foresight and willingness to tend to new land. In their own nations, they'd known what land could give: full bellies, community, safety. In the Americas, Black people started anew. Bishop Richard Allen, founder of the African Methodist Episcopal (AME) Church, the nation's first independent Protestant denomination by and for Black people, wrote in 1827, "This land which we have watered with our tears and our blood, is now our mother country." A motherland away from motherlands. A new place to spread roots.

After decades of working this land, backs and spirits were broken from the forced labor. Black people realized that they knew the land better than the white men. For the folks who decided to escape, the land—and the sky's stars that guided them south to Mexico and north to Canada—seemed to be choosing and colluding with enslaved Black people. Storms erased the tracks of fugitives; mushrooms, berries, and fish were foraged along a long and strenuous journey; and constellations served as bread crumbs, guiding Black folks to freedom across borders. For Black people who remained in the Deep South, the land that may have once felt like a captor was now beginning to feel like a fellow hostage yearning to be free. A kindred relationship was reborn.

I come from a line of Black people who saw their liberation in the land. Many of my ancestors were born in a time when agriculture *was* the economy. But beyond that, they saw a path to self-determination in raising children and grandchildren in safe enclaves away from white people. "For a former[ly] enslaved person, land signified independence, namely the ability to provide food and resources for one's family," writes Dr. Alaina E. Roberts. She goes on to assert that Black Americans wanted to "[maintain] some sort of relationship with the nation that they had helped build." Freedom was all of this, and I come from a legacy of people who wanted to be free by any means necessary.

Louis Baker—my paternal great-great-great-grandfather—was born enslaved around 1820 in Warren County, North Carolina, and lived most of his life in the county of his birth. We don't have many records that add color to Louis's life or that tell us what his experience in captivity felt like— this is yet another act of violence, erasing Black people of the antebellum South from their own story—but much is said of Warren County, where he purchased his first parcel of land.

According to the 1860 census, over 10,000 Black people were enslaved by approximately 162 slavers in Warren County alone. Many of those enslavers were vicious overseers. In the 1930s, thousands of formerly enslaved people were interviewed as part of a Federal Writers' Project initiative to document first-person slave narratives. One interviewee from Warren County, Chana Littlejohn, described there being little reprieve for even praying Black folks, let alone those who dared dream beyond the limits forced upon them. "Dere wus no churches on de plantation . . . When we sang we turned de wash pots an' tubs in de doors, so dey would take up de noise so de white folks could not hear us."

Using their brutal realities as the antithesis of freedom, Black people like my great-great-great-grandfather began to question: *What do I want out of this life?* Freedom, then, sounded like unfiltered ululation; a volume that no one could quell. It looked like a house pushed back from the road where one could see everything coming and going. It felt like grass beneath your bare feet and dirt underneath your fingernails. It tasted like a home-cooked meal, fully seasoned, using the ingredients grown in one's very own backyard or bartered from neighbors. It smelled a little funky—mixing the smells of the various animals with one's own sweat—but the stench, and all the bounty that accompanied it, was yours.

Freedom was autonomy, and in America, that level of independence could only be achieved by having land of one's own. To own land, one needed to first be seen as human in the eyes of the law.

———

As debates over slavery gained wider recognition and global abolitionist movements chipped away at columns of power, white Americans looked for a way to dispose of, rather than coexist with, the Black and Indigenous peoples they had been extorting. The American Colonization Society

(ACS) was a group of powerful former slave owners and racists who refused to imagine, let alone truly consider, a country where Black people had the same liberties as they themselves did.

They worried among themselves, *What if they realize we're outnumbered and try to get revenge?* The many rebellions and uprisings on plantations across the country had seeded that fear. *What if they ask for back pay and reparations for the centuries of enslavement they've endured?* This young country, already in debt to allies like France, refused to cede land and money to former footstools. Many ideas about what to do with the Black population were thrown at the wall to see what would be least costly. How to spend as little as possible on Black America?

It is true that many abolitionists and Black people in the first half of the nineteenth century believed that Black people, in order to achieve true autonomy and safety, both needed and deserved a nation to call their own. Therefore, with ACS's offer, some Black people jumped at the opportunity to "repatriate" to the African continent, their pain and loss fueling a colonizer mindset. Imperialism is imperialism, even with brown faces at the helm. Whose land were they "returning" to and with what resources and blessing? What would be done with the people who met them at the shores? Sadly, in Liberia, these formerly enslaved African Americans would eventually transform into a new elite class, exerting political and economic power over the Indigenous Liberian people.

In addition to Liberia, wealthy white people deflected responsibility for their crimes by sending Black Americans to other nations, including Panama and Haiti. The "where" mattered far less than the speed. White Americans rushed to relocate the Black people who had built the economy that made the United States a global power, in order to continue hoarding the fruit of their labor and avoid having to pay out reparations from the global power's coffers. While some Black people wanted nothing to do with their former enslavers or their so-called democracy, others looked on with contempt as they imagined needing to start over, yet again, in a new nation. As Katherine J. Harris recounted in her essay "Colonization and Abolition in Connecticut," free and enslaved Black people began to resist efforts of removal, "view[ing] colonization as a means of defrauding them of the rights of citizenship." The newly "purchased" land to the west was explored as the potential site for an autonomous and isolated Black reservation. In the end, those self-ordained white men who made up the federal government decided they didn't want to choose between having an all-white society and expanding as far as the eye could see. Why have one when you could have both?

In an 1837 speech, former vice president and secretary of war John C. Calhoun notoriously defended these practices, once stating that "there never has yet existed a wealthy and civilized society in which one portion of the community did not, in point of fact, live on the labor of the other." Thirteen years prior to his white supremacist monologue, Calhoun, the grandson of an Irish immigrant, founded the Bureau of Indian Affairs, without approval from Congress or the Indigenous people themselves, to manage Indigenous people and land in relation to the new federal government.

The Bureau of Indian Affairs implemented violent, assimilationist policies across Indigenous communities, including family separation, tribal police forces, and boarding schools as indoctrination sites. All of these practices stripped Indigenous people of spiritual and cultural connections to one another and the land they saw as kin.

Though he didn't directly preside over the growth and expansion of the bureau, Calhoun's track record and words tell us that he likely would have been aligned with those policies. As the son of a proud "Indian fighter" father who passed on his love for states' rights and his disdain for his new home's original residents, Calhoun was nothing if not consistent across his career.

Calhoun was deeply inspired and molded by his studies and connections made at Yale College, where he graduated as valedictorian in 1804. His views were typical of most of the student body and the world they were being groomed to lead. Therein lies the problem. As the first Yale alum to be elected to federal executive office, Calhoun represented what Yale was designed for: consolidating influence in service of oneself. It's an extension of Yale's inception story and colonial ties to both slavery and land theft. Established before the Declaration of Independence was ever signed, Yale's physical structures—including what now makes up Connecticut Hall on Old Campus—were quite literally built through the backbreaking labor of enslaved African peoples and funded through profits made via the British East India Company, the private firm behind British imperialism worldwide. It's no wonder that later alums would continue the family business.

More than a century after his graduation, Yale named a residential college after Calhoun: a monument to his critical role in removing Indigenous people from their land and forcing Black people to work it. This decision would be protested for decades to come, by students, alumni, staff, and faculty alike. Unfortunately, it wouldn't be until 2017—the year after my own graduation from the university—that administrators would finally bend to demands to rename the college.

At the 2016 protests demanding the renaming of Calhoun College (ALEX ZHANG).

For Indigenous communities, staying out of land redistribution was (oftentimes) an intentional choice. Vehemently opposed to their removal from ancestral lands, Indigenous people were equally resistant to the idea of American citizenship. To accept it was to accept this apartheid state and white men's right to divvy up the land. And like Black people, most Indigenous people were simply trying to survive.

While Indigenous people were battling a violent process of border creation, most Black people were still trapped in the belly of the antebellum South and rightly fearful of the consequences of running or fighting. Many enslaved Black people worked solely to live another day. Similarly, many free Black people were too busy looking over their shoulders, defending themselves against re-enslavement and exploitation by unjust court systems. Even if the enslaved and the displaced managed to break away, their loved ones would remain ensnared, and the threat of recapture would loom over them. Black people and their Indigenous neighbors began to understand that the only limit to American westward expansion would be the Pacific Ocean. In other words, the limit to American greed didn't exist.

To "win" at this colonial game as a Black or Indigenous person required a shark-like mentality, a complicity with the system that was designed to swallow them, and a mindset that went against everything they had been taught to be. On some level, then, Black and Indigenous people knew they could never truly win or be free until the entire system was abolished. Its genesis was too evil to be reformed. To believe in reform was to believe that some element of the system deserved redemption. To be a patriot was to find beauty in a founding story that is only ugly.

For both groups, their resistance often began with small acts of self-preservation and intra-community building. They needed a more vigorous strategy in order to have a chance at survival. To be a citizen and member of their new world, there were prerequisites built around ownership and monopolies; a way of being far more individualistic than Black and Indigenous people particularly cared for. To survive, they had to adapt to this new economic system while never losing sight of the living thing on the other end of the transaction.

In "Touching the Earth," an essay for *Orion* magazine, bell hooks reminisces: "Before I understood anything about the pain and exploitation of the Southern system of sharecropping, I understood that grown-up Black folks loved the land." She goes on to state that "the vast majority of Black folks in the United States lived in the agrarian South. Living close to nature, Black folks were able to cultivate a spirit of wonder and reverence for life."

Some *still* find beauty in the crawlers that come up for air after heavy rain, a testament to the natural rhythms all around us. The petrichor ema-

Bakers' Acres.

nating from the grass and snaking its way up to the nose. The freshness all around. Some haven't lost hope for leisure, and for children running around without a care in the world beyond a few chores. Some still believe that life is too miraculous to only survive. They never gave up on the dream of land ownership because they never gave up on those who survived before—or after—them. Many Black people carry an intergenerational love for the land of the Deep South, passed on by our elders and ancestors who fought hardest for it.

SO MUCH FOR FORTY ACRES AND A MULE

(1862–1876)

═══

The slave went free; stood a brief moment in the sun; then moved back again toward slavery.

—W. E. B. DU BOIS

All struggles are essentially power struggles. Who will rule? Who will lead? Who will define, refine, confine, design? Who will dominate?

—OCTAVIA BUTLER

Contrary to what Kanye West may believe, slavery was not a choice. Enslaved, Black people were surely in distress—but they were no damsels. The mainstream narrative around emancipation brushes past the robust abolitionist movement of the nineteenth century, so when we hear, again and again, only a few names—Frederick Douglass, Harriet Tubman, Abraham Lincoln—we believe that a small few convinced an empathetic majority to "free the slaves," when in fact Black people freed themselves. Long before the Civil War began, the fight for freedom and equity was being waged and led by those who knew the brutality of enslavement up close. Black hands took up arms against enslavers at great risk to themselves and their families. Black feet ran as far as the wind would carry them. Black lips parted so that the liberatory language of their movement would reach the farthest corners of this planet. Black people disrupted the convenience and profit of the trade of enslaved people, and, in doing so, broke apart the chains shackled upon them.

There was no question of whether we had the guts to come to our own defense. The question was, and remains, how much are white Americans willing to do the same? Time and time again, the answer has been "not nearly enough."

In a speech over ten years after Lincoln's assassination, Frederick Douglass reminded audience members who attempted to whitewash history that "you are the children of Abraham Lincoln. We are at best only his step-children . . . children by forces of circumstances and necessity."

Many white people at the time, including Northerners supposedly loyal to the Union and all her residents, vehemently opposed the risk of laying down their life for that of a Black person. In July 1863, working-class white men across Manhattan turned the city upside down in what is now known as the New York City Draft Riots.

Men who initially refused to take up arms for the liberty of the United States were eager to do so *against* free Black people who represented the anti-racist future they feared. While Northern politicians were busy sitting atop their self-erected moral pedestals, their constituents were lashing out against the Black workers they claimed were stealing their jobs. One New Yorker who served as a Union soldier later stated, "I am willing to let them fight and dig if they will; it saves so many white men."

Others across the Union let their racism slip when questioning whether Black people were capable of fighting. "I won't trust niggers to fight yet. I have no confidence in them and don't want them mixed up with our white soldiers," General Sherman once said. Ironic, knowing that Black agents would come to play indispensable roles in the Union victory. Harriet Tubman, for example, would go on to lead the Combahee River Raid, setting Confederate plantations ablaze and freeing more than seven hundred enslaved Black people who would go on to enlist as soldiers themselves.

But most white Americans saw Black skin and equated it with inferiority. Even their so-called allies. This distrust and vitriol came from the same General Sherman who later issued Special Field Orders No. 15, the foundation of the famed "forty acres and a mule" promise. The order was revoked the same year it was introduced by President Johnson. To give General Sherman some credit, in the following breath after painting Blacks as inept, he stated that "the first step in the liberation of the Negro from bondage will be to get him and family to a place of safety . . . then to afford him the means of providing for his family." If only his country agreed more with the latter statement than the former.

Regardless of debates and resistance, when the Emancipation Proclamation authorized enslaved and/or emancipated Black people to "be received into the armed service of the United States," Black people overwhelmingly took freedom into their own hands, deciding that if they wanted something done right, they'd have to do it themselves. While emancipation wasn't the central goal of the Union, it soon became the secret weapon that would turn the tides quickly. According to the National Archives and Records Administration, approximately 94,000 Union soldiers were former slaves from states that had seceded from the Union. Another 44,000 were freemen from the border states, and more than 50,000 others were "recruited from the northern states and the Colorado Territory, many who were ex-slaves that went north on the Underground Railroad." Two of those freedom fighters were my ancestors.

Edmond T. Jones was born enslaved in Franklin County, North Carolina, and traveled a few counties north to Norfolk, Virginia, where he enlisted in the army. He was nineteen. In December 1863, two years after President Lincoln was sworn in, Edmond officially enlisted to serve with the Union Army. Flyers and advertisements had been raining down on the country offering "freedom, protection, pay, and a call to military duty" to any Black men who would serve. As a Black teenager, this was likely Edmond's first opportunity to take his life into his own hands. With the Civil War in full swing, some of the bloodiest battles were still to come and the Union needed all the help it could get.

With the swipe of his pen, President Lincoln emancipated enslaved people in the Confederacy, particularly those willing to serve in the army. In doing so, the president gave the Union a second wind and a real shot at disrupting the Confederate economy. The 1st Regiment of the U.S. Colored Cavalry, according to Second Lieutenant Frederick W. Browne, "being the first colored cavalry regiment, had in its ranks a rather better class of men than the infantry regiments had; some being from the North and some being the outlaw negroes who, in slavery times, had been able to maintain their liberty in the swamps of Eastern Virginia and North Carolina." It is unclear whether Edmond fled through those swamps or simply served alongside men who had called them home, but what is known is that those same "dismal" swamps that housed maroons for centuries prior had now become both a battleground and a recruitment center.

While Edmond was fighting in the eastern theater of the war, my maternal great-great-great-grandfather was working up the courage to join comrades in the West. Under the alias Thomas Johnson, William H. Carter served in Unit C of the 5th Regiment, United States Colored Cavalry. There were only a few cavalry regiments for "colored troops" and the 5th Regiment was certainly one of the more notable ones. Organized out of Camp Nelson, the third-largest recruiting center for Black men during the Civil War, the 5th Regiment's strategic placement in Kentucky allowed it to attract both escapees and freedmen. Ironically, this would come to include enslaved Black people within the state, as Kentucky had not been mandated to emancipate Black people. Only those held captive in Confederate states were freed through Lincoln's Emancipation Proclamation.

William "Thomas
Johnson" Carter's
enlistment papers and
pension records
(NATIONAL ARCHIVES
AT WASHINGTON).

Many were unhappy about Camp Nelson becoming a site of Black resistance and what that would mean for the rest of the region. Some felt that it jeopardized economic interests across the state. Others who considered themselves advocates against slavery felt that Camp Nelson attracted too many fugitive Black people and should focus on legal liberation efforts. In May 1865, an anonymous letter was sent to the editors of the Louisville *Journal* expressing the writer's disdain:

> Runaways are still received at Camp Nelson, and protected and harbored . . . I wish to see free freedom obtained according to the law and the Constitution, and not in violation of it. Not that I desire the freedom of the slave *less,* but I love the Constitution of the county and the integrity of the Administration of the Law and Government *more* . . . I don't wish the morals and ultimate welfare of Black women, girls, and children sacrificed even for their present freedom, when it is certain to come in a few months at most without any such sacrifice.

Just eighteen at the time, William was still a boy standing at five-six with dark hair and eyes to match his complexion. His entire life up until that point had been spent on the farms of Scott County, Kentucky, but when the war broke out William got his chance to trade his hoe and hammer for a Colt revolver and Springfield musket.

On April 1, 1865, two weeks before the assassination of President Lincoln, William arrived at Camp Nelson, which at the time was also serving as a refugee center for the families of Black soldiers. Under the leadership of Commander Louis Henry Carpenter, William would have been trained in the dangerous art of fighting on horseback. A real cowboy!

Though the war would end a little over a month after William enlisted, he would continue to "serve" for almost a year after the final surrender. Many other Black veterans would volunteer and continue playing out their cowboy fantasies as so-called Buffalo Soldiers, a nickname given to Black cavalry members who served in the U.S. Army. Some acted as peacekeepers following the war as the country worked to rebuild. A few others worked as the nation's first national park rangers before such a role even existed. In fact, it was Buffalo Soldiers (not Smokey Bear) who first popularized the famous wide-brimmed Ranger flat hat.

The vast majority of Buffalo Soldiers, though, did the bidding of the federal government during the "Indian Wars," cleaning land, laying roads, and evicting Indigenous people from newly acquired land. Most other veterans were busy trying to understand their role in this scathed nation. They felt lucky to be planning for a future at all.

In the end, one in five Black soldiers laid down their lives in a country they didn't ask to be kidnapped to, for a Union whose preservation they'd never get to see. Countless others were assassinated through lynchings and other forms of white supremacist violence. They took their liberation into their own hands and hoped full citizenship and protection would come with it.

Historian W. Caleb McDaniel described the period right after the Civil War, noting that "slavery did not end cleanly or on a single day. It ended through a violent, uneven process." There was no one mode of communicating to Black people at the time that they were free, and many depended on the same white people who had been enslaving them to deliver the news.

While researching for this book, I visited Historic Stagville, a former plantation in present-day Durham, North Carolina, now serving as a museum preserving and honoring the legacy of the Black people who lived and worked there for centuries. (I rarely visit preserved plantations, as they tend to present beautiful estates without examining the truth of what ugliness made it all possible.) After driving down a winding dirt road, my research assistant, Hannah, and I approached a clearing in the trees with a small building, maybe a welcome center or gift shop. As I entered to check in for the tour, a bookcase greeted me with titles like *Wake: The Hidden History of Women-Led Slave Revolts* and *A Mind to Stay: White Plantation, Black Homeland*. To the right of the bookcase was more shelving with a bright yellow sign; I leaned in closer and read, CREATED WITH LOVE BY LOCAL BLACK-OWNED SMALL BUSINESSES. A tall and thin white man with curly blond hair greeted me from behind the register, letting me know he would be my tour guide and that we'd get started in about ten minutes.

Hannah and I waited in the car, unsure of what to expect. I tried my best to ignore the grounds' beauty. It's difficult for me to acknowledge the sheer natural radiance of sites of violence like former plantations, but Stagville was undeniably breathtaking. Trees surrounded us and the lush greenery felt all-encompassing. Oddly enough, once the tour started, the trees were one of the first things pointed out as distinctly different from antebellum times. "These trees wouldn't have been here. This was all clear-cut and you would have been able to see all the way down to the Flat River." I hadn't realized we were standing atop a hill until he said this. Our guide made it clear that removing the trees that separated the fields and slave cabins from the overseer's housing had been a power move. "If you're down in those fields, anytime you look up, you see what's important . . . You look at this white house."

No words were minced and no history was sugarcoated during our two-hour walking tour of Historic Stagville. In fact, we lost several tourists along the way, disappointed by the curriculum. That didn't stop the radical honesty pouring out as we walked from big house to wooden cabin and everywhere in between. Standing outside of two-story lodgings previously inhabited by enslaved laborers, our guide shared the story of when the Union Army first arrived at the plantation, days after its owner, Paul Cameron, fled.

The first Union officer was met at the door by an enslaved Black woman, Ella Jordan. The Union soldier demanded all of the gold or silver that the former owner had. When Ella confessed that she didn't know where the wealth was being hoarded, the Union soldier—allegedly there for the emancipation of all enslaved Black people—threatened to kill her rather than leave empty-handed. Our guide didn't sugarcoat things: "Just because the Union was here does not mean there was safety."

A second Union soldier arrived not long after the first, also seeking to get rich but this time finding a young Cy Hart and his mother, two Black people also enslaved at the Stagville plantation. Cy recalled that the soldiers were dirty, tired, and hungry, but fairly nice. When they realized there was no money to steal, they asked for a feast. The Black staff—at the mercy of these servicemen and still believing themselves enslaved—showed the soldiers the smokehouse overflowing with hams and other meat. The

Union soldiers packed as much meat as they could carry, instructing Cy's mother, Nellie Hart, to cook them dinner, and filled their bellies. After indulging, the soldiers notified the Black people they'd just forced to serve them that they were free, gave them the remaining meat from the smokehouse along with some money, and left. "That's how it went down," noted our guide.

Charity Austin, a formerly enslaved Black person living in North Carolina, told an interviewer of the Federal Writers' Project that she actually met Abraham Lincoln once, prior to his presidency. Charity described Lincoln as "the raggedest man you ever saw" and didn't recognize Lincoln until he was later elected. Years later, when Lincoln was assassinated, Austin recalled that "boss tole us Abraham Lincoln wus dead and we were still slaves . . . We stayed there another year after freedom. A lot o' de niggers knowed nothin' 'cept what missus and marster tole us. What dey said wus just de same as de Lawd had spoken to us . . . When de nigger wus freed dey didn't know where to go and what to do. It was hard, but it has been hard since."

Others lived in communities where white people used the threat of rope—or worse—to dare Black people to test their newfound "freedom." In his book *How the Word Is Passed,* Clint Smith quotes Susan Merritt of Rusk County, Texas, who recounted that "lots of Negroes were killed after freedom . . . You could see lots of Negroes hanging from trees in Sabine Bottom right after freedom."

Emancipation wasn't living up to the glimmering visions many had imagined. For all those who made it to the other side of the war, the fighting had just begun.

———

After having done the seemingly impossible, newly freed Black people turned their eyes and ambition toward the country they'd built. The fields they'd sowed and harvested. The economy they'd unwillingly expanded, churning out billions of dollars in revenue. Few imagined they would have the chance to partake in the full wealth of this land, but they dared to dream about a parcel for themselves and their loved ones. They were right to be cautious.

In doing away with chattel slavery, the U.S. economy was forced to transform and everyone—white people, Indigenous people, and Black people—projected their hopes and fears onto the land. Felix Haywood said, "We thought we was goin' to be richer than the white folks, 'cause we was stronger and knowed how to work, and the whites didn't and they didn't have us to work for them anymore. But it didn't turn out that way."

Back at Stagville, as we stood outside a wooden cabin in a semicircle, our tour guide broke down the ways that sharecropping became a forced racial and economic identity for many formerly enslaved Black people and their children. "The folks that were able to get off the plantation the fastest are those with skills, domestic artisan, and the field hands are going to take the brunt of the abuse. They want a piece of this land. They need a piece of this land to start out. And that's what they asked Paul Cameron for. And he says, no, you will never have a piece of this land. And there is this standoff until June when the food runs out. And then the sharecropping contracts begin." Their former-enslaver-turned-new-employer rented sharecropping families the mules, tools, seeds, food rations, and housing that they needed to survive and work for him. Unlike in slavery where these costs were treated as Cameron's investment into his farm operation, the burden now fell to the sharecroppers.

"They had to give Paul Cameron two-thirds of what they grow. They keep one-third after they pay supervisors who are here to make sure the Cameron interests are upheld. The supervisors were formerly called overseers, and now the sharecroppers have to pay them. This goes until November, when there is a strike." In the midst of a critical wheat harvest, Black sharecroppers refused to work until more equitable contracts were drafted. Paul Cameron and the overseers he'd hired pulled out all the stops to crush the strike. In the end it was a call to the Union Army that was most effective, again proving that many who fought for the Union were more committed to peace with Confederates than justice for newly freed Black people.

"New York 125th comes out. They find the organizers of the strike. They expel them from the plantation permanently, and they change the contract—instead of getting to keep one-third, sharecroppers can now keep one-quarter. And they are told, don't you ever try this again." Our tour guide reveals that his great-grandfather was a Union soldier, and it's clear that he's grappled with the tension between what many want to believe versus what was actually true. While heroic tales of Union saviors and military victories fit a convenient narrative about a compassionate North, many Union officers weren't abolitionists at all. Our tour guide was honest about this. "Most of them were ambivalent or annoyed by freed Black people. They wanted to go home. That's all they wanted to do. And they calculated that the easiest way to get home is to keep the peace by siding with the former planter class like Paul Cameron every time. And that sets up ninety years of sharecropping."

———

With Black people no longer part of white America's inventory, white Americans scrambled to regain their footing at the top of the sociopolitical hierarchy. Again, they looked to landholdings to fill the gap, breaking treaties with Indigenous nations almost as quickly as they'd been signed.

By positioning their imperialist conquests as successful efforts to explore, tame, and subdue the "Wild, Wild West," they gained widespread buy-in from politicians *and* civilians—not unlike the fifteenth-century patronage by royalty and the Catholic Church that sent "explorers" like Christopher Columbus around the world. White supremacy has never been abolished anywhere on this planet. It has always evolved and shapeshifted. Especially as the railroad industry exploded onto the scene, making transportation of "settlers" even more streamlined, white flight was incentivized every step of the way.

In 1968, Dr. Martin Luther King Jr. spoke about his reasons for co-organizing the Poor People's Campaign and reminded us of the government's weaponization of affirmative action to aid white people in taking ownership of fifty million acres of land formerly held by Native Americans:

> At the very same time that the government refused to give the Negro any land, through an act of Congress, America was giving away millions of acres of land in the west and the midwest, which meant that there was a willingness to give the white peasants from Europe an economic base. And yet it refused to give its Black peasants from

Africa, who came here involuntarily in chains and had worked free for 244 years, any kind of economic base. And so emancipation for the Negro was really freedom to hunger . . . It was freedom without food to eat or land to cultivate and therefore it was freedom and famine at the same time. But not only did they give the land, they built land-grant colleges with government money to teach them how to farm; not only that, they provided county agents to further their expertise in farming; not only that, they provided low interest rates in order that they could mechanize their farms; not only that, today, many of these people are receiving millions of dollars in federal subsidies not to farm and they are the very people telling the Black man that he ought to lift himself by his own bootstraps. And this is what we are faced with, and this is the reality.

Dr. King was referencing the Homestead Act of 1862, which divided up land for "American citizens." As Indigenous Americans rejected America's nationhood as a whole and Black Americans were lynched for trying to move ahead, white Americans were positioned to benefit. As the federal government broke treaties and continued expanding farther south and west, land was divided into parcels and disseminated among (mostly white) homesteaders.

In *I've Been Here All the While,* Dr. Alaina E. Roberts tells us that "the Homestead Act of 1862 formalized the migration that was already occurring and provided additional motivation to settlers in parts of the West . . . at first, settlers could claim . . . 160 acres of free land [beginning] January 1, 1863." The requirements? American citizens who were heads of households, at least twenty-one years old, or military veterans. When all was said and done, over 160 million acres were taken from Indigenous people and given to American citizens, which at the time only included white Americans.

After emancipation, many Black people would attempt to take advantage of this purported free-for-all, which, like most things in this nation, would turn out to be free-for-whites-only. Dr. Roberts recounts that "Black Americans were largely denied assistance in using these avenues to obtain and maintain land and wealth. On the other hand, with the full strength of

the U.S. government on their side, white Americans soon became the largest landowners in the region and triumphed in the narrative of civilization
that justified their colonization."

Ten percent of what we now call the United States was all but shot out
of T-shirt cannons for salivating white men and their investment portfo-
lios. Generational wealth was secured for white men and their descendants, while the rest of the nation fought for scraps. According to the
National Park Service and the University of Nebraska, less than a million
acres were issued to Black people. That's a fraction of a fraction of all
270 million acres of land that had been redistributed while the Homestead
Act was in effect. Environmental devastation as an act of economic warfare; the United States has used this tool consistently, and never in favor of
the disenfranchised.

In fact, the only semblance of reparations for formerly enslaved Black
Americans came not as an act of benevolence or self-accountability. Rather,
it was one of anti-Indigeneity meant to hurt the Five Tribes by appointing
white Americans as executors of justice. According to Dr. Roberts, "[Black
people who were formerly enslaved by Native Americans] became the only
people of African descent in the world to receive what might be viewed as
reparations for their enslavement on a large scale."

In an echo of how Indigenous communities aligned with the British
during the American Revolution, the Five Tribes' loyalties were torn during the Civil War between Northern capitalists who represented an expanding Union and Southern racists who were willing to make peace with
Native Americans if it meant the extension of slavery. The Confederacy
spun a web of empty promises, vowing to respect the sovereignty of Indigenous soldiers who would fight alongside them. Not all agreed, and some
chose to move farther southwest, proactively anticipating that no matter
who won, their people would suffer. Many others had grown comfortable
in a plantation economy and wanted to retain their economic stakes in the
trade and ownership of enslaved people. The Fives Tribes who allied with
the Southerners, whether by choice or coercion, would soon regret that
decision.

While rebuilding the South and readmitting Confederate states into
the Union was a postwar priority, Northern aggression was targeted at Na-

tive Americans who dared deny the call to fight with the Union. Never mind that the federal government had done nothing but make and break pacts for almost a century. Now emboldened, it was ready to punish the tribal leaders who stood against it by taking more of their land.

William Loren Katz succinctly described this aftermath: "Emancipation also was imposed from outside. The U.S. government and white citizens had once demanded Native Americans adopt slavery and hunt runaways. Now they demanded that all [enslaved people] of Indians become free and equal. The white man had again spoken with forked tongue." Rather than implementing land redistribution across the board, only Black people enslaved by Indigenous Americans were deemed worthy of restitution. Nothing for those who endured the lash and cruelty of white evangelical Christians.

Only the Choctaw and Chickasaw tribes resisted strongly. Seminole, Cherokee, and Muscogee peoples quickly freed the Black people within their ranks and worked to more equitably integrate those freedmen into their society. To this day, freed people still battle for tribal citizenship and the benefits extended to other tribal members.

———

While a "postwar exodus," as Dr. Alaina E. Roberts called it, existed with large swaths of Black Southerners migrating north, many Black people were unwilling to start over. My ancestor, Louis Baker, remained in Warren County, as did the three generations to follow him, with a commitment to rebuilding a community built by and for Black people.

For Black people who did own their own land, like my paternal ancestor Louis Baker and my maternal ancestor William Carter, cultivating it was familiar, but managing and profiting off of it was another thing entirely. They'd need to get up to speed in order to have a shot at all. In addition to learning the new language of commodifying land, Reconstruction offered a moment to be ambitious for the first time in their lives, and to reinvent themselves in God's image. Omnipotent. All-powerful. At once, land became both currency and self-portrait; the more land one had, the more wealthy and powerful they were.

This country's obsession with picking oneself up by one's own bootstraps—especially if that someone wasn't white—became blatantly obvious during this time. Land was initially intended to be confiscated from former slavers and redistributed to the formerly enslaved through the Freedmen's Bureau. The rumor of "forty acres and a mule," which stemmed from that field order by General Sherman, was derived from a conversation he had with Gullah Geechee people. Those who General Sherman met in the final years of the war communicated that they only wanted the land they'd been working. The "mule" aspect was meant to be a creative use of the now-idle livestock from wartime.

In 1867, a disabled lawyer and abolitionist from Pennsylvania, Representative Thaddeus Stevens, introduced H.R. 29, which sought reparations "to four millions of injured, oppressed, and helpless men, whose ancestors for two centuries have been held in bondage." The bill goes on to state that "nothing is so likely to make a man a good citizen as to make him a freeholder. Nothing will so multiply the productions of the South as to divide it into small farms."

But President Johnson disagreed with these "radical" policies and did not believe the *federal* government had the jurisdiction to enforce civil rights legislation across the country it was constructed for. He had "returned" land to former Confederate owners and, in 1866, vetoed critical bills designed to strengthen reconstruction. His resolve to stand in the way of progress would reverberate for decades to come.

Though the Freedmen's Bureau supported families in reuniting after forced separation by former owners, provided free medical care, and established several universities, it did not end up disseminating any land. By 1872, the bureau was terminated after just seven years of service. Less than a decade was dedicated to undoing three centuries of exploitation.

This failed first attempt at land redistribution meant that slavery had been dismantled in name only. Racial capitalism still reigned. Most formerly enslaved people remained too poor to have options beyond living with and working for their former slavers. Thus, the enslaved were transitioned into landless sharecroppers, many living in the same rickety, wooden shacks from before the war.

Others, who lived on plantations that had been pillaged and burned during the war, traveled as far as they needed to, searching for a new employer. One might have hoped that as workers, free Black people would have the right to negotiate their pay. But with limited choices, masters-turned-bosses maintained the upper hand. They set the rates, work conditions, and living arrangements, and the threat of violence ensured very few questioned that dynamic. What did it mean for families stripped of everything to be expected to "join society" and compete with land-owning white men without the same rights?

My grandmother's people come from Candor, North Carolina, where the dirt is dark and sandy—perfect for growing the juiciest peaches around. Candor is known for its peach festivals and not as much for the Black people who have made the town's agricultural economy go 'round. My grandmother recalls "peach parties," a tradition taught to her by her grandparents, who learned from their own elders. This was the art of turning the chore of growing fruit and vegetables into a family affair. Aunts, uncles, parents, and children would gather in tight quarters to collectively peel baskets upon baskets of peaches. Sweet, round peaches that needed to be preserved or packaged for customers. Occasionally, they'd also pickle the peaches, transforming their flavor.

My father visited Candor with his mother several times. "Candor felt like the beginning of the Deep South—really rural and small towns. I remember the watermelons lining the road so big and bountiful, you almost couldn't see the houses behind them. And boy were they sweet." My grandmother remembers Candor in much the same way, though not because of the small towns; she associates Candor with hard labor and racism. My grandmother's least favorite crop was cucumbers. She recalled, "They were so low to the ground, it made your back hurt and you didn't get much money. You had a wire basket and they would give you ten cents a basket. That was a bushel of cucumbers that you're picking for only ten cents. You'd be picking all day to make a dollar." Cucumbers are also some of the harshest crops for a farmer, because they had to be picked in entirety during the hottest few weeks of the year. The exploitation was even further exacerbated if you couldn't read, do math, or otherwise prove that your employer was cheating you. Many sharecroppers went into debt working for former enslavers who continued turning a profit by cheating their "employees" out of the literal rightful fruits of their labor.

Another Federal Writers' Project interviewee was Silas Abbott, born in Mississippi but living in Brinkley, Arkansas, at the time. After the Civil War ended, his parents continued living on the land of their former enslavers. The arrangement was supposedly that Silas's parents received twenty acres to run a cotton gin. One evening, the gin was mysteriously set on fire and "[Master Ely] had to take our land back and sell it to pay for four or five hundred bales of cotton [that] got burned up that time." Silas shared that he and his family "stayed on and sharecropped with [Master Ely]."

The system of sharecropping was designed to make it nearly impossible for a Black person, who was reliant on white landowners for shelter, wages, and tools, to do better than breaking even. One had to be both prepared and lucky to beat these odds. Mitchell and Josephine Ross were both born enslaved by William D. Elams, who was assumed to also be Josephine's biological father. Being Black on a plantation in the late nineteenth century instilled a deep desire for agency that the Rosses would remember post–Civil War.

Assuming the expected role of sharecropper following emancipation, Mitchell worked the land until he had saved enough to purchase some acreage for his own family. When he had accumulated enough money, he approached his former owner—not as a serf but as an equal seeking a mutually beneficial transaction. In the winter of 1888, Ross walked away proudly with fifty acres to call his own. The sale was so momentous for him and his loved ones that the date became an annual family holiday commemorated with a feast to rival Christmas dinner. Loved ones near and far traveled to northwest Littleton and stared out at the Roanoke River while standing on Ross land. Finally.

Louis Baker and his first wife, Nancy (née Harris), were two of the lucky few Black people to become landowners in the late nineteenth century. Just five years younger than Louis, Nancy is described in census records as a "mulatto" Black woman, meaning that she was likely born of sexual violence against her mother, Emily. I can imagine how the dream of autonomy guided Nancy's every move; being able to own one's body not only in the context of labor, but also in being able to love and be loved free of duress.

She and Louis had five children together, and in 1882 they handed over $1,634—likely their life savings—in exchange for 344.5 acres of land known then as the B. B. Baker Tract. Their children, and later Louis's children with his second wife, Nellie, would benefit from their resilience for generations to come.

The same year that he procured land for his family, Louis deepened his roots even further by joining Lovely Hill Baptist Church, which had been founded two decades prior by twelve free Black people. Lovely Hill, true to its name, began atop gorgeous, elevated grounds in a simple clearing amidst towering loblolly pine trees and makeshift pews. By the time Louis joined the congregation in 1882, an acre of land had been purchased for five dollars and an official building was constructed. The local newspaper noted the expansion with just a sentence: "The colored brethren have commenced work on their new house of worship at Lovely Hill." Louis, a landowner, had joined a community of Black people who prioritized property ownership, and understood it as critical to both their success and safety.

Louis and Nancy weren't the only ones thinking in this way. Black people nationwide chose to handle their business with or without the federal government. Many of the first Juneteenth celebrations involved voter registration drives and efforts to pool resources and purchase land. The first recorded celebration, which took place in 1866, was initially referred to as "Jubilee Day" and served more as a political rally than a festive party. Emancipation Park in the Third Ward of Houston, Texas, was a by-product of this movement.

The story behind its founding isn't the feel-good story we'd like to believe. The writer Clint Smith sat down a few years ago with Jacqueline Bostic, the great-granddaughter of Jack Yates, who was central to the creation of the park. In Smith's book *How the Word Is Passed,* he details their interview and the harrowing story of Yates's insistence on freedom by his own definition. After surviving enslavement himself and being separated from his wife, who worked on another plantation, the Emancipation Proclamation was signed and Black people hoped for a smooth transition. What they'd get was anything but.

While Yates's Virginia-based slaveholder complied with the newly signed legislation, his wife and children's enslaver intentionally moved to Texas to avoid compliance. Not willing to be even farther from his family, Yates sold himself back into slavery. Texas became their new home. After being eventually freed *again,* Yates was determined to build a strong Black community that could fend for itself and be insulated from the racism that engulfed them.

He and his family settled in Houston, and Yates became a well-revered minister whose theology couldn't be separated from his politics. According to Smith, "In 1872, this piece of land was purchased by a group of formerly enslaved people in the hopes of providing Houston's Black community with a place to celebrate Juneteenth . . . working together with other community members, they collected eight hundred dollars to purchase the land—the first public park in the city of Houston and in the state of Texas."

Most of us can't imagine the levels of depravity and degradation that people like Jack Yates were vulnerable to. The violence was so severe that one would understand if a survivor were only able to look out for themselves afterward. For people like Yates, who had already scaled insurmountable mountains, the willingness to still center community is awe-inspiring.

Landed Black families were both well respected and well positioned to cushion white supremacy's blows. Similarly, in securing their own parcel of land, Mitchell and Josephine Ross became both beacons and mentors for their community. The Rosses did not settle for their personal slice of the American dream and continued finding ways to establish cooperatives, or mutual aid, among Black farmers. Once they'd gotten their farm up and running, they would share any surplus crops with nearby Black families who were more food-insecure than they were. They had intentionally, yet informally, filled in the voids created and exacerbated by state and national government agencies.

Additionally, for other farmers trying to get on their feet, the Rosses shared equipment and technology that was otherwise hoarded by powerful white farmers. As the industry transformed, depending less on field hands and more on machinery, the Rosses ensured Black farmers didn't get left behind. They traded goods with other Black families who would barter with produce, eggs, milk, or other products of value. By engaging in this way, Mitchell, Josephine, and the community around them resisted the capitalist urge to exist on an island of their own choosing, and instead leaned on one another. They taught their children, including Georgianna Ross, to seek and watch out for their kinfolk, the only loyalty Black Americans trusted in this land of trickery and cruelty.

The same government that endorsed and institutionalized their enslavement couldn't also be a liberator. Black liberation has always been at odds with federal aspirations for a greater republic and more power on global stages. At every turn, when the U.S. government has had the option to meaningfully repair the trauma and theft of white supremacy and chattel slavery, it has instead chosen to build up industries that depend on widespread access to stolen, hoarded land and cheap or free labor, to maximize profits.

Black Americans soon learned that inheriting land and building an autonomous life was one thing; maintaining it was another entirely.

CHAPTER

4

WHERE
BIPARTISANSHIP GOT US

(1876–1877)

═══

**Slavery was bipartisan. Jim Crow was bipartisan . . .
When colleagues talk to me about bipartisanship, I ask:
At whose expense? Who is being asked to foot the bill?**

—SENATOR RAPHAEL WARNOCK

"They . . . they roundin' up white folks."

The words were first spoken incredulously, as a whisper. Then again more matter-of-factly.

"They roundin' up white folks!"

Again and again until the words were broken up into a staccato interspersed with laughter. The joy was palpable and communal, as the sea of sharecroppers gathered together to praise God for sending their salvation. People danced, cried, hugged, sang. Some pinched themselves and mumbled to themselves in disbelief. This country that had never shown itself to care about Black life before was suddenly and miraculously prioritizing their safety. It felt too good to be true, but they were sure to give God the glory anyhow.

In the background, rounds of ammunition were being fired as Union men rode horseback—fleeing overseers, former slavers, and Confederates. White men ran frantically in every direction, caught off guard by accountability in action. Their wives dared not intervene lest their own roles be revealed. White children huddled together, wondering if the world was ending. And it was. Their world at least.

Back in a corner of the barn, an elder sat alone, marveling at the energy around her. Kinetic. Infectious. Hopping from person to person like the Holy Ghost. She stood up slowly and began walking to the front of the barn slowly reciting Psalm 9 for only herself and God to hear. Soon the room fell into a hush as they listened intently to the scripture that had shown itself to be a prophecy realized:

> "I will praise thee, O Lord, with my whole heart; I will shew forth
>   all thy marvelous works. I will be glad and rejoice in thee: I will
>   sing praise to thy name, O thou most High.
> When mine enemies are turned back, they shall fall and perish at
>   thy presence . . .
> The Lord also will be a refuge for the oppressed, a refuge in times
>   of trouble . . . He forgetteth not the cry of the humble.
> The Lord is known by the judgment which he executeth: the
>   wicked is snared in the work of his own hands . . . For the
>   needy shall not always be forgotten: the expectation
>   of the poor shall not perish forever . . .
> Put them in fear, O Lord: that the nations may know themselves
>   to be but men. Selah."

Those lucky enough to have seen this unprecedented moment up close would join a small and dying class. They would be some of the few Black people in this country to feel *protected by* rather than *in opposition to* their government—the Confederacy had fallen, the Civil War was ending, and the Union was in a stage of reinvention and self-discovery.

———

From the late 1860s, President Ulysses Grant had been warning white Southerners that their reign of terror would soon be ending. No one held their breath. White wealth was being salvaged post-Abolition, and the plantation economy was being reimagined into new industries. Core to these efforts was the need for white domination and Black subjugation, which gave way to immediate and powerful whitelashing following the fall of the Confederacy. Terror became like oxygen for white Southerners, and the victims were often Black landowners or laborers who dared demand the freedom they'd been promised.

In 1871, President Grant signed the Ku Klux Klan Act to stop the heinous crimes of the terrorist group, and sent Attorney General Amos Akerman to enforce it personally. By any means necessary. In many ways, Akerman was a shocking choice for such a powerful and new position. In fact, *The New York Times* marked the appointment with a headline that read, "Universal Surprise at the Choice." For some, it was the choice to put a Southerner in the presidential cabinet. The North always remembers, you see. But Akerman was actually born in New Hampshire and had only been calling Georgia his home in the years leading up to the war. A former slave-owning attorney who opposed secession, yet had enlisted in the Confederate Army anyway, Akerman was paradoxical enough to be seen as an olive branch, but willing to critique his own party and work with "the opposition." Just what President Grant needed. But what could Black people expect out of such a man?

Akerman wasted no time in fulfilling the projected duties of his post. Immediately after assuming the office, he instructed federal officers to prosecute *every* anti-Black civil rights violation. Violations ranged from whippings and theft to murder, hangings, and sexual violence. In York County, South Carolina, more than six hundred violations were reported, including hundreds of whippings and eleven murders. And these were only the instances that people were brave enough to report. Akerman believed that, in his own words, "[Klansmen] take all kindness on the part of the government as evidence of timidity, and hence are emboldened to lawlessness by it." His explicit goal with the Justice Department was "to terrify evil doers."

When the Klansmen called Akerman's bluff, they expected the federal government to fold. These were not powerless vigilantes. They were incredibly well-connected and expected those connections to shield them from any real consequences. Unfortunately for them, there was a new sheriff coming to town. President Lincoln had (begrudgingly) made a promise on America's behalf when he signed the Emancipation Proclamation into law through executive order. "That on the first day of January, in the year of our Lord one thousand eight hundred and sixty-three, all persons held as slaves within any State or designated part of a State, the people whereof shall then be in rebellion against the United States, shall be then, thence-forward, and forever free." What words. That anyone standing in the way of freedom for formerly enslaved people was an enemy of the state. And here was a glimmer of America holding up its end of the bargain. Moments like these gave Black people in the South hope, however short-lived.

Though one may be inclined to praise Grant's efforts and intentions regardless of their ultimate impact, this book isn't here to sanitize the leg-acy of former presidents, who each, in some way, made this empire stron-ger. Ulysses Grant was no exception. Despite advocating at times on behalf of a community in desperate need of a champion in the White House, his commitments rarely weathered the test of time. Like many self-proclaimed allies across history, and certainly today, President Grant's efforts were more a reflection of what was most convenient for him and his party, rather than what was truly needed to effect sustainable change.

For all intents and purposes, the vast majority of Grant's party had a white savior complex. It allowed them to do good in some instances, but they ultimately had more bark than bite. The Republican Party had, in many ways, leaned into the political branding that made Lincoln so popu-lar. Remember that, prior to the Great Depression, the Republicans were concentrated in the North and defined first and foremost by their empha-sis on business opportunity. For many Republicans of the era, resisting the expansion of slavery began as a way to ensure their industrial pursuits wouldn't be thwarted by slave owners buying up all the land for agricul-ture. When they realized abolition was convenient, they jumped behind it, but only so far as it would serve their other endeavors.

One doesn't need to compare President Grant to modern thinking to know that his beliefs and commitment did not align with those of true abo-litionists and progressives of the time. In the same breath that Grant would recite that "the Creator did not place races of men on earth for the stronger to destroy the weaker," he was also enforcing his will through genocidal "wars" and assimilationist "peace" policies that conveniently freed up large swaths of land. Though he saw himself on moral high ground, in the end he served American business and exceptionalism above all else. And at this time, America's pockets only went as deep as her borders went west.

Meanwhile, Akerman's investigations were both time-consuming and expensive. Attorneys tasked to support his undertaking were drowning in grievances submitted by Black people, while white communities mobilized to crowdfund the legal defense of "our boys that have been kidnapped by the Yankees." One campaign raised $10,000—the modern-day equivalent of over $300,000. With those hurdles in their way, Akerman and his team were taking three steps forward and ten steps back. "If it takes a court over one month to try five offenders," hypothesized Akerman, "how long will it take to try four hundred, already indicted, and many hundreds more who deserve to be indicted?"

Grant's lack of commitment to the espoused values that won him the election revealed itself when railroad tycoons demanded a less diligent attorney general and Southern Democrats called for more autonomy to terrorize Black people. Southern terrorism freed up land and guaranteed a workforce of sharecroppers who would feel beholden to their former enslavers. Railroad tycoons needed someone in charge who would grant them large swaths of Indigenous land to expand their industrial pursuits from sea to shining sea. Ironically, both sides were acting based on their vision for the future of land ownership. President Grant was asked to let Akerman go, and he did just that.

When Akerman was replaced by Attorney General George Henry Williams, the prosecutions of Ku Klux Klan members were drastically reduced for fear of public perception and in favor of bipartisanship. The next year, the 1872 elections went by so peacefully that Grant took it as a sign that his year-and-a-half-long project of dismantling white supremacy was successful, and no further vigilance would be necessary. In June of the following year, Grant ordered the outstanding prosecutions to be suspended, and in 1874 many federal civil rights statutes were deemed unconstitutional. Yet again, the safety of Black people was negotiable.

But President Grant's betrayal was just the beginning. America would continue to renege on its promise. America would continue to decide it was okay that Black people were not only dying but also being relegated to a non-citizenship, non-human class in this country. And as such, most Black families in America carry a story of unspeakable white supremacist violence that changed the trajectory of their lives. Lynchings. White mobs.

Bombings. Mass incarceration. Surveillance. Police brutality. All of these stories in some way point back to the failed Reconstruction, and all are part of the legacy of the 1876 presidential election and subsequent compromise.

———

The contentious presidential election of 1876, in which Republicans and Democrats made a backroom deal, resulted in Rutherford Hayes becoming president and the withdrawal of all federal troops from the South. This "compromise" led to some of the first Jim Crow laws and unleashed unspeakable violence on Black Americans nationwide—especially in the Deep South, where the future of Black generational wealth and political participation was determined. Land was a large factor in how this played out.

White Southerners were desperate for a win, and if they couldn't legally own slaves, then they wanted to at least be able to retain social and economic control that was only possible through land ownership and legal impunity. As historians have long noted, had the Confederacy succeeded in becoming its own nation, it would have been the fourth-richest country in the world in the early 1860s. This didn't need to change so long as land remained in the possession of white folks. It didn't matter that Black and Indigenous people were free on paper. Their livelihood depended on the white people who employed them. Legal impunity was a tool for protecting that way of life.

Meanwhile, Northerners and Midwesterners were happy to be back in control federally and would do anything to ensure it remained that way. Civil wars were costly, and many were abolitionists in name alone. Bipartisanship, unity, and their pursuit of wealth mattered far more than the quality of life for free Black people.

Two candidates from each party were put forth as a reflection of the weaknesses they sought both to address among their respective political parties and to highlight in the competition. The Northern Republicans knew they'd need to retain the newly powerful Black vote while also appealing to the more economic-focused concerns of white men nationwide. They selected Rutherford Hayes, a politician from Ohio who had served as governor and U.S. congressman. Hayes had served in the Union Army and advocated for Black suffrage, but he was a businessman first and foremost, with the potential to reach across the aisle more than Grant had. Meanwhile, the predominantly Southern Democrats wanted to build a party that was less geographically centered and could build a new identity beyond the failed Confederacy. After having been shut out of politics postreunification, they needed a real shot at governing again. They chose Samuel Tilden, the governor of New York, as their candidate.

One may question why a group of people would go through so much trouble to disenfranchise another group, and to answer that, you have to understand how dominant an industry agricultural production and land ownership had become. As the most exported U.S. commodity of the time, cotton ruled, and it propelled America into the stratosphere as a global economic leader. The more land, the more production. This land lust fueled the genocide of Native Americans, colonial expansion westward, and the continued assault on Black autonomy. The only thing standing in the way was this election, and Tilden's party came fairly close to winning.

Rutherford Hayes lost the popular vote, but twenty electoral votes were in dispute. It's unclear exactly how valid the official results are. Accusations of voter fraud were rampant on both sides, and of course there was the violent and relentless voter suppression of Black people. Hayes and his party argued that if Black people weren't being terrorized, it wouldn't have been nearly as close in states like Louisiana, South Carolina, and Florida, which represented nineteen electoral votes in total. Black support should have made it a landslide for Hayes. But that's not what the popular vote indicated, and white Southerners were willing to fight for this tooth and nail. If Reconstruction continued any further, their oppressive ways of being would be steamrolled and it would take great effort to regain the stronghold they'd built after centuries of slavery.

The fight was on, and an extralegal "election commission" was formed by President Grant and the then-split Congress. This commission was made up of five senators, five House representatives, and five Supreme Court justices. All white men, and one more Republican than Democrat. Two and a half months after the initial election, this commission voted along party lines, 8 to 7, for Hayes to win the presidency. Things wouldn't end that easily and Democrats doubled down, refusing to accept the ruling of the commission. Tilden supporters threatened to take up arms and march on Washington. Sound familiar?

A clandestine meeting was held to solve this dilemma and the Compromise of 1877 was born. There's little official record of this meeting, and many have contested who was involved and how formal it was. Some believe no elected officials participated in the commission, but rather railroad and oil tycoons who controlled the economy at the time. What we do know is that several white men gathered in a five-story hotel in Washington, D.C., and didn't leave until a decision was made. Ironically, the Wormley Hotel, where this caucus convened, was owned and operated by a free Black man, James Wormley, who traveled the world studying culinary arts and was rumored to have been at President Lincoln's bedside the day that he died. That latter point has been widely disputed, but the fact that the rumors were remotely believable says a lot about the type of man James Wormley was. He was entrepreneurial and community-focused, helping to establish the first school for Black youth in Washington, D.C. The hotel would be one of his most successful ventures, a home away from home northwest of the city, frequented by diplomats. Who knew that the Wormley Hotel would also host a meeting of the minds to change the course of American history? A shift that would make it significantly harder for people like Mr. Wormley to own much of anything.

Hayes self-identified as a "staunch abolitionist" who had defended free Black people in court proceedings during the antebellum years. Yet he was all too willing to negotiate a backroom deal, surrounded by other white men, which ended federal support for Reconstruction and cemented the same system he claimed to be dismantling. Ultimately, Hayes's oration and well-wishes were ineffectual and meaningless, leading to a mass exodus of Black people out of the South and rural America as a whole. Some argue that Hayes had no choice and that it was better for him to make small concessions to keep Tilden out of office. Those same historians argue that a Tilden presidency would have been more disastrous, or that even with Republican control of the White House, a Democrat-controlled Congress would never approve funds to add true federal protection for Black people. In doing so, Black Americans were pushed farther away from the land that was their birthright, paid for in sweat equity.

By 4:00 A.M. on March 2, 1877, as dawn rose over the city, the Senate president declared Hayes president-elect. As Lin-Manuel Miranda puts it in *Hamilton*, no one else was in the room where it happened . . . and that is often the case for political decision-making. What we do know is that in exchange for Democrats' agreement to a peaceful transition, President Hayes would end Reconstruction with no pushback from Republicans. All white men involved in the compromise hoped their savviness would lead to political stability, with no regard for the Black communities they had just used as bargaining chips. When the Republican Party of 2020 cited this 1876 election and the subsequent compromise in their attempts to sow discord and uncertainty, it spoke volumes about the sort of outcomes they aspired to.

Two months after his inauguration, Hayes kept up his end of the bargain and ordered the removal of all federal troops from the South, allowing rampant racism a clear path forward, with nothing standing in its way. If, just six years earlier, white supremacists were literally and figuratively running for the hills, this compromise offered them cover to return to their communities with assurance that the criminal justice system would no longer be a system of checks and balances, but a tacit accomplice. Southern Democrats had Hayes's word that he would not federally intervene, which allowed Jim Crow to become law and the second wave of the Ku Klux Klan to proliferate.

And proliferate, they did. Black people—specifically property- and/or land-owning Black people—became the targets of violence in rural communities across the country. The sons and daughters of the Confederacy had received the green light they needed to take (back) "their" country. Under the cover of masks, midnight hours, and white power, organized mobs terrorized Black communities.

As the night of October 6, 1878, gave way to the early morning of October 7, a sixty-year-old farmer and landowner named Stephen Wade became yet another casualty of Hayes's compromise. A *Pittsburgh Commercial Gazette* article dated October 10, 1878, tells the gruesome story of how the white community of Darke County, Ohio, deputized themselves to either exile or execute Mr. Wade. On June 14 of that year, Wade and his three adult sons had been "advised to leave . . . within thirty days, or suffer the penalty." Wade was unmoved and exactly three months later another letter arrived, this time with a picture of a man in a coffin. The letter warned Wade "to leave this county, in haste." Wade remained unmoved.

Less than thirty days from that second letter, as Wade slept beside his wife, terrorists surrounded his home and pointed weapons at every entrance and exit. When they had assumed their positions, a single shot whistled through the night sky, piercing the air and severing the silence. The newspaper article documents what happens next in sordid detail:

> In terror [Wade] got out of his bed and fired once into the mob, but without effect . . . First he ran to the north window and looked out, but the wolves were plainly seen watching for him with ready weapons. Seeing all was in vain, and in a fit of desperation he ran to the back door and intended to escape, but no sooner had he opened it than he received a heavy charge from a shotgun in his left eye, penetrating his brain. He fell saying, "Oh, Lord!" And died without a struggle. At 1 o'clock, when the murderers left, three children and a woman, Wade's housekeeper, came out of the house unhurt but crazed by what had occurred, and ran as fast as they could . . . Wade's three sons were not at home, or it is probable they would have met the same fate.

Reading the article, I'm struck by the level of detail. Who would have known how the mob assembled if Wade, his family, and his staff were fast asleep? Were the killers so brazen as to boast of their conquest? There certainly wouldn't be justice in this case. In fact, a few short decades later, the fairgrounds and county seat would become convening centers for Ku Klux Klan members across the country. The *Pittsburgh Commercial Gazette* article concludes by noting that "no arrests have been made, but some are suspected of being connected with the mob . . . there is a secret organization of a desperate character in Darke County, and the lives of peaceful inhabitants are in danger. The extinction of such an organization has become a necessity." If only the president of the United States at the time believed the same.

My maternal line carries such a story. One that took place almost fifty years after the fateful 1876 election and that has been passed on through oral tradition and corroborated through census and local records. I didn't grow up knowing the sinister experiences that my ancestors had endured, but I felt it in the heavy-handed parenting that sought to keep us out of trouble—seen and unseen. While the cultural emphasis on oral tradition and the waning memories of elder storytellers makes it difficult to parse out all the facts, the fear at the root of this hand-me-down memory is all too real.

My maternal great-grandfather, Robert Howard Carter, grandson of William H. Carter, lived in New Castle, Kentucky, with his parents, Louise and Robert Timothy, and several of his siblings. Together they worked to acquire their piece of the American dream: land.

It is likely that Robert Timothy had been born to the children of "Exodusters," who launched the first wave of mass movement out of the South and toward safety and perceived prosperity. Some Exodusters left the country altogether for places like Liberia, but most went out west to places such as Kansas, Kentucky, and Ohio. In all cases, a fear of the known as well as a hopefulness of the unknown goaded my ancestors out of their Southern homes and toward this abyss. The unknown had to be better than a law weaponized against them, right?

The policy of the Midwest (at the time) was that whoever cleared the land, kept the land. Never mind that the grounds were only overgrown in the first place because those who tended to the land had been forcibly removed. Unfortunately, a former slave's only shot at economic independence involved reappropriating stolen land. Robert Howard, the son of "farm laborers," a nicer term for sharecroppers, must have known how different one's quality of life could be when they owned the land they worked. He had been born into labor just one town over in Campbellsburg, Kentucky. But there in New Castle, there was a new shot at life in a small town where everyone knew everyone and a man could provide for his loved ones. A farm to call your own . . . for the time being.

Born three years after the infamous movie *Birth of a Nation* debuted, Robert Howard Carter was raised with the fear of God *and* white men deeply instilled in him. It was widely known to Black people that white men were lying in wait to snatch the newly cleared land right from under them, and by force. All the work and none of the harvest. Families developed and shared tactics on how to defend themselves against such acts of manipulation—a sort of verbal *Green Book* for owning land while Black. This wouldn't help them in a white man's court of law, but perhaps a show of force could keep them from being taken advantage of.

The flaw in such wishful thinking is that it all boiled down to who could get away with fighting back. It was one thing to talk among yourselves about keeping white folks off your land, but it was another thing entirely to actually attempt to enforce ownership—let alone succeed at it. Having been property themselves only decades before, it was a bold move to assert oneself against any white person—from a child to a grown adult. Word of mouth was all that was needed to keep most Black people "in their place." But in new territory, many hoped a new way of being could be possible.

For weeks leading up to harvesttime, Louise, Robert Timothy, and their sons alternated holding watch. Rain or shine, day or night. Someone was always on watch, prepared to sound the alarm or fight for the land themselves. One dark autumn evening, while the men of the family were out to town handling business, Louise stood watch. Her frame may have been small, but her vigilance didn't falter. Her resilience would surprise everyone—including herself. But the white men lurking in the shadows couldn't have known that, their racism blinding them so. Perceiving her to be an easy target, a gang of white men strutted up to her wooden porch demanding that she get off the land they were now claiming as theirs.

Louise was no dainty woman. Hardened by life in the South, and generally life as a Black woman, she was all too familiar with the entitlement of white men, especially when it came to land and labor. Louise was prepared to defend what was her family's or die trying. When it was clear she wouldn't go down without a fight, that gang of white men picked up their weapons and attacked Louise until they had beaten all resistance out of her.

Thinking her dead, the white men abandoned Louise's body in order to officially lay claim to their new land. Before that could happen, Louise was found by Robert Timothy and her other sons. Traumatized by her broken body, yet motivated by her unscathed spirit, they sought the only justice Black people could hope to find in their world: revenge. It's no shock to me, or anyone well versed in the historic inevitability of righteous youthful rage, that it would be one of the youngest family members to re-fuse to accept brutality as a way of life. Robert Howard saw a clear harm and sought to rectify that with his bare hands. Armed with a description of her attackers, Louise's teenage son, my great-grandfather, located one of the men responsible and killed him.

Just looking in the wrong direction of a white person was an excuse for them to plan a lynching. There's no telling the price that would have been paid if the Carter family remained in the state of Kentucky, let alone New Castle. While I'm sure the whole family affirmed Robert's need to avenge the attack of his mother, they also knew it would cost them the farm Louise had paid for in blood. In the end, white supremacy won, and the land was relinquished, as the entire family fled Kentucky with little besides their lives.

The terror that originally brought them to Kentucky had compounded, carrying the family north to the Ohio River. The next time Robert Timo-thy, Louise, and their children showed up on a U.S. Census, they were in Dayton, Ohio. New Castle was a distant, bitter memory.

Today, New Castle remains a small town with far fewer Black and brown faces. A winding Campbellsburg Road is now peppered with coun-try clubs, wineries, and ponds that stretch out. The sprawling green hills, fenced in, belong to white-operated corporations.

Prior to hearing this story, I didn't know our family tree had any ties to Kentucky. Ohio was all I'd known, and that wasn't by accident. After flee-ing the state, there was no returning . . . including for the descendants. No one set foot in Kentucky again until decades later, when my great-grandfather sought to show his family where he had grown up, and where his children might have grown up, had their lives not been uprooted by white terrorism. Even now, when I ask my maternal grandfather and his siblings about the land left behind and whether they had ever considered returning for it, it is clear that the apprehension of their childhoods was just as present today. *You never know who's holding a grudge.* Years of agricultural investment and generational entrepreneurship were disrupted, but there's no way to calculate the totality of the loss our family paid.

We can only imagine the world where my great-grandfather and his parents felt protected by the criminal legal system, but in the visions I have of that world, that gang of white men would have thought twice about employing such violence against a Black woman and her family. I imagine that the same way my ancestors pass down stories of unspeakable violence, they would have passed down stories about Attorney General Akerman and the Ku Klux Klan members he forced into submission. Elders would have regaled us with stories of how their government committed to their safety through the ensuing decades of continued enforcement of Reconstruction.

To dig even deeper, it's hard to say how much violence could have been thwarted had the election come to a different conclusion, but one thing that cannot be ignored is that rescinding the only show of force against anti-Blackness was the moment America deprioritized equity and justice. When your livelihood and inherent safety are at the whim and will of disgruntled white men on power trips, building economic stability will always be forced into the backseat.

Their confidence in getting away with such brutality would have faltered, but if they chose to ignore the warnings of the federal government, my grandfather might have felt he had options in safeguarding his mother. Had the government chosen the hard work of repair over the convenient work of bipartisanship, they might have fortified the agencies Ulysses Grant established, and the Department of Justice might have been a credible source of protection for Black people of the early twentieth century. Perhaps my family would never have traveled to Kentucky at all if the South had been a home to them as opposed to a purveyor of violence.

But this wasn't the course of action taken. Instead, law enforcement was deputized to protect and serve wealthy landowners, and as a result, the criminal legal system became a public debt collector for those whose fortunes were made before the war. They took and redistributed Black and Indigenous wealth to any white man who was willing to receive it. These

acts did more than victimize specific individuals; they sent Black and Indigenous families into economic holes that couldn't be clawed out of while
white families and businesses made off like literal bandits. This is what's at
stake when powerful people feign helplessness.

In his essay "Nothing Personal," James Baldwin wrote: "I know the
myth tells us that heroes came, looking for freedom . . . but the relevant
truth is that this country was settled by a desperate, divided, and rapa-
cious horde of people who were determined to forget their pasts and determined to make money." The wealth gaps cemented during this era
would only widen over the next century, and the acts of terrorism needed
to maintain this hierarchy unleashed unspeakable trauma on generations
of Black people.

PART TWO

===

THE PHOENIXES

Hope is a discipline.

—MARIAME KABA

CHILDREN OF THE DARK ARE WISER

(1865–1900)

═══════

I was resolved to fight.

—FREDERICK DOUGLASS

Even with the odds stacked against them, as the nineteenth century drew to a close, Black Americans continued to chip away at inequity, carving out corners of the country for their safety and sanity. Page Harris of Maryland was born in 1858, on a plantation infamously known as "Blood Hound Manor" because of their vicious canines, bred for the sole purpose of tracking fugitive enslaved people. Following emancipation, Page attended some of the first segregated schools for Black children before working in a naval shipyard as a waiter. By 1897, Page had voraciously tucked away his earnings and used that savings to purchase a 120-acre vegetable garden.

Berry Smith, known affectionately as "Uncle Berry," also knew the violence of slavery intimately. "Born an' bred in Sumter County, Alabama," he picked cotton both as an enslaved child and as a free young man. When the Emancipation Proclamation was signed and Uncle Berry attempted to claim his freedom, his former enslaver threatened to whip him, causing Berry to flee. While hiding in nearby woods, Berry found work cooking for soldiers and working for railroads when he could. After years of working, Uncle Berry purchased forty-seven acres and a quaint home.

In less than a decade, people who had been treated as property in the eyes of the law asserted their right to own rather than to be owned. In the aftermath of the Civil War, according to a study by Dr. Loren Schweninger, one in five free Black heads of households had become property owners. People like Monroe Brackens, who was born in Mississippi in 1853 and was freed from bondage at the age of six or seven. He worked most of his young life as a cowboy, wrangling and breaking wild horses for white employers. He eventually bought eighty acres of land in Medina County, Texas, where he raised sugarcane, grew watermelon, and rode horses. In his thirties, Monroe married and settled down in Oklahoma after leveraging his Texas farm to purchase a new one. Proof of life.

Dr. Schweninger writes, "It is difficult to view this period without being struck by the remarkable expansion of [B]lack property owning." These rates were highest amongst Black men, urbanites, and mixed-race Black people, which speaks to the pervasive nature of patriarchy, colorism, and the consolidation of white power in small towns. Green Willbanks was a fair-skinned man who called Georgia home all of his life. He recalls never having any money of his own during slavery because "children were not allowed to do much work . . . and had few opportunities to earn money." This carried into post-emancipation, where Green recalls very few Black people owning land just after the war by nature of their lack of capital. He and his wife, Molly, purchased a plot of land and farmed it most of their adult lives. "In fact," he recalled, "I have never done nothing but farm work." It was easiest to access capital and buy land when you were someone white men wanted to do business with. And yet, the fact remains that Black people were surviving every scheme intended to destroy them.

In each of these cases, Black people sought land ownership as their path to controlling their own destinies. Beatrice Black was born free and married young in Biscoe, Arkansas. Her father-in-law served in the Civil War and used his earnings to purchase forty acres from the government. Into her old age, this plot of land became a refuge—somewhere all of her children and their extended families were able to sustain themselves. White people couldn't starve you if they weren't your source of produce. They couldn't make you homeless if they didn't own the land you lived on. They couldn't deprive you if you didn't depend on them in the first place.

As far as contemporary political frameworks go, socialism may seem too steeped in theory to be materially helpful to marginalized people. But across the nineteenth and early twentieth centuries, socialism was the de facto way that Black communities organized themselves and lived. Safety in numbers and evenly distributed resources. The first Black American landowners held land communally with siblings, parents, adult children, and extended loved ones. William Williams was born into slavery to two Black parents living on two neighboring plantations. Just after Williams's birth, his father was sold away; three years later, so was William. Thankfully, they were one of few lucky Black families able to find one another post–Civil War. By then, Williams's father had acquired more than a hundred acres, several mules, and plenty of food. A bounty for his newly reunited family. Land was something generations of Black people had access to and benefited from. The greatest antidote for white resentment and jealousy was Black solidarity.

My own ancestors did the same when purchasing land alongside fellow parishioners and distributing among siblings and grandchildren. My family, based in northeastern North Carolina just on the outskirts of the former capital of the Confederacy, knew this well. Louis's son, Frank W. Baker, inherited his parcel of the Baker tract and set out to turn it into a profitable farm capable of sustaining his growing family. On a crisp fall day in 1892, Frank W. married his second wife, Annie B., in Warren County, North Carolina. Both Frank W. and Annie B., the daughter of Civil War veteran Edmond T. Jones, came from families who had the foresight not only to envision, but also to fight for, their liberation. Louis would pass away less than a decade after their union, but his legacy lived on through the piece of earth his son and daughter-in-law cultivated together. To paraphrase Dr. Maya Angelou: Still, like dust, they rose.

You can't take land with you when you pass away, but in this physical world where land is a form of capital, you can create an economic impact for future generations. The ability to bequeath capital limns the racialized chasm separating the haves and the have-nots in America. Those who had the capacity to grow their landholdings, and who exercised their right to leave that land to their descendants, enjoyed far greater economic opportunities/freedoms than those who did not.

In many instances, finding someone from whom to purchase land was easier said than done. As Dr. Schweninger documents in *Black Property Owners in the South, 1790–1915,* "In many sections of the Mississippi Valley if a white man or woman sold land to a [Black person] he or she might be physically attacked. Every effort was made to 'prevent negroes from acquiring lands' . . . One Alabama planter boasted during the early months after the war, 'it won't need any law for that. Planters will have an understanding among themselves: you won't hire my niggers, and I won't hire yours.'" A similar experience of economic isolation was felt across Delaware, Maryland, and Virginia. "In portions of Delaware and Maryland, white vigilante groups scoured the countryside, burning [B]lack churches, schools, and farmhouses."

Yet, in spite of the exclusion placing them at an extreme disadvantage, Black landowners continued to rise. According to Schweninger's research, by 1870, Mississippi and Georgia "led all states in the total number of [Black] property owners." He goes on to report that "in rural areas of the Trans-Appalachian West, former[ly enslaved people] in the upper tier of states possessed advantages over their brethren in the Deep South. In some areas, whites were not opposed to [B]lack proprietorship. Some even assisted freedmen and women in their quests for self-sufficiency." In 1860, there were 775 Black realty owners, and in just ten years that number had jumped to more than 6,500. The number of rural landholders in Kentucky, Tennessee, and Missouri rose a staggering 744 percent.

The growth of Black wealth and Black landholdings increased even more exponentially from 1870 to 1890. Generally, the percentage of Black farm owners across the South rose by over 500 percent with some states, like Texas, boasting a surge of 1,391 percent and Virginia seeing a rise of 1,490 percent. What exactly was the monetary value of this growth? According to Schweninger, by 1910, fewer than 150,000 Black owners controlled land valued at $165 million. Adjusted for inflation, this is a whopping $4.7 billion! (Yes, that's billion with a *b*.)

———

Not too far from Frank W. and Annie B., another (seemingly unrelated) pair of Bakers were also building their life in northeastern North Carolina. Though their upbringings felt worlds away, Blake and Georgianna Baker's love brought them together in the 1890s. While Blake came from a family of sharecroppers, Georgianna's parents—Mitchell and Josephine Ross— were not only Black landowners, but also literate. As a community pillar and Baptist preacher, Mitchell had learned quickly how to advance in the U.S. South. Blake and Georgianna met in school, where they quickly bonded over their love for family and their ambition to circumvent the roadblocks placed before them. They committed to doing so together.

While expanding their farm, Blake and Anna never lost sight of community. There was a notion at the time—and to this day—that successful or wealthy Black families should distance themselves from other Black Americans once given the chance. For some, this stemmed from ego and the desire to be seen as different from the many negative stereotypes associated with predominantly Black spaces. For others, it was a survival tactic. But the reality was that Black people were far safer in community with one another than they were in their silos.

Georgianna and Blake certainly knew this to be true, and it was this sense of commitment to working-class Black people that they would later pass on to their three surviving children, including future freedom fighter and civil rights leader Ella Baker. After purchasing land from their former enslaver in 1888, the Rosses—Ella's maternal grandparents—became well-respected for a "kinship-based system" through which they leveraged their resources for the benefit of every Black family around them. According to John Horhn in "They Had No King: Ella Baker and the Politics of Decentralized Organization Among African-Descended Populations":

> Their land resources enabled them to help smaller families who were either unable to support themselves, or did not have access to farming equipment. Baker explained that at certain points her grandfather would allow access to their wheat threshing machine to enable black farmers who were unable to afford the cost of such machinery or services elsewhere, the opportunity to process crops. The family also engaged in a kind of barter and trade system with the local community. This system provided food security and guaranteed the needs of the local African-American community were met. This process had the added benefit of enhancing group coop-

eration and social cohesion as a by-product. Ella Baker noted these dynamics and later put them to use as National Director of the Young Negro Cooperative League (YNCL) years later.

Ella Baker credited her maternal grandparents for her emphasis on grassroots organizing. This socialism-in-practice was reminiscent of the maroon communities that sprung up across the antebellum South. In some instances, plantations abandoned by disgraced Confederate soldiers were reclaimed by free Black people and transformed into all-Black settlements.

A *Chicago Tribune* article from 1865 describes one such example of "occupancy and improvement by freedmen" of "abandoned lands of rebels" not too far from Hampton, Virginia. A former plantation of approximately four or five hundred acres was discovered to have been settled by over eight hundred Black families totaling five thousand people, with over a thousand children. Each family had constructed their own home, along with communal spaces for worshiping, working, and playing. They built five churches and two grocery stores. The community even elected a governing body and raised communal funds for legal representation to defend their rights to the land. Where the government had failed them, Black people filled the cracks on their own.

While most Southern Black people would need to wait for the end of the Civil War to partake in land ownership, the North had already opened the door to self-determination. One of the most widely known yet tragic examples of early Black American land ownership (and later, expulsion) took place in what is now the most visited urban park in the nation: New York City's Central Park. Before Manhattan elites decided they needed a green oasis, from 1825 to 1857 the area was known as Seneca Village, home to hundreds of people, the majority of whom were Black.

Clint Smith wrote that "the historical significance was not simply that the Black people living there were free, or even that the community eventually became peacefully integrated; it was also that many of the Black residents owned property. Owning property gave them stability, some measure of economic security, and, as per law passed at the 1821 Constitutional Convention, the right to vote." This was not mere happenstance. In fact,

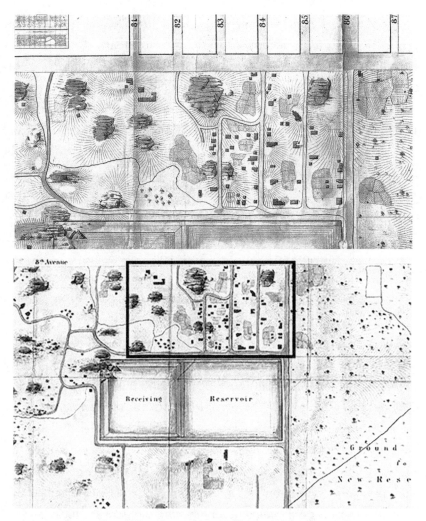

Maps of Seneca Village drawn up by Egbert Ludovicus Viele,
Central Park's chief civil engineer.

Seneca Village became the premier destination for landed Black people. One in five property-owning Black people in New York City at the time lived in Seneca Village, a foreshadowing of what was possible if Black people were given the chance to participate economically and politically.

Initially home to the Lenape or Delaware tribe, the area had formerly been called *Manahatta,* translating to "hilly island." Lenape peoples experienced a lush green field overflowing with fruit trees, nuts, and biodiversity until the fifteenth century, when Dutch migrants tricked the Indigenous people out of their land and violently expelled them. (Which is redundant, because to push someone out of their home is inherently violent.) A wall was quickly constructed to prevent Lenape people from returning to reclaim their ancestral home. That is how Wall Street got its name.

Over the next two centuries, *Manahatta* would be renamed Manhattan and would change hands between Dutch, British, and white Americans until a white farmer named John Whitehead came to own it in the early 1800s. He and his wife broke the land up into lots and began marketing the approximately two hundred available parcels. One of the first recorded buyers was a Black man named Andrew Williams, followed by the AME Zion Church, a Black congregation. About ten years later, a similar and nearby Black community known as "York Hill" was destroyed when the city claimed their land for the creation of a new water system. With that, the floodgates opened and Seneca Village became home to Black families who were pushed out with few other options.

For a few decades, Seneca Village was prosperous and peaceful. The majority of the community remained a Black enclave but, over time, many European migrants, especially Irish people, moved in, eventually making up about a third of Seneca Village's residents. By the 1850s, white ire set its sights on the Black residents taking up space in the center of their city. Seneca Village had become colloquially referred to as "Nigger Village" by wealthy white people. These influential people and their publications (including what we now know as *The New York Times*) launched a narrative campaign to taint public perception, opening the door for local government and city planners to step in. The city used eminent domain—the right of a government to discriminately seize private property for public use—to kick the mostly Black residents out, forcing them to start over from scratch, without even the full value of their previous landholdings.

Before this coup, Seneca Village had been a beacon of hope, a testament to what is possible when those of different races and ethnicities live in true community with one another. Seneca Village's demise signaled to Black people that to sustain land ownership, they'd need a buffer from white neighbors whose jealousy might threaten their collective livelihood. Dr. Alaina E. Roberts noted this when she commented, "Because white farmers refused to include them in farming cooperatives, African American farmers did not homestead alone. To support one another, they settled near each other's farms." What would start as one or two families seeking refuge would swell into entire all-Black towns based on the desire—and need—for proximity. Many were founded away from the East Coast in more sparsely populated parts of the country where self-governance was still possible, even for Black Americans. Today, a small sign in Oklahoma reads: A FEW ALL-BLACK TOWNS SURVIVE BUT ALL ARE REMEMBERED, a legacy of economic and political freedom.

————

The journey to land ownership for most Black people in the nineteenth century began with monetizing their work ethic, which had previously only been profitable for white people. For as long as Black people had lived in the Americas, work had been expected from them for nothing in return. Here was the chance to put a dollar amount on their labor. The ability to navigate workplaces without being cheated by employers or corporate buyers could mean surplus funds for buying land, building homes, and investing in a family's future. Thus, Black land ownership was directly tied to the fast-changing labor movement and the ability to earn a fair wage for one's work.

George Washington Carver was one of the more prominent Black leaders who made it his mission to ensure Black farmers understood their economic power, as tied to the land. A scientist by trade and an environmentalist by soul, Carter traveled throughout the South teaching Black sharecroppers and landowners about the many uses for the crops they were growing, and about some they hadn't considered before. Peanuts, he offered, could be affordably processed and sold as soaps, rubber, paper, flower, and even cosmetic products. Carver also cautioned against soil depletion and taught the practices of regeneration as opposed to maximization. He disseminated knowledge like this to prove that we could accomplish a lot independently by developing our relationship with the land.

Unfortunately, Black Americans weren't just competing against the greed of wealthy white people who wanted to retain cheap (or free) labor; they were also up against working-class whites who now blamed the influx of Black workers for their own unemployment. Instead of blaming racial capitalism for treating human beings like commodities, many white-led unions attacked Black workers who didn't always have the option to with-hold labor for better rates. Many that weren't openly antagonistic were unwilling to openly collaborate with Black farmers and barred them from union membership.

A few predominantly white groups did, however, see the opportunity to build a cross-racial movement on behalf of all agricultural workers. Richard Manning Humphrey opened up his farm and community plat-form to the Black farmers in Texas who founded the Colored Farmers' National Alliance and Cooperative Union. The Colored Farmers' Alliance offered trainings, organized strikes, and worked with members to help them become (and stay) debt-free. The Agricultural Workers' Organiza-tion (AWO) pooled resources to extend credit and start-up equipment to Black farmers for the creation of cooperative grocery stores, mills, credit unions, and farms. Some groups even retained legal representation to ad-vocate for fair wages, and organized labor strikes when necessary. But they were a minority.

In her book *Collective Courage: A History of African American Coop-erative Economic Thought and Practice,* Jessica Gordon Nembhard docu-ments this legacy of collaborating for survival. "If [Black] household members pooled their energies to make a good crop, and if communities collectively provided for their own welfare, then poverty and oppression ruled out most of the alternative strategies. Individualism was a luxury that sharecroppers simply could not afford." Through the late nineteenth cen-tury and early twentieth century, Black land ownership existed in Black-owned faith spaces, schools, and homesteads that entire families could benefit from. Collective ownership was key for people who couldn't afford to purchase land on their own, or who wanted to build something that could enable their whole community to thrive. This was especially true for Black landowners surrounded by white Americans who resented their sta-tion in life.

Overwhelmingly, one of the most influential and most consistent forces driving Black land ownership and wealth building was the Black church. Black churches began as spaces of emotional reprieve to cope with the toll of white supremacy. Post-emancipation, preachers rushed to secure acreage that could house their congregations. These Black churches were at the front line of fulfilling urgent needs for the Black community, from financing childhood education to recording oral history. They were crucial spaces in which to educate the community, acting as a buffer between violent white America and church members who were attempting to carve out a life.

Black churches have helped ensure the stability and prosperity of Black people. Many scholars have rightfully criticized the ways Christianity was both introduced to and weaponized against Black Americans, as well as the oppressive role evangelical Christianity has played in American politics. Still, many Black clergy and faith leaders re-appropriated the Christianity of their masters into a tool toward liberation, and they extended tangible support to their parishioners.

There is something to be said about how the church has specifically helped finance Black land ownership. In some instances, churches complemented the work of the Freedmen's Bureau in uplifting and expanding Black banking institutions. As John Hope Franklin and Alfred A. Moss Jr. reiterated in *From Slavery to Freedom,* "The church served as an agency for the improvement of the social and moral conditions among Negroes . . . In Atlanta, H. H. Proctor's Congregational Church organized a day nursery, kindergarten, gymnasium, school of music, employment bureau, and Bible school."

Karen Cook Bell explores this phenomenon in her book *Claiming Freedom,* where she recounts that the "church became the center for everything and played a major role in holding the community together . . . land and religion had complementary roles in that these two elements structured the community." Common fundraising tactics that originated in late nineteenth-century Black churches include building funds, which have remained a staple in the community. Growing up, as the daughter and granddaughter of Pentecostal and Baptist pastors, I saw posters with drawn thermostats measuring the status of fundraising efforts. Building funds maintained the church facilities and expanded them. My church home in New Haven, Connecticut, was host to blood drives, extracurricular activities for children, and many other community services for the predominantly Black area. My grandparents' church in New York also served as a food bank, with plans to build affordable housing for the elderly. These institutions were always more than places of worship.

Building funds are a way that churches and other houses of faith crowdsource the finances needed to acquire land, build edifices, and/or maintain property. Typically signified with a publicly displayed marker of fundraising progress, these funds are characterized by community accountability and community ownership. Everyone contributes and everyone watches the fund grow over time. "In the process of institution building," Bell expounds, "nearly every African American community in low country Georgia sought to secure title to land for church purposes. In the AME Church, as well as in other churches, committees on deeds and homesteads were established in each district of South Georgia for this purpose." According to W. E. B. Du Bois's 1907 report on economic cooperation among "Negro Americans," in 1876, the AME church raised $169,558.60 in one year.

Bell goes on to share the story of First Bryan Baptist Church and a Black woman parishioner, Elizabeth Edy. Edy made monthly contributions to the building fund of her church, paying three dollars regularly toward rebuilding on a new site. In instances like these, churchgoers become stakeholders in land and edifices they wouldn't have been able to afford alone. These churches became venues for celebrations, sources of emotional comforts, and eventually even burial sites. Further, the building funds proved incredibly successful both for the expansion of Black churches and the inspiration implanted in the minds of participants. Many Black Southerners hadn't even dared to dream of a life beyond sharecropping until their pastor showed the power of collective action. If these all-Black organizations could raise capital and hold deeds to land across the South, what was stopping their patrons from exerting their own power in similar ways?

———

At the eastern edge of Warren County, North Carolina, just before reaching Halifax County, about a ten-minute drive from Lovely Hill Baptist Church, sits Judkins Township. The township used to be encapsulated in what was colloquially known as "the Baker community," because much of the land was part of the tract of land purchased by Louis Baker. As of the 2020 Census, Judkins Township had just under seven hundred residents and is an even smaller community than it was almost a century before.

Within the township, which begins at Halifax Public Road, is a school for Black children, one of the first in the county.

There are very few records on nineteenth- and twentieth-century schools serving Black students, so it's been difficult to imagine what the school looked like in its prime. If you let my Aunt Sue tell it, she and her siblings used to visit throughout her childhood. "It was a one-room building and we called it the 'primary' at the time. I believe it went up to the ninth grade, that school." If you were to look at a 1993 edition of the Baker family-reunion book, you'd read that "around the turn of the century, Louis' son Albert realized the need for a school for young [Black people] and deeded a portion of his land to the Warren County Board of Education for a school." A deed from Warren County confirms that on October 28, 1901, Albert Baker gifted an acre to the "colored" Public School Committee in exchange for a symbolic five dollars, far below its market value even back then.

Albert Baker and his wife, Pinkie Baker.

Land meant autonomy. Landless people were at the mercy of local, racist governments but those with deeds had the ability to build a school, set their own hours, and ensure the classroom was physically accessible to the entire community. Albert's yearning to extend a true education to the young people of his community was not an isolated act. In the early 1900s, a grassroots educational movement led by Booker T. Washington lit Black, rural America ablaze. As the goalpost shifted, it was no longer enough to know how to care for land. One needed to profit from land and avoid trickery, which would require being able to read and keep ledgers. This would be especially critical for Black landowners looking to do more than break even and actually run enterprising and competitive businesses.

The public commitment to education was an act of assimilation into "American" ideals of success and legitimacy while also ensuring a unique cultural experience for Black children. With the Baker School, Louis and Nancy's lifework carried new meaning, not only providing for their children but for all of the Black children of the township. This is the legacy that Albert helped to expand, just as education was becoming the new frontier of economic mobility for Black people. In her book *South to America,* Dr. Imani Perry underscores for readers that "the reach of institutions that nurtured Black children in the wake of a white supremacist order is much broader than most of us, even in African American studies, realize."

Thousands of Rosenwald Schools, named for the main financier, Julius Rosenwald, were built nationwide. One to three teachers taught as many Black students as the schoolhouse walls could squeeze into the classroom. Many of the physical buildings looked more like wooden cabins or trailer homes, yet they brimmed with groups of students thirsty for even a sliver of what was readily accessible to their white "peers." Some schoolhouses, constructed of brick, were spacious enough to fit more than two or three classrooms, and they mostly depended on access to land. In a world of separate and extremely unequal, Black children couldn't depend on government-funded schools being available to them. Townships and counties with few resources regularly prioritized building schools for white children with no thought toward what Black students would do. Many schools serving Black children were situated in larger cities, leaving the millions of Black people in rural areas with long commutes, often on foot.

The few schools available to rural Black children often opened and closed around the planting and harvesting schedules, proving that their labor was prioritized higher than their right to education. Even when school was in session, if there was a need, a Black child could be pulled out of class by a parent or the white farm owner that the family sharecropped for. (This happened more often than one would think.)

Educational institutions for Black students of all ages began to pop up across the South in order to meet the need created by segregation. In less than a decade, one in three rural Black children was being educated in a Rosenwald School. These and similar schools helped Black towns and communities achieve their identity as spaces of Black independence and social status. Several of these institutions specifically focused on providing Black youth the education needed to compete in the agrarian economy. Many built school schedules that completely revolved around planting and harvesting. The vast majority of students at the Baker School would have needed to ensure their education didn't get in the way of helping out at home.

Several Negro Schools Begin Work for Year

In order that there may be a recess to allow children to pick cotton several of the four-months negro schools of Warren have begun there 1930-31 session and others will open next week ,it was learned yesterday at the office of the superintendent of schools.

Schools which opened on Monday include Jordan Hill, Mayflower, Fork Chapel, Stony Lawn Vaughan, Johnson Baltimore, Baker, Axtelle special.

Schools to open on Monday are Pine Grove, Shocco Chapel, Young, Oakville, Rising Sun, Ridgeway.

A Warren Record *article from 1930 mentioning the Baker School.*

According to research conducted by Andrew Feiler for his book *A Better Life for Their Children: Julius Rosenwald, Booker T. Washington, and the 4,978 Schools That Changed America,* many civil rights leaders were products of Rosenwald Schools, including Maya Angelou and John Lewis.

While over eight hundred Rosenwald Schools were built across North
Carolina—more than any other state could boast—it's difficult to say
whether the Baker School was a Rosenwald School built on donated land,
or someone else was responsible for funding its construction. As is the
case with many rural schools for Black children, the building no longer
stands and few records were preserved for state archives. What we do
know is that the school served the local community for about four decades
as one of few opportunities for Black children to receive a robust education from teachers who looked like and be-
lieved in them. Until its closing in 1953,
hundreds of families depended on Albert's
benevolence to fill in the gaps that Jim Crow
created.

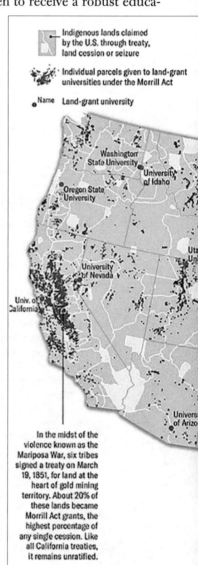

Indigenous lands claimed
by the U.S. through treaty,
land cession or seizure

Individual parcels given to land-grant
universities under the Morrill Act

Name   Land-grant university

It was easy to project one's hopes and
dreams onto education, as had occurred with
the land. After centuries of being barred from
reading and writing, the turn of the century
presented some of the first non-clandestine
paths to being Black and educated in America. Where did land tie into things? The
American economy was still agrarian and
most students were being educated to lead
profitable farming enterprises. Additionally,
students needed schools and those buildings
needed land.

Enter the twentieth-century apartheid
education system where quality instruction,
facilities, and resources were reserved for the
white and wealthy. Many predominantly
white institutions founded before the 1900s
benefited from legislation designed to replace
Indigenous people with white settlers, and
schools became a great vehicle to do so. The
Morrill Act of 1862, sponsored by a representative from Vermont and signed into law by

In the midst of the
violence known as the
Mariposa War, six tribes
signed a treaty on March
19, 1851, for land at the
heart of gold mining
territory. About 20% of
these lands became
Morrill Act grants, the
highest percentage of
any single cession. Like
all California treaties,
it remains unratified.

President Lincoln, stole and sold more than eleven million acres of land across the Midwest that was previously home to more than two hundred Native American tribes.

High Country News completed a years-long assessment of "Morrill Act acres," and its findings were damning. The U.S. government raised more than $17 million on the backs of displaced Indigenous people and redistributed the money through grants that served as the foundation for college endowments at more than fifty universities. Some land was never sold

---

The Morrill Act gave **79,461 parcels of Indigenous land,** totaling about **10,700,000 acres,** to **52 land-grant universities (LGUs)** to fund their endowments

In Gage County, Neb., 40% of the land was given to Morrill Act parcels, the second highest amount of any county. The lands were acquired through the June 3, 1825 Treaty with the Kaw.

The Treaty of 1837 contributed 1,062,334 acres, more than any other land cession, to 33 LGUs. The result for LGUs was $3,257,230 paid to their endowments, the highest profits gained from any one cession.

North Dakota State University

University of Maine

University of Vermont

Univ. of New Hampshire

University of Massachusetts

Cornell University

South Dakota State University

University of Minnesota

University of Connecticut

MIT

Univ. of Rhode Island

Iowa State University

University of Wisconsin

Michigan State University

Penn State University

Colorado State University

University of Nebraska

Purdue University

Ohio State University

West Virginia University

Rutgers University

University of Delaware

University of Maryland

University of Illinois

Kansas State University

University of Missouri

Kentucky State University

Virginia Tech

University of Kentucky

Virginia State University

North Carolina State University

University of Arkansas

University of Tennessee

Clemson University

Mississippi State University

University of Georgia

South Carolina State University

Alcorn State University

Auburn University

Texas A&M University

Louisiana State University

University of Florida

SOURCES: Andrews 1918; GLO, BLM; Royce 1896–1897; USFS; USGS; Natural Earth.

Map by Margaret Pearce for High Country News.

and at least a dozen predominantly white universities are, even today, the legal owners. As was shared in the study by Tristan Ahtone and Robert Lee, "Today, these acres form the landscape of the United States. On Morrill Act lands there now stand churches, schools, bars, baseball diamonds, parking lots, hiking trails, billboards, restaurants, vineyards, cabarets, hayfields, gas stations, airports and residential neighborhoods . . . In Missoula, Montana, a Walmart Supercenter sits on land originally ceded by the Pend d'Oreille, Salish and Kootenai to fund Texas A&M."

Only three Black institutions profited from the initial Morrill Act by nature of the legislation being passed when most Black people were still enslaved: Alcorn State University in Mississippi, Claflin University in South Carolina, and Hampton University in Virginia. In 1890, a second Morrill Act was passed to include Black institutions like Tuskegee University. The unprecedented federal funding was welcomed by many in the Black community, yet made the institutions complicit in ongoing efforts to displace Native Americans and train Black students to better serve the agricultural economy. Blood money. Dr. Alaina E. Roberts describes similar points in American history as "rare moment[s] when settler colonialism worked in favor of Black people."

In their defense, though, it was white hands and minds that begot most historically Black colleges and universities (HBCUs). So it makes sense that white supremacy would fund white visions of the world, even if the target clientele were Black students. Take Hampton University, situated in Virginia, the heart of the former Confederacy. It was first called Hampton Normal and Agricultural Institute and then simply Hampton Institute. Like many of the first and most prestigious HBCUs, Hampton was founded and funded by a white man on Indigenous land.

Samuel Chapman Armstrong was a major nineteenth-century white philanthropist who founded what is now known as Hampton University. Armstrong initially collaborated with and mentored many prominent Black Americans, including Booker T. Washington. His focus was the education of Black and Indigenous people. Armstrong was deeply influenced by his father, Richard, a missionary—or colonizer—known as the "father of American education in Hawaii." Richard Armstrong and his wife had ten children and their third, William Nevins Armstrong, would later become the attorney general of Hawaii as well as the president of the state's Board of Immigration for a handful of years. Their sixth child, Samuel, would take what he had learned about assimilation to the mainland United States.

Samuel Armstrong had a specific vision for the sort of education Black people needed. Local Black Virginians, including Hampton University students, were calling for sovereignty and self-determination. Armstrong believed he knew better and pushed back. Instead, he would accommodate the creation of a colonized, agrarian South in which Black self-improvement would take place within a model set by elite whites, and within a world controlled by them. Armstrong sought to educate the future laborers of the agricultural South, not to empower a subjugated class to resist their oppression. Workers only, never owners. Students, never teachers. Audre Lorde's warning about the master's tools being insufficient comes to mind.

At Hampton and other white-helmed educational institutions, the white gaze reigned supreme. Though initially focused on training Black people, the university soon set its eyes on Indigenous youth. With displacement and rapid settlement of land across the Midwest came the issue of what to do with the survivors. Many believed schools were the perfect place to de-radicalize righteously angry Native young people and assimilate them into white American culture. Armstrong realized that Native youth might resist these efforts if they came from white men, sparking the idea that perhaps Black Americans could teach their Native peers about the virtues of Christianity. In turn, Indigenous students were expected to teach their tribes the good news of what whiteness had done for them. Armstrong described this dual mission in 1888: "You see I've only . . . boosted darkies a bit, and so to speak, lassoed wild Indians all to be cleaned and tame by a simple process I have invented known as the 'Hampton method.'" All this in the pursuit of more land and more labor to sustain America, the newest global power.

The first seventeen Indigenous students were brought to Hampton as prisoners of war from Florida. In their first several years at Hampton, Indigenous students were pulled from their families and tribes to learn under Armstrong's watchful eye. Most were Lakota, Iroquois, Seneca, and Cherokee, but more than sixty tribes would come to be represented on the burgeoning campus. All students were expected to complete "apprenticeships," a euphemism for continued forced labor at the university's farms and workrooms. On any given day, one could find Black and Native Hamptonites tilling land, sewing clothes, and constructing furniture with wood, tin, or iron.

While Armstrong's vision wasn't what either community wanted, it made for a great fundraising strategy. White Americans from all walks of life—Christian missionaries, Union veterans, and nonprofits—rushed to hand over whatever they could afford toward the enrichment of these "undisciplined races," as university administrators referred to them. In an 1885 overview of Hampton's growth and development, two high-ranking white women instructors at the Institute reflected on the university's wins. "To Negro and Indian alike the gospel of work comes as a revelation, and while it is not always accepted without a struggle, yet none the less is its

Louis Firetail (Sioux, Crow Creek), wearing
tribal clothing, in American history class, Hampton Institute,
Hampton, Virginia, in the late 1890s
(LIBRARY OF CONGRESS'S FRANCES BENJAMIN JOHNSTON COLLECTION).

influence healthful and strengthening, and the record of our graduates of both races shows that Labor and Prayer are weapons of which most of them have learned, in part at least, the unconquerable power."

White guilt was transformed into green dollars as Northerners raced to make themselves feel better through narcissistic humanitarianism. Sending money to educate Black and Indigenous children of the South was easier than looking inward at how those above the Mason-Dixon Line profited from and enabled the violence happening in the South. Their donations were self-soothing, self-serving, and very influential. By the turn of the century, Hampton was the wealthiest school serving predominantly Black students.

———

The end of the nineteenth century and beginning of the twentieth left Black and Indigenous communities at a crossroads. Both groups felt distinctly un-American and yet they started down separate paths toward making the best of an undeniably horrific situation. The brilliant poet, and my sister-friend, Terisa Siagatonu reminds us that "America happened to so many of us without consent." But the nation building had, indeed, happened. Now what? Many Indigenous tribes had tried armed resistance as well as diplomatic treaties, and both tactics had ended in their displacement. The thirst for land proved to be insatiable as promise after promise was broken and tribes were moved, and then moved again, until it was abundantly clear that a white man's word meant nothing.

Black Americans had never even been offered the illusion of negotiation or promise of equity, so there were few feelings of betrayal. Instead, Black folks wondered how to make the white man's government work for them. How to trick a trickster. How to convince a thief to share his spoils. How to shuck and jive in order to lull white America into believing we cared to belong.

As westward encroachment continued on violently, the U.S. federal government attempted to again assuage Indigenous fears by opening up allotment processes to Black and Indigenous families. Many Native Americans (understandably) refused to participate in the outrageous exercise. Black Americans saw this as a chance to even out the playing field and finally carve out a piece of this land for themselves.

With each new piece of legislation—the 1887 Dawes Act, the Dawes Commission of 1893, the 1889 Land Run—Black folks claimed more and more acreage, though never more than the white Americans for whose benefit the legislation was intended. Further, as white America descended deeper inland to newer territories and states, Black people reclaimed the coastal South that was left behind. Some former plantation owners abandoned land that had been destroyed by the Union Army in favor of a fresh start. Others were beginning to see the signs of the land being too stripped from overplanting and not enough crop rotation.

The University of Maryland estimates that about 60 percent of Southern plantations were deserted post–Civil War. A different paper, in the *American Economic Review*, affirms that white slaveholding families lost a significant amount of wealth directly following emancipation but then recouped those losses within one or two generations. Seeing more economic opportunity out west, and an easier path to those frontiers through the railroad boom, many prominent white families sold their land in Virginia and the Carolinas, as well as along the lower Mississippi River in Arkansas, Louisiana, and Mississippi, for pennies on the dollar to whomever they deemed foolish enough to purchase it. Other former slavers shifted their remaining fortunes from agricultural investments to textiles, manufacturing, and other industries up north that were beginning to boom.

Property values across the South dropped and white people scrambled to salvage their net worth while Black people saw green—not money, but a new beginning. In his book *The Land Was Ours,* Andrew Kahrl documents this moment in time where preparation met opportunity: "Coastal lands that once generated considerable wealth for the South's slavocracy and sold for upwards of $5,000 per acre before the war could, by the 1870s, be fetched for $50 an acre or less. Other stretches of southern coastlines remained, as they were before war and emancipation, forsaken and forgotten—the land of mosquitoes, predatory animals, dense forests, and sandy, non-arable soil. As a result, coastal zones became ripe for Black landownership."

The Black people who settled there were no fools; they knew the land was in need of rehabilitation, but some land was better than none. Accustomed to making a dollar out of fifteen cents, as we say, these new Black

A 1910 advertisement (MPI/GETTY IMAGES).

landowners got to work restoring the land. Some continued farming, whether for self-subsistence or as their primary family business. Others ventured into new terrain, opening resorts, beaches, and other spaces of recreation.

Against all meticulously designed odds, by the turn of the century, Black Americans owned almost one million farms, making up approximately 14 percent of the nation's farmland, mostly across the South. Many Black folks hoped it was just the beginning of their newfound prosperity. Most white folks were betting on the opposite.

ANYTHING YOU CAN DO,
I CAN DO BETTER

===

**Freeing yourself was one thing,
claiming ownership of that freed self was another.**

—TONI MORRISON

Black women—based on their unique experiences at the intersection of race, class, and gender in the twentieth century—were focused on survival and resistance, which ultimately pushed them toward land ownership. Though erased in many ways, Black women were as much part of the land-owning movement as Black men. When Louis Baker purchased more than three hundred acres in 1873, he didn't do it alone; Nancy Harris was right there with him. When Louis later married Nellie Williams, my great-great-great-grandmother, it was the land he purchased with Nancy that would be passed down to his children with Nellie. My family line benefited from Nancy's labor and foresight.

When Louis's son Frank W. came of age, he expanded upon that inheritance with his wife, Annie B. Jones. Together and over the course of many decades, the two purchased land and Annie ensured that her name was on those deeds. History would know she was an integral part of their marital team, as opposed to a silent beneficiary. Frank W. and Annie's children were now the third generation of free Black people. Their daughters, Pattie Lee and Hattie Bell, born in 1893 and 1897 respectively, lived on their parents' farm their entire lives. This birthright would ensure they joined the ranks of land-owning Black women in the early twentieth century who didn't need to depend on men for financial security. As is the case with many Black women born prior to the mid-twentieth century, little is known about Hattie and Pattie except that they lived very peculiar lives. Though four years apart in age, the girls were raised almost like twins and were deeded land by their parents in 1940. Sadly, Hattie died just ten years later, in January 1950, and Pattie would follow her to the grave just a few months after that. The sisters lived and died together, leaving their landholdings to their only remaining sibling.

Frank L., the baby boy of the family, was born in January 1905. Over the course of his life, he inherited land from his parents and his sisters, leading him to own a large chunk of Louis and Nancy's initial endowment. To work all of that land, Frank acquired new tractors and other machinery to aid in the harvesting process. When he wasn't using it himself, he'd rent it out to other farmers. While Frank L. was certainly well-positioned, his soon-to-be-wife, Martha, wasn't easily impressed.

"Grandma Martha was maybe five-eight but felt six-foot. She always felt so stately to me," recalls my father, reminiscing on his father's mother. "She had a red bronze skin color and a country twang. She rarely spanked us grandkids but would always threaten to give us a 'North Carolina hook' if we acted up. I only remember sweet coming from her." Martha truly was a sweetheart, nurturing her children and bestowing cute nicknames on them, like "Apple Dumpling" and "Bunny," according to my grandmother Jenail. "I wanted to be a mother-in-law just like Miss Martha," Grandma said with a smile. "Alfred would be talking on the phone with her and she would actually ask to speak with me. And I said, 'Hi, Miss Martha, how you doing?' She said, 'You know I'm fine, how are you? Is he treating you right? If Alfred is not treating you right I'll come up there and get him.'" We both laughed at the thought.

Jenail remembers Miss Martha, her mother-in-law, as someone who seemed always to be on her feet, yet never complained. Even as teenagers and young adults, most of the Baker children could only pick around a hundred pounds of cotton per day, two hundred max. Martha was known to pick upward of three hundred pounds, all while still mothering and keeping the family fed. "Mister Frank would be sitting down telling Martha to get him water or medicine even though she was working. One day, I told Miss Martha, 'You've been working all day long. How about I send Alfred to the store and I'll cook?' She was worried that Mister Frank wouldn't eat the food unless it was Miss Martha who had cooked it. So we didn't tell him that I cooked it. I made blackberry stew, fried chicken, potatoes, and greens. When Mister Frank came in asking for dinner, she told him it was ready. He ate the whole dinner while Miss Martha and I silently smiled at one another."

Though my father wouldn't have seen that up close, he remembers the stories. "Grandma Martha was one of the better people that worked the field. She was so fast that she could do her task and then help other people. During harvests, she'd pick an entire row by herself, break to feed her children lunch, and then come back to help others finish their rows." My Auntie Deanna confirms Martha's work ethic with her own recollections. "Grandma would collect slop in the kitchen and throw it out to the pigs through the window. I remember the garden and going out there with her." My Auntie Karen, the second youngest of her siblings, was born two months after Martha passed away but recalls the many stories told of her by her father. "Grandma Martha would order chickens through catalogs and trade her eggs for other things she needed." Back when bartering was the norm, Martha maneuvered through the agricultural playing field with ease, knowing that her brain and brawn were backed up by long-term economic independence.

Martha, like Frank L., descended and profited from Black land-owning ancestors, so she'd always known what autonomy looked like up close. Her grandparents, Tony and Polly Spruill, were born into slavery and lived long enough to see emancipation, the rise and fall of reconstruction, and the early twentieth-century golden age of Black land ownership. While Polly was Tony's second wife, she treated all of Tony's children like her own. After all, family separation in the Black community was unfortunately a normal occurrence so close to the fall of chattel slavery. Polly was mostly referred to on official deeds (and indentures) as "Tony's wife," though she was an integral partner in their journey to ownership. Polly passed that work on to her children and "step"-children, like Martha's father Plummer, an educated Black man who always dressed the part.

When Martha approached the figurative marriage table, she wasn't empty-handed, creating a unique power dynamic that not all Black women were able to achieve. Martha didn't need Frank L., she wanted him; but with or without him, her economic future was set by both her parents' savviness and her own capabilities. "My mother kept my father afloat," my Uncle Ernest once told me.

Interestingly enough, Black women tended to have more employment opportunities post-emancipation due to their perceived ability to work both in fields and inside homes. On our visit to Historic Stagville, the tour guide reiterated just how common it was across late nineteenth- and early twentieth-century North Carolina to see Black women with disposable income. "A lot of domestic formerly enslaved people signed contracts with white widows who had no idea how to cook or clean or do anything. Actually, domestically, formerly enslaved women had the most economic power because of that. There are stories of these white war-widows having to sell their dresses to get extra money. And the only people who had the money to buy these dresses were the formerly enslaved domestic women who were working for them. And these white women, you could tell, were not very happy." The more disposable income one had, the better the chances of owning land versus sharecropping or renting from someone else. Though many Black women at the time needed to purchase land alongside or through a male proxy, the money was their own.

In *Slavery, Land Ownership, and Black Women's Community Networks*, Karen Cook Bell documents land ownership patterns in nineteenth-century Georgia and puts a magnifying glass to the role of Black women specifically. Her research concludes that women who worked as seamstresses, launderers, and cooks were able to save money and purchase land. While most Black women owned small plots of land—between five and ten acres each—their acreages were known to benefit families for generations. "Women often took great care to include their children as co-owners of land . . . women assumed a vital role in establishing political platforms, often through mutual associations in religious institutions, which reflected their concerns as women, mothers, and workers . . . women sought to alter power relations." One such example of this was the

Georgia Colored Farmers' Alliance, which served as a union for Black farmers to ensure equitable pay. Boasting ninety thousand members, the Alliance was widely supported by Black women.

In a 1908 issue of *The Plantation Missionary,* a local newspaper published by the Industrial Missionary Association of Alabama, evangelical Christians report on a research trip taken throughout the South and West. In one recorded anecdote, the unnamed author recounts a trip to Oklahoma where she interviewed Black women who "made conspicuous successes in market-gardening and poultry-raising." One former dressmaker, recently moved from St. Louis, saved two hundred dollars in one year from her sewing work and used it to rent five acres from a local farmer. The farmer thought he was getting it over on the young dressmaker because he had rented her the worst land on his farm, yet in a few short years the woman and her husband had made enough money to buy the land "ten times over."

Another Black woman pioneer was Lucy Hicks Anderson, born in Northern Kentucky in 1886 to a loving, working-class family. From the age of fifteen onward, Lucy found odd jobs mostly as a domestic worker and traveled from Kentucky to Texas to New Mexico, before ending up in Oxnard, California. During her first marriage, Lucy saved enough money to purchase property, where she ran a boardinghouse and brothel. Lucy's business took off and she quickly climbed the social ladder, known for throwing exclusive parties for wealthy and influential Californians, as well as for supporting charitable efforts.

During Prohibition, Lucy's brothel also became a speakeasy, selling liquor to those who couldn't find it elsewhere. This was dangerous business for anyone—let alone a Black woman—but Lucy's connections allowed her business to expand in spite of conservative scrutiny. On one occasion, a local banker bailed her out in time for her to host his dinner party that evening. Anytime Lucy was arrested, a powerful friend came to her defense. That is, until 1945 when a Navy man accused one of the sex workers employed at Lucy's brothel of giving him a sexually transmitted disease. All women who worked there, including Lucy, were required to be medically evaluated, and there was no one to save her from the unrelenting eye of the military. During her evaluation, doctors discovered that Lucy was a transgender woman.

Lucy and her second husband, Colonel Reuben Anderson, were both immediately arrested and charged with perjury (lying on their marriage certificate), while Lucy bore the added charge of impersonating a woman. With their marriage voided by the courts, more charges came down from the federal government for defrauding the state in evading the draft and collecting benefits for wives of soldiers. Many at the time were shocked that Lucy had maintained her secret for as long as she had. During her trial, Lucy reiterated this: "I have lived, dressed, and acted just what I am—a woman." As a child, when Lucy first began expressing her desire to dress in what was deemed "girls' clothing," a doctor told Lucy's parents that it was best to raise the child as the girl that she was. And they did.

Unfortunately, the judge and jury in California weren't as open-minded as that Kentucky physician. Headlines across the state used Lucy's name and pronouns in quotations and announced, "Ventura cook unmasked after 20 years." The local *Ventura County Star* newspaper referred to Lucy in 1946 as "the Oxnard Negro who masqueraded for years as a woman." Lucy and Reuben were quickly found guilty and served time in prison as well as probation. Lucy was sent to a men's facility and was barred from wearing dresses or skirts.

Upon their release, the two remained a couple and lived together in Los Angeles, as they were strongly discouraged from ever returning to Oxnard by the local police chief. Lucy sold her Oxnard property in 1949 in order to be released from probation and said goodbye to her home of nearly thirty years. But during the approximately fifteen-year period when Lucy moved through the world as an entrepreneur, socialite, and philanthropist, she was a beacon of hope for what Black transgender women could hope to aspire to: a loving relationship where she could be her full self, and a prosperous career that gave her autonomy.

Far too often, though, when we imagine a group of Black people facing off with injustice and marching toward victory, we envision men. Black men in suits at the front lines of protest. Black men in overalls tilling the land. Black men on pulpits leading congregations. But what of Black women and our role? In being part of a chorus, women's voices have been drowned out.

But Black women and other gender-marginalized Black people have also trodden the stony road and let their voices resound loudly in the pursuit of justice. To paraphrase a question that Oprah Winfrey asked Meghan Markle in their 2021 interview, Black women and LGBTQ+ people have been *silenced,* not silent, despite playing pivotal roles in burgeoning Black land ownership.

RISING UP

(1900–1915)

═══════

I don't buy much, I buy land bro.

—KENDRICK LAMAR IN THE INTRO OF
BABY KEEM'S SONG "THE HILLBILLIES"

While initial efforts to own land revolved around collectivist models, over time Black people were incentivized to build personal wealth, giving way to a more individualistic and capitalist attitude toward land owner-ship. In some ways, this was a natural evolution. Purchasing property with others was common when few Black people had the means to buy on their own. As opportunity increased, families began to carve out spaces for themselves. On the other hand, private ownership was incentivized as a prerequisite to civic engagement and true power. The right to vote in this country was initially only accessible to landholding white men. As poor white men pushed back against their disenfranchisement, the right to vote was ostensibly expanded to include all men regardless of race or class, though this wasn't truly the case. White settler American democracy was conceived as being made up of white men citizens who owned private property, and capitalism wouldn't change that for quite some time. Collec-tive ownership among Black communities made it so a truer form of de-mocracy had to be practiced among them.

In "Land of the Freeholder: How Property Rights Make Local Voting Rights," Boston University professors document how property qualifica-tions for voting, serving on juries, and otherwise engaging in local politics persisted well into the twentieth century. Their paper reports that "almost 90 percent of property requirements restrict[ed] voting and office holding at the local level. Most centered on local bond referenda, school districts, and land use—suggesting that homeowner citizens were granted particular control over local taxation and public services. These requirements were largely clustered in the American South and West—emerging alongside Jim Crow laws and mass availability of federal public lands."

The rules were constantly being shifted to box Black people out. The imperative would be finding a way to work with or around those rules without allowing them to change you. Unfortunately, capitalism inherently changes you the moment you become an active participant. Visible Black leaders began to set their eyes and intentions and mirrored white attitudes in ways that would prove successful in the short term and detrimental in the long haul. Booker T. Washington became one of the most well-known advocates for Black capitalism and this "bootstraps mentality," often coupled with an almost condescending critique of Black people who couldn't or wouldn't follow suit. Washington was often found emphasizing land ownership "like the white man" and building relationships with white funders who could expand those goals.

Washington and W. E. B. Du Bois disagreed on this topic, and in his essay "The Talented Tenth," Du Bois writes that "if we make money the object of man-training, we shall develop money-makers but not necessarily men." Later, in *The Souls of Black Folk,* Du Bois explores the double consciousness of being Black in America and needing to reconcile "warring ideals in one dark body." To be Black is to feel responsible for those around you, knowing that we are stronger together. To be American in a capitalist society is to think first of yourself, your needs, and your desires. To be both at once is an almost impossible task; one set of values must win in the end. Toni Morrison would later reflect on double consciousness as a strategy rather than a curse; to be in this world (America), but not of it or changed by it, would allow Black Americans to maintain our integrity in the face of unspeakable injustice. Trauma and the need to survive changes us all, though, so this was certainly easier said than done.

Du Bois wrote that his desire was to be Black in America "without being cursed and spit upon by his fellows, without having the doors of

Opportunity closed roughly in his face." He criticized those who attempted to obfuscate the demand for total liberation as a request to bring good fortune to a select few. That dilution of the more robust goal of freedom for all "shirk[ed] a heavy responsibility . . . when in fact the burden belongs to the nation."

Despite the pushback, Washington remained steadfast in asserting that political activity alone would never lead Black people down the path toward true equity. Believing deeply that we must have property, skill, and character to achieve equal footing in America, Booker T. Washington advocated for individual success that would lift the entire community. After gaining economic independence, Washington declared, *then* Black people could push for political agency from a place of power. Demanding versus asking.

———

It's tempting to dub any place with a concentrated community of wealthy Black people as "Black Wall Street." The term has been used endearingly in reference to places like Wilmington, North Carolina, and Tulsa, Oklahoma, when in reality these cities were so much more—so much better— than the eight-block former slave market and modern-day monument to greed.

On Wall Street, it's mostly white men who make themselves rich. In late nineteenth-century Wilmington, a city where more than half of all residents were Black, people made one another feel safe, heard, and cared for each day. All but one Wilmington restaurant were Black-owned. One could find Black people in all levels of politics, from aldermen to superintendents and beyond. There were Black jewelers, Black barbers, Black mechanics, Black coroners, Black carpenters, and Black tailors. The Wilmington *Daily Record,* owned by the Manly brothers, was one of the only Black newspapers across the entire state of North Carolina.

If you had taken a stroll through Wilmington in the 1880s or '90s, you would have found Black men in top hats and Black women with perfectly coiffed hair and long beautiful dresses riding around in horse-drawn carriages on their way to work. Their work didn't require them to bow or cower; Black Wilmingtonians led lives full of dignity and brimming with ambition. Aspiration was encouraged, not stifled. Residents of

Wilmington—Black and white—lived in seemingly miraculous harmony, serving and spending money with one another.

While there are countless examples of this prosperity, few exemplify it as much as local butcher Ari Bryant. Having been born around 1853, it's likely that Bryant was enslaved somewhere in southern North Carolina. For most of his teens and young adult life, he called Wilmington home and was a beloved son-turned-mentor for the community. He gave speeches celebrating other Black businesses, served as president of the Cape Fear Steam Fire Engine Company, and held office as a First Ward poll holder overseeing local elections. Bryant at one point even managed a local baseball team, the Mutuals, and was known for his fine clothing and extensive community service. This occasionally made him a target for petty theft, but that never stopped him from opening his home and heart to Black Wilmingtonians.

Wilmington was home to dozens of Black-led churches, cemeteries, barbershops, and theaters. There was the Academy of Music on North Third Street and the City Market that ran across both Front and Market streets. A community tennis court later became a practicing ground for internationally recognized athletes like Althea Gibson. The entirely Black firefighter team, Cape Fear Steam Fire Engine Company, began with a small station on Ann Street, later expanding to a larger one on the corner of Sixth and Castle streets. The Wilmington *Daily Record* office began at the corner of Water and Princess streets but moved to South Seventh Street when they, too, needed more space. Their new office space was just around the corner from the YWCA, lovingly named for America's first Black published poet, Phillis Wheatley. There was the mattress factory, the canning company, the ballparks, and the Wilmington Colored Library.

But Wilmington's pride and joy was the Freeman Beach, later known as the Seabreeze Resort, juxtaposed by nearby (and predominantly white) Carolina Beach. Located off of U.S. 421 South, the waterfront property was derived from a larger parcel owned by Alexander and Charity Freeman, a couple of Black and Indigenous heritage. They passed 180 acres on to Robert Bruce Freeman Sr., who increased the beachfront landholdings more than tenfold so that, by his death, the plot included more than five thousand acres. Some of the land was donated for the creation of a school and church. The remaining acreage stayed in the Freeman family, who developed the pristine grounds over the course of decades, making it into one of only two beaches available to Black people in the entire state.

By the 1920s, Freeman Beach had become a hot spot of leisure and joy for generations of Black people from both near and far; many literally waded through water to dine, dance, and spend money at the mostly Black-owned attractions in the area. Being able to walk the pier and access delicious local seafood made the area popular for families and young people. Thanks to the fairly shallow water of Myrtle Grove Sound, guarded from the Atlantic Ocean by barrier islands, vacationers could literally swim up to Seabreeze Resort. Just imagine barefoot Black boys and teen girls in circle dresses stepping into the water until it had reached their waists. Clothes clinging to their brown skin as they made it to the other side, the sun always trusted to dry them off.

Bop City, as the area was quickly nicknamed, became a thriving ecosystem of hotels, restaurants, nightlife parlors, bathing facilities, and an amusement park within larger Black Wilmington's prosperity. The limitless space dedicated to doing "grown folks' things" brought many Black military men to Wilmington who were happy to spend their hard-earned salaries at places like Seabreeze the moment they got some time off. The Black artistic and musical scene at Freeman Beach began to spill over to nearby white-run resorts that attempted to re-create the vibe and magic. It would be white Seabreeze patrons who introduced white jukebox owners to Black records, ultimately desegregating the Carolina Beach airwaves.

Situated along the Cape Fear River, Wilmington was influential and anything but afraid. The Black community of Wilmington was so strong that, when the Ku Klux Klan attempted to intimidate residents through antagonistic "rides" around town, Black people communally patrolled the streets with guns. The KKK didn't return. There are few other cities in the country, then or since, where Black people were represented in all aspects of day-to-day life, and where wealth seemed to be shared.

As a port city, Wilmington teemed with opportunity. Formerly enslaved people found great demand for the skills they'd honed on plantations as the need for lumber mills and naval stores exploded. Emancipated Black people flocked to Wilmington to be able to receive wages for work, and the

Freedmen's Bureau followed them, knowing that they were fleeing coercive conditions. Initially tasked with designating the promise of forty acres and a mule as reparations for chattel slavery, the federal government quickly reneged on that vow and the Freedmen's Bureau instead extended medical, banking, and family reunification services.

> Harry Nixon (Freedman) states that he worked on the plantation of Mr John Sanders situated in Robeson Co, since 5th June 1865 . . . Harry & family left the place on the 13th of August last, states his reason for so doing that he & family were not given enough to eat.

> John Caldwell "Freedman" states that he with four other "freedmen" worked on the plantation of Mr Edmond Caldwell of Sampson Co since 27th April 1865 . . . Mr Caldwell promised to give them a fair share when the crop was gathered—He has now from no cause driven them off his premises & refuses to give them any thing for their services.

> Edmond Newkerk "Freedman" states that he with four other freed persons worked on the plantation of Mrs Mary Ann Wells of Duplin Co . . . Edmond states that he furnished the Teams and that the "Freedmen" fed themselves & team all the time & that now she claims half the corn & all the fodder & schucks & tried to force her claims by having them put in jail a few days since.

In almost every instance, the Freedmen's Bureau wrote to the white employers demanding restitution. No response from any of the named landowners has ever been found. That the bureau was unable to repair transgressions that had already taken place didn't stop Black Wilmingtonians from asserting their vision for the city they wanted to build and live in.

Outside of fielding complaints, the Bureau office in Wilmington also operated two hospitals—a general hospital and a smallpox clinic—and several schools until the 1870s, when the Bureau was dissolved. By then, Wilmington was well on its way to being the pinnacle of Black excellence.

Farm laborers in Wilmington grew prosperous working the "light and loamy" soil of Wilmington, as the North Carolina Department of Agriculture described it. The 1896 report goes on to say that "the strawberry business alone engages the attention of many farmers" and that "the potatoes, asparagus, lettuce, [and] tomatoes are only some of the sources of revenue." To be a resident of Wilmington in the late nineteenth century was to know abundance at a time when most Black people only knew strife.

Across the country in "Indian Territory," Black people in Greenwood, a predominantly Black neighborhood in Tulsa, Oklahoma, were also carving out their slice of heaven on Earth. Both Black and Indigenous people attempted to make Oklahoma a refuge for their communities through widespread land ownership and entrepreneurship. Their efforts had been thwarted when the federal government broke treaty after treaty and organized a land rush in the region for white settlers. That didn't stop Black leaders from quite literally preaching the gospel of Oklahoma as a potential "Promised Land" for Black Americans.

D. B. Garrett first traveled to Oklahoma from Kansas seeking something—anything—better than the violence and systemic exclusion he'd witnessed growing up. Alongside more than three hundred others dubbed "the Emigrant Society of Topeka," Garrett trekked southward until he reached the area where the colored colony was given permission and homesteads to settle. According to a May 1889 edition of *American Citizen*, "46,920 acres [were] owned by colored people from Topeka." And this was just one of many budding colonies across the state. An *American Citizen* article from June of that same year stated that "the majority of those who have taken claims in the Oklahoma Territory express themselves as well pleased with the 'Promised Land.'"

Soon advertisements were popping up across the South and Midwest, encouraging Black people to leave behind their troubles in favor of this oasis. One such appeal, a letter titled "To the Colored Men of the South," boasted that "there was never a more favorable time than now for you to secure good homes in a land where you will be free and your rights respected . . . give yourselves and children new chances in a new land where you will not be molested and where you will be able to think and vote as you please."

Thousands of Black people heeded the advice of those first Black transplants to Oklahoma, including O. W. Gurley, a Black man from Alabama who had amassed wealth in Arkansas but knew the South would always impose a ceiling to his success. Gurley moved to Oklahoma in 1893 and finally made it to Tulsa about thirteen years later. Tulsa neighbored oil fields that had proven to be incredibly lucrative, flooding the area with barons and creating many businesses for the workers to patronize.

Gurley soon opened one of the first grocery stores and hotels in town. He then purchased large swaths of land that would later be cut into smaller lots to be sold to other Black newcomers for both residential and commercial uses. It wasn't long before those lots sold out and what became known as Greenwood was a hub of business and excellence. Gurley then realized that many would need loans to expand their business. Those loans couldn't be accessed through white banks. The mogul created a new stream of income for himself and others by becoming one of the primary lenders for Black businesspeople.

The wealth of Tulsa's oil industry showed no signs of slowing down, and neither did the Black enterprises of Greenwood. It is believed that a dollar spent there circulated thirty times among other Black businesses. In that way, money was rarely hoarded and everyone could enjoy the affluence that Greenwood had to offer. More than thirty city blocks became home to doctors' offices, beauty shops, pool halls, strong schools, and a large theater. As the community swelled, Booker T. Washington took notice, dubbing this area in Tulsa the "Black Wall Street."

Gurley's handprints seemed to be on every part of the city, whether he had directly supported the business or not. Due to his fatherlike role in the community, Gurley was appointed a deputy of the local police force, called on to help establish an AME church in the city center, and boasted an investment portfolio of over a hundred properties as well as a net worth of a million dollars. For his instrumental work in ensuring new residents had a place to gain their footing, Gurley is considered a founding father of Greenwood.

The key to success for communities like Wilmington and Greenwood was strength in numbers. Consolidation of wealth often had little to do with classism and everything to do with a safety only found in groups. A

Black person in the late nineteenth or early twentieth century was only as powerful as their neighbors. Otherwise, anyone—no matter how rich or famous—could be isolated and picked off. Even someone as prosperous and beloved as Gurley. Money alone wasn't enough to save a Black person and, actually, being the only one with money was more a hazard than an accolade.

The Gulf Coast sugar region of the South—namely Louisiana—saw this reliance on community proliferate through widespread union organizing. Dissimilar to Wilmington and Greenwood, where many Black people were owners of businesses and land, working-class Louisianians were more likely to be sharecroppers. They didn't live on lush estates or have time for leisure. Many resided in cabins constructed by and for enslaved people, working for those former enslavers. These workers were more likely to be in overalls and clothes suitable for the fields than in three-piece suits. Yet they, too, took part in cooperative economics and efforts to protect one another from wage theft, retaliation, or worse. Alone, they could easily be replaced by another worker. Together, they felt unstoppable and capable of receiving fair pay for safe work. Little more, nothing less.

Khalil Gibran Muhammad documented this history at length for *The 1619 Project*:

> Given the large Black populations in these areas, freedmen made significant gains overnight, electing Black state officials and inspiring economic changes and labor organizing on sugar plantations . . . [White] planters frequently complained that when they dismissed one worker, the others "would immediately quit work and threaten to leave the place." As new wage earners, Black sugar workers acting in solidarity negotiated the best terms they could, signed labor contracts for up to a year, and moved from one plantation to another in search of a life whose daily rhythms beat differently than before.

At one point, more than ten thousand Black sugarcane farmers in Louisiana embarked on a strike demanding a better share of the wealth they were making possible. After all, Louisiana was responsible for more than

95 percent of all sugar exports in America. Surely, the planters who employed these Black workers could afford to pay them at least one dollar a day, which would have more than doubled their salaries.

W. H. "Hamp" Keys, a community leader and former legislator, was instrumental in sustaining the strike for as long as it lasted. In their most notable action in 1874, Keys led a march from plantation to plantation, ensuring that the white growers who refused to bargain with them saw the might of their collective. For his work as an orator and organizer, Keys was called the "reputed leader of the mob" and an "instrument of great evil" in articles for *The Times-Picayune.*

The strike was off to a strong start and lasted approximately three weeks before police were called in by the wealthy white planters to quell the nonviolent acts of the strikers. Not only that; white civilians were also authorized to take up guns to end the strike once and for all. And squash it, they did. In parishes across the state, Black strikers were intimidated and killed. Thibodaux saw the worst of the violence, which can only be described as a massacre. Limp Black bodies were dropped in unmarked graves. Reverend T. Jefferson Rhodes, a Baptist minister from the area, recalled later that "there were several companies of white men and they went around night and day shooting colored men who took part in the strike." Even those not involved in the strike became prey for the bloodthirsty vigilantes.

Notoriously, a white Louisiana widow named Mary Pugh commented post-massacre that "this will settle the question of who is to rule[,] the nigger or the white man?" The message was clear: White wealth would not be threatened by Black organizing, whether explicitly political or not. Any areas of concentrated Black wealth, landholdings, and political power would be squashed in the years to come. Wilmington would be first. A warning of the bloodshed to come.

PART THREE

THE HEIST REVISITED

Within white supremacist capitalist culture in the United States, there has been a concentrated effort to bury the history of the Black farmer.

—BELL HOOKS

WHITELASHING AGAINST
BLACK WEALTH

≡

**The America of my experience has
worshiped and nourished violence for as long
as I have been on earth.**

—JAMES BALDWIN

In the 1890s, just before the turn of the century, over a thousand Black Wilmingtonians owned real estate in the city, comprising almost one in four Black landowners statewide. This high concentration of Black wealth was perceived as a threat, and the resultant whitelashing was swift and violent.

Elite white men across the state of North Carolina, enraged by the political and economic advancement of their former footstools, plotted to disenfranchise Black Carolinians once and for all. "Red Shirts" set out to harass and assault Black people who either engaged in political activity or were known to be wealthy and influential. This militia functioned as the paramilitary arm of the Democratic Party.

But the core white supremacist strategy used by the wealthiest and most powerful white men across the state was wielding the word, both written and spoken. From Goldsboro to Laurinburg to Wilmington and beyond, the Democratic Party's chief strategist, Furnifold McLendel Simmons, sowed seeds of hatred into the minds of white people across backgrounds. Poor or rich, attorney or farmer, adult or child, suddenly all white North Carolinians feared "negro domination" and became emboldened to

One of the only known photos of Red Shirts taken in
Laurinburg, Scotland County, North Carolina, in 1898
(COURTESY OF THE STATE ARCHIVES OF NORTH CAROLINA).

protect white supremacy. These buzzwords traveled far and wide, from urban centers to rolling farmlands—and by no accident or coincidence.

Journalists, artists, and orators were strategically dispatched to fan the embers of violent intolerance and move people toward the next phase of their plan: outright violence. Charles B. Aycock, considered by historian H. Leon Prather to be "the Democratic Moses," regularly delivered roaring speeches with salacious tales of Black men terrorizing white women. "White men have neglected poor and long-suffering white women . . . It will be up to them whether Negro supremacy is to continue . . . In South Carolina one white man ruled two negroes, but in North Carolina the thing was reversed and one negro rules two white men. Oh! The shame of it! Will not white people come together and put down negro rule?"

Aycock's words were reprinted over and over by allies in the media, ensuring that his venom would permeate, as were the words of Rebecca Latimer Felton. Felton fought for women's suffrage while regularly fighting *against* funding for Black schools, alleging that more educated Black people resulted in higher rates of sexual violence and rape. In 1898, the Georgia native took it a step further, delivering a speech declaring that "if it needs lynching to protect woman's dearest possession from the ravening human beasts—then I say lynch, a thousand times a week if necessary." *The Wilmington Messenger* regularly shared excerpts of her speech, disseminating her vitriol throughout the community where Black and white residents had previously peacefully lived and worked side by side.

To create longevity for this fearmongering, local reporters sensationalized their reports and amplified alleged crimes committed by Black men. Headlines like "A Negro Insulted the Postmistress Because He Did Not Get a Letter" and "Arrested by a Negro: He Was Making No Resistance" and "Unbridled Lawlessness on the Streets," all written by Josephus Daniels of the Raleigh *News and Observer,* stoked the fire further. These articles, alongside racist political cartoons depicting the potential consequences of "Negro rule," worked in tandem to ensure that a critical mass of white people would either actively participate in the violence to come, or at the very least not stand in the way.

NORTH CAROLINA—Wake County.

John Hubbard, being duly sworn, deposes and says: That while working the public roads some days ago, he heard several negroes in Mark's Creek Township, Wake County, talking about the Constitutional Amendment, and one of the negroes, a preacher and neighbor of H. H. Knight, by the name of Offee Price. said they, referring to the white people, may pass the Amendment, but that they would have to fight, and that the right way to do them, the whites, would be to kill them from the cradle up.

JOHN HUBBARD,

Sworn and subscribed before me this the 29th day of June, 1900.

A. T. MIAL, J. P.

Anti-Black political cartoon drawn by Norman Bennett and published in the Raleigh News and Observer *on July 4, 1900.*

Amid the fabricated uproar, Alex Manly of the Wilmington *Daily Record* typed out a response to white North Carolinians' so-called fears. Manly sought to set the record straight that it was ironic for white men to decry rape, considering they were so often perpetrators of sexual violence against Black women. What he had said was true, no doubt, but publicly calling famous white men hypocrites . . . men had been lynched for less. To have left it at that would have been a daring test of his autonomy as the editor and owner of his own paper. Manly continued writing:

> [O]ur experience among poor white people in the country teaches us that the women of that race are not any more particular in the matter of clandestine meetings with colored men than are the white men with colored women. Meetings of this kind go on for some time until the woman's infatuation or the man's boldness brings attention to them and the man is lynched for rape . . . You set yourselves down as a lot of carping hypocrites in that you cry aloud for the virtue of your women while you seek to destroy the morality of ours. Don't think ever that your women will remain pure while you are debauching ours. You sow the seed—the harvest will come in due time.

The response to Manly's editorial was swift.

Article titled *"A Horrid Slander,"* which was published in the
Wilmington Star *(Wilmington, N.C.)* on October 15, 1898. The article states,
*"The infamous assault on the white women of this State which appeared
on the 18th of August in the* Daily Record *has aroused a storm of
indignation from one end of the State to the other* (COURTESY OF UNC LIBRARIES).
Article titled *"Vile and Villainous,"* which was published in the News and
Observer *(Raleigh, N.C.) on August 24, 1898* (COURTESY OF LIBRARY OF CONGRESS).

Senator Ben Tillman of nearby South Carolina irately probed, "Why didn't you kill that damn nigger editor who wrote that?" While many wanted immediate revenge, the white strategists masterminding everything knew that the more sustainable regime change would require patience. Just under three months, to be more precise. If this were truly about white women's safety and Manly was considered a real threat, he'd have been killed before sundown. This was about power and ownership. So long as Black people remained in office and economic equals to white men, revenge would always be short-lived. The Democratic Party needed to ensure only the white vote was counted in the statewide November 1898 elections, in order to cover up Step Two: the pillaging. Step One was stealing the election and organizing for white supremacy.

In Wilmington, this campaign was widely supported by the most powerful and elite white people in the county. When money was being raised to fund printing, equipment, and weapons, most white-owned businesses across Wilmington contributed. In a special 2006 edition of the *Star-News* remembering the 1898 massacre, historian Timothy B. Tyson noted that "Wilmington's elite directed the charge. 'The Secret Nine,' as an admiring local white historian called the cabal that helped hatch the violence and coup in Wilmington, included J. Alan Taylor, Hardy L. Fennel, W.A. Johnson, L.B. Sasser, William Gilchrist, P.B. Manning, E.S. Lathrop, Walter L. Parsley, and Hugh MacRae." Corroborating this story, the *Charlotte Daily Observer* noted after the fact: "The business men of the state are largely responsible for the victory. Not before in years have the bank men, the mill men, and the business men in general—the backbone of the property interest of the State—taken such sincere interest. They worked from start to finish, and furthermore they spent large bits of money on behalf of the cause."

These nine men and their families were among the dozen or so who benefited most from the massacre. No doubt, historians could read their donations as investments. For a small fee, they could destabilize an entire community and free up precious land and businesses for the taking. But they wouldn't be doing the work alone. Local alderman Benjamin Keith recalled that membership for what became known as the White Government Union was made mandatory under threat. "Many good people were marched from their homes . . . and taken to headquarters and told to sign." These so-called "good men" didn't seem to push back enough for threats to be made real.

How does one steal the election if they aren't in charge of counting the results and with too little time for gerrymandering? Voter intimidation. According to Manly, "gatling guns," the closest thing to what we now have in automatic weapons, were paraded in the streets and gunpowder was purchased in bulk by white men. Stores refused to sell any to Black men. Red Shirts rode through every county in the state, putting the fear of white retaliation into the heart of any Black person even thinking of voting. Former congressman Alfred Moore Waddell spoke regularly during evangelizing meetings for Red Shirts. The day before the election, Waddell directed the group assembled before him: "If you find the Negro out voting, tell him to leave the polls, and if he refuses, kill him, shoot him down in his tracks. We shall win tomorrow if we have to do it with guns." Black turnout that November was dismal to say the least, and Democrats won by a landslide.

While the newly elected officials began moving in and ousting their opponents, Hugh MacRae, an MIT graduate and one of the "Secret Nine," held a public meeting. Present were lawyers, doctors, reverends, salesmen, and other well-to-do white Wilmingtonians. Once everyone settled in, the meeting's purpose was revealed in the form of a manifesto—"A White Declaration of Independence," drafted by MacRae, Taylor, Fennel, Johnson, Sasser, Gilchrist, Manning, Lathrop, and Parsley. In the Declaration, the nine men called for the resignation of the mayor, chief of police, and entire board of aldermen. They also demanded the abolition of the Wilmington *Daily Record* and the exile of Alex Manly and several other Black business owners.

After the Declaration had been read—to the sound of whoops and cheers—the men gathered thirty-two prominent Black community leaders, all men and mostly clergy. At gunpoint, these thirty-two were read the Declaration and scrutinized for any signs of anger or self-defense. At the conclusion, the men gathered were given twelve hours to respond affirmatively to each of the demands. The "or else" was implied.

By this point, Manly had left town under advisement that it was the only way for him to remain alive, and so the *Daily Record* had already ceased publication. The men raced to warn their families, parishioners, and named exiles about the warnings, attempting to design a response that might prevent bloodshed. Most of those who were marked for banishment fit one of three categories, according to later reports. "Those local citizens slated for banishment [were] . . . African-American leaders who insisted on citizenship for their people or who openly opposed the white supremacy campaign; black businessmen whose prosperity offended local whites; and white populations who had a 'political record of cooperating with the Negro element.'" In a community like Wilmington, with a biracial legislature and vibrant Black community, numerous Wilmingtonians fit this bill, making everyone fearful of what was to come, even if they met every demand.

The majority of the list were Black attorneys, Black clergy, and the wealthiest Black landowners. For Black legal professionals like W. E. Henderson, sitting in a courtroom and arguing against a white lawyer and their white client—especially on behalf of a Black person—was risky. Despite being trained and qualified for the task, being so knowledgeable and equal in status went against everything that white supremacy stood for. Henderson knew this well because he had moved to Wilmington after fleeing Salisbury, where he'd defended a Black man who was accused of killing a white person. Now here he was being kicked out again; Henderson knew the risks and did his work anyway, because it mattered. After fleeing Wilmington, Henderson settled in Indianapolis, where he restarted his legal practice and took on cases addressing segregation, workers' rights, political disenfranchisement, and lynching.

Several Black ministers of the time were both faith leaders and community organizers, some far more outspoken than others. Long before the Declaration was drafted, Rev. J. Allen Kirk had attracted the ire of white Wilmingtonians by calling on his congregation to support Manly and the *Daily Record.* He, too, was on the list of exiles, alongside Thomas C. Miller, the mortgage lender. Through his line of work, Miller became powerful not simply through his wealth but more so through his standing in the community. White people as well as Black folks were indebted to him.

I can imagine Miller making his rounds each month to collect payments with interest, and how much white residents seethed at the thought of owing a Black man anything. Further, Miller regularly expanded his landholdings through courthouse auctions, where his access to capital made him one of the more competitive buyers in town, often outbidding white peers. Miller was arrested by the new police chief for "safekeeping" on the night of November 10. A foreshadowing of what was to come.

White Wilmington, led by the not-so Secret Nine, was already gearing up for violence that was no doubt imminent. Judging from their actions in those next twelve hours, there had been only the illusion of choice. In the early morning of November 10, white women and children were discreetly taken to safety away from the city as their husbands, fathers, and sons prepared for battle. Or rather slaughter, because there was no opponent resourced enough to fight back. Black Wilmingtonians wanted to be left alone and made sure to respond to the demands by the deadline. Black leaders drafted a letter, and were so worried about not making it in time that they hand-delivered their white envelope to Waddell's mailbox, hoping it would be enough to call for a truce. Waddell was nowhere near his mailbox. He and two thousand men were marching through town toward the *Daily Record* office. After saturating the building with kerosene and watching the flames dance, the mob thirsted for more. It was clear to anyone still within city limits that there was no turning back.

The Daily Record *office after a white mob burned it down* (LIBRARY OF CONGRESS).

Deeds and surveys attributing land to Black business owners and families were burned, while the Black community was terrorized and turned into refugees. Clusters of white men posted up on street corners, killing anyone they wanted. Manly, always the journalist, compiled stories relayed to him by survivors into a secondhand account of the day. "On a corner the mob met a number of colored men. The white men ordered the frightened Black men to disperse and began firing upon them, killing three and wounding others . . . Halsey, a highly respected colored man, was driven out of his own house and into the yard and there shot him down and his wife and children." A boat in the Wilmington port was outfitted with a Colt gun, and anyone attempting to leave town was shot down.

Those murderous men were so bold that they called in their own journalists to bear witness to their white supremacist revolution. Reports from *The Wilmington Messenger* later wrote that "a volley tore off the top of a [Black] man's head and he fell dead about 20 feet in front of the news-hawks." Hiding in one's home wouldn't be enough to keep a Black family safe, especially if that home was coveted by whites. Trying to thwart the violence was an even worse offense. A local Black politician, Daniel Wright, was accused of self-defense and shooting at burglars from inside his home. After being dragged out of his front door and bludgeoned with a pipe, jeering vigilantes told him to run for his life. No sooner than Wright had made it fifteen yards away, forty bullets tore through his skin, ripping him to pieces.

Many survivors lived to see another day only by fleeing to the nearby woods, cemeteries, and swamps with nothing but their loved ones and, in some cases, bedding. Black elders lay there on the moist ground, faces pressed to soil, stifling cries of their children and grandchildren. Cries that were a natural response to the day's tragedy but would have surely led to their discovery and death. After enduring weeks of bone-chilling cold and wilderness, many survivors who did return to their homes and businesses found new inhabitants had wasted no time moving in.

When all was said and done, hundreds of people had been killed, well over a thousand fled the county, and hundreds left North Carolina altogether. There were few funerals, as most of the bodies were dumped in the river. Waddell had prophesied "the current of the Cape Fear choked with

RICHMOND, VIRGINIA, SATURDAY, NOVEMBER 19, 1898.

HORRIBLE BUTCHERIES
AT WILMINGTON.

THE TURKS OUT DONE.

Innocent and Unarmed Colored Men Shot Down.

Hundreds Run to the Woods

**The Mob Captures the Town.--White Ministers
Aiders and Abettors of Murder.**

THE GOVERNOR POWERLESS AND THE PRESIDENT OF THE UNITED
STATES SILENT. GOD'S AID IMPLORED. THE CRIES OF DEFENSE
LESS.--ANARCHY RULES.

A clipping about the Wilmington Massacre from
The Richmond Planet, *an African American publication.*

Negro carcasses" a month before the massacre. Indeed, the river ran red
that November.

To ensure "peace" post-massacre, church services were banned for
three weeks, a curfew was implemented, and Black ministers were forced
to walk around town quelling the rage of the survivors. When church services did eventually pick back up, all sermons at Black churches needed to
be pre-approved and white men stood watch to ensure no one went off
script.

While Black communities covertly mourned their dead and all they'd
lost, traditional media and white North Carolinians rejoiced. *The Wilmington Messenger* declared that "the year 1898 marks the restoration of
white man's supremacy after it had been submerged for years in the Dead
Sea of corruption and vice." Many key architects and spokespeople for the
massacre only grew more powerful after its success: Several leaders, including white supremacist orator Charles Aycock, later became North

Carolina governors. Alfred Waddell, after having been instrumental in the murder and intimidation of more than half of Wilmington's residents, served as Wilmington's mayor for seven years. Furnifold Simmons stopped strategizing behind the scenes and became a U.S. senator, holding his seat for three decades alongside many other massacre participants. Rebecca Felton was also appointed to the U.S. Senate, becoming the symbolic first woman senator (serving for exactly one day). Of all members of Congress, Felton was the last to end her personal enslavement of Black people. Her disdain for emancipation and social equity was palpable.

Reverend Charles S. Morris, who was turned into a refugee post-coup, lamented the destruction of his beloved city: "What caused all this bitterness, strife, arson, murder, revolution, and anarchy in Wilmington? We hear the answer on all sides—'Negro domination.' I deny the charge . . . In the legislature there are 120 representatives, seven of whom are colored. There are 50 senators, two of whom are colored—nine in all out of one hundred and seventy. Can nine Negroes dominate 160 white men?" The truth is that one would have been one too many for those white supremacists. There were thirty-nine Black government workers in Wilmington in 1897; a little over a year post-massacre, only nine remained. But to truly understand the story of Wilmington, and white supremacy in America as a whole, one must understand that violence like this was rarely about Black people in power, but more so Black people who leveraged their power toward equity for all Black people. One wealthy Black person isn't a threat, but a community of autonomous Black people is.

According to Sue Ann Cody, whose thesis "After the Storm" documented the violence of 1898, "Several African-American family narratives of the violence acknowledge white protection during the violence as a sign of their higher status." Interviews taken in 1973 by anthropologist June Nash confirm these findings as survivors and descendants of survivors recall white protection. Some of the Black people spared included the Freeman family, who owned thousands of acres of beachfront property, which was later developed into Seabreeze Resort. The Freeman family was well-known among poor white people for selling or even giving them land—a self-preservation tactic that later saved his life when grateful mobsters ensured he was excluded from the violence. Others, including more con-servative Black ministers and businessmen, recall receiving warnings and even protection during the massacre.

While this level of white protection may have been something to boast about, everyone knew these were convenient and self-serving exemptions. For the most part, Black people lost businesses, property, and their life sav-ings in the fires that raged that November day. Reverend Kirk, one of the exiled ministers, later wrote that he and other clergy were "exiled and scat-tered over the country from our pulpits and our people, without having time to get our property or our money or any other means of protection for our families." He went on to describe many of the victims as "property holders, averaging from five to forty thousand dollars, respectively." Yet, over a century after the massacre, when a commission was established to create a comprehensive historical narrative and assessment of the impact of the massacre, those present came to a different conclusion. The Wil-mington Race Riot Commission reiterated what Black Wilmingtonians had been saying and passing on for centuries with one notable difference: The commission found "no evidence" of land theft. The commission ex-plicitly states that "analysis of deeds and tax records indicates that most Black property owners in Wilmington retained ownership of holdings after 1898." Sue Ann Cody acknowledged that oral tradition asserts prop-erty loss, yet she similarly declared that this was mostly a myth.

In the case of Wilmington, it's baffling how anyone could come to the conclusion that no property was lost/stolen, considering the destruction of records and forged documentation that became rampant during and after the massacre. Even if we were to ignore that intentional erasure from the historical record, why is it not enough to hear directly from the im-pacted people—and their descendants—on what was stolen during the violence? How, knowing that many prominent residents were forced to flee with no more than they could carry, do we assume that they lost no property holdings?

Kavon Ward, CEO and founder of Where Is My Land—an organiza-tion that investigates cases of land theft and advocates for restitution—once shared with me: "Black oral history is enough." She's seen firsthand as families' pleas were discredited for lack of a paper trail, despite having very consistent and meticulous anecdotal evidence of the land they and their loved ones once owned. To discredit the stories passed down by Black elders as myth is an act of white supremacy.

The Black people of Wilmington were not killed because they voted or served in office. They were killed because of what they did with that power, what they owned, and how it forced white America to consider that if Black people had managed to become their equals with all of the cards stacked against them, what did that say about them and poor white people? Theft of both life and assets was central to the mob's aims. A. J. Mc-Kelway, the then-editor of the North Carolina *Presbyterian,* confirms this in an article where he wrote, "The effect of their fellows [Black people] in places of political power turned the heads of the whole negro population—the serving class. They demanded the whole of the sidewalk as a matter of right, white women learning soon, for fear of insult, to step out into the street to avoid collision." Were white people actually superior or was white supremacy all a lie? And without the power to lie, cheat, and steal both labor and wealth, what would their lives amount to? They wouldn't wait to find the answer to those questions.

Alfred Moore Waddell gave a speech at the Wilmington Opera House on October 24, 1898, praising colonization and asserting his intention for white people to retain absolute power: "It is just, and right, and absolutely best and wisest for both races that the white people, who settled this country, and civilized it, and made it the grandest country on the globe, and who have done more for the negro race than all the other peoples that have ever lived upon the earth, should alone govern it, as a whole, and in all its parts." Through Waddell's words we understand that this has always been about white supremacists' self-serving vision, which depends on their belief in their divine right to rule the land. And that vision came to pass.

In 2006, Timothy B. Tyson wrote that "those who favor amnesia ignore how the past holds our future in its grip, especially when it remains unacknowledged. The new world walks forever in the footsteps of the old." Up until 2020, a public park not far from downtown Wilmington, equipped with tennis courts, picnic sites, and nature trails lined by longleaf pine trees, bore the last name of Hugh MacRae, co-engineer of the massacre. Lauren Krouse, a writer who both studied and taught at the University of North Carolina at Wilmington, described the site as a spacious plot of land where she went to de-stress after classes, unaware that it was a monument to white supremacy. In fact, MacRae loaned the land to the City of Wilmington on the condition that the space remain accessible only to white people. Today, the park has been renamed and now bears a Black Lives Matter mural, yet this symbolism doesn't erase the reality of who is allowed to exercise autonomy and build wealth in the city.

Over a century after the massacre that decimated the Black population of Wilmington and pillaged their wealth, less than 20 percent of Wilmington residents are Black, compared to the more than 55 percent of residents who were Black in the late nineteenth century. The report drafted by the race "riot" commission in 2006 found, based on city directory data, that segregation expanded and the city center became almost exclusively white post-massacre.

On a trip to Wilmington, I visited one of the few remaining Black-owned restaurants in Wilmington: Truck's Chicken 'n Fish. The redbrick building is unassuming from a glance, yet as you inch closer the ghosts of Wilmington are omnipresent. A black-and-white poster with mugshots and protest imagery calls on you not to forget the Wilmington Ten, a group of Black political prisoners wrongfully convicted of setting a white-owned grocery store on fire. Stepping through the entrance, you're greeted by a corkboard with newspaper clippings announcing the restaurant's inception story as a soup kitchen, as well as more recent initiatives to offer affordable meals to community members. Over a hot meal of fried chicken, catfish, and French fries with a side of Kool-Aid, I ear-hustled as the two elder Black women behind the counter vented about the economic disenfranchisement of the city—a product of both the COVID-19 pandemic and racism.

A few days later, while visiting one of the only memorials honoring victims of the massacre, constructed in 2008, I met Nikki and Eddie, who come from generations of Black Wilmingtonians. As I read the faded words on the stone semicircle, I noticed the Black couple walking toward us and wondered if it would be intrusive to ask them about the legacy of the massacre. As I wrestled with whether to approach them, Eddie glanced at us and said, "Y'all looking at us like 'I think they can tell us something.'"

I smiled at his discernment and asked if they were from here or simply passing through. We stood there for more than an hour as they shared their intimate knowledge of the city. Nikki pointed out a building one block away where bullet holes from 1898 can still be seen. That was only one remnant of the massacre. The more insidious evidence has been how twenty-first-century gentrification has continued to push Black residents out.

"This area was the Black area; nobody wanted to live here. Standing here, you used to be able to see the river," Nikki says, motioning toward an area full of tall buildings and clusters of trees. "No lie, straight down to the river. Oh, it was gorgeous. I mean, especially when it was sunny. Now the only way to see the river is to actually go down." Eddie nodded, reflecting that "now they own all the property." "They" is undoubtedly white Wilmingtonians, whether they've been in the city for generations or recently moved from larger Northern cities. Waterfront condos have continued to pop up on land that once belonged to Black business owners, politicians, and community advocates. Eddie continued: "They're moving middle-class families across the bridge . . . There was a Black beach near Carolina Beach called Seabreeze. All of the land and everything was owned by the Wheelers, the Freemans, and the Wade family. The town of Carolina Beach started taking and using the land little by little. And now they have a predominantly white beach down there called the North End and they have been in litigation over that land for the past I think ten or fifteen years—even longer than that." Nikki, without missing a beat, jumped in and noted that "you have to pay to go to North End, you can't just go there."

"There are about four or five families that are really, really, really anchored in this town. They have a lot of political power. They have a lot of the money." He didn't need to say the names for me to know that these families descended from some of the Secret Nine conspirators and other leaders of the coup/massacre.

Eddie repeated what refugees had said over the years: Property seizures were rampant during the massacre. "[The white mob] burned down the newspaper, and then they started seizing all the buildings. They started burning deeds down at the courthouse so there would be no records of who owned it. All of Third Street," he said while pointing down a main road, "a lot of the more historic houses—the big ones—were owned by Black people." Nikki picked up where he left off: "Wilmington was multiracial, so you could have Black families and businesses beside white families and businesses because Black people were just as successful. And that made a lot of people mad because they'd come by and see successful Black people, like 'Why do you have more than me?'" Both Nikki and Eddie made it clear that land theft was essential to the intention and success of 1898. Wilmington was just the beginning.

Many racist rampages were inspired by the Wilmington Massacre, America's only successful coup and the first of many onslaughts of violence against Black wealth-building. The Wilmington Race Riot Commission's report noted that the tragedy "marked a new epoch in the history of violent race relations in the United States." Less than ten years later, white Georgians would literally consult with architects of the massacre for advice on how to replicate the outcome in their own state. Michael Hoke Smith, who later became the fifty-eighth governor of Georgia, successfully stole the election and laid the groundwork for the 1906 Atlanta Race "Riot" by following the blueprint shared with him by prominent North Carolinians: calling for the protection of white womanhood, planting seeds of violence through speeches, and arming white residents. Smith encouraged his fellow white vigilantes to "handle them as they did in Wilmington [where the woods were left] Black with their hanging carcasses." Shortly after his election, that is exactly what happened.

Thirteen years after dozens of Black Atlantans were killed in cold blood came the Red Summer of 1919. Across America, Black communities burned, Black assets were seized, and Black lives were taken. It was just as Du Bois said: "The advance of the freedmen had been too rapid and the South feared it." A reign of terror was unleashed from sea to shining sea to ensure that those who were able to rise above their station were hammered back into place. By the time 1921 had come around and Greenwood Tulsa was leveled to the ground, massacres had been almost normalized. There were few places to hide and evade the terrorism that seemed to wring Black people dry. And in almost all instances, working-class white people were merely doing the bidding of the more elite and powerful white men who had orchestrated the scheme.

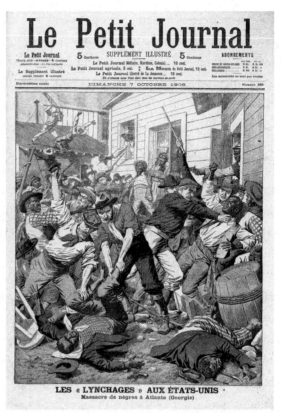

Cover of Le Petit Journal, a Parisian newspaper, on October 7, 1906, with the headline "Les Lynchages Aux États-Unis: Massacre de Négres à Atlanta (Georgia)," which translates to "The Lynchings in the United States: The Massacre of Negroes in Atlanta."

Even without the presence of pitchforks and armed mobs, white supremacist violence has been a norm in this country, and especially in the face of Black ownership. Black-led attempts at sovereignty have almost always been met with white violence in America. Five years before the Tulsa Race Massacre, Anthony Crawford, a formerly enslaved Black person who had acquired a 427-acre cotton farm, was beaten, lynched, and then shot for good measure. His offense? Refusing to sell his cottonseed at the insultingly low price offered by a white man. The more than four hundred acres, which Crawford had worked his entire life to have, were technically deeded to his children, but they lost the land to a local bank when their fear of facing a similar fate kept them from returning.

For the 1619 Project, journalist Trymaine Lee told the story of Elmore Bolling, an Alabaman who ran a general store, gas station, and catering business on a leased plantation where he also grew cotton, corn, and sugarcane. His many businesses had proven to be quite lucrative and, over time,

Bolling accumulated a savings of $40,000, which is the twenty-first-century equivalent of almost half a million dollars. In 1947, Bolling was shot seven times and left in a ditch by a group of white men who hadn't bothered to disguise themselves at all. While their motivations may not have been clear in the darkness of that cold December night, the months to come would surely reveal them. White people, some posing as creditors, stole most of Bolling's savings as well as the money made from selling the assets he left behind. A friend of Bolling's told a newspaper his theories for what had taken place. "He was too successful to be a Negro." As Lee put it, "Today's racial wealth gap is perhaps the most glaring legacy of American slavery and the violent economic dispossession that followed."

———

Black people weren't the only ones being pushed off of land that had been hard-fought-for. Indigenous people across the nation were still being re-moved and forcibly relocated—some tribes for the third and fourth time. In regions like the West Coast, Indigenous Chicanos who had called California, Texas, New Mexico, and other regions home for centuries were also lynched and forced off the only land they'd ever known. White su-premacy didn't care; Chicano families were rounded up and put on trains or flatbed trucks headed south to Mexico. It's why many Mexican Ameri-cans today reiterate that they didn't cross the border but rather the border crossed them. Almost two million people were illegally deported through federally funded programs like Operation Wetback, to make space for white settlers.

In a handful of instances, resistance efforts successfully warded white supremacists away, but these were few and far between as most white mobs had local police and the National Guard on their side. During the Great Depression, as the prices of cotton and tobacco plummeted statewide, In-digenous Lumbee people of Robeson County, North Carolina, established a mutual aid cooperative to weather the scarcity together. Lumbee people were incredibly vulnerable to predatory interest rates that threatened to take even more than they'd already lost. A journalistic article by historian Ryan K. Anderson describes how Lumbee people were often forced to mortgage their farms to pay off debt, but the kinship system developed in the 1930s allowed for families to be fed and community networks to be built with community in mind more than profit margins. The network, named the Red Banks Mutual Association, was so successful that it remained in place long after the Depression ended and well into the '50s.

Local Ku Klux Klan leaders became upset at their inability to exploit the tribal members and the power they were demonstrating through their mutual aid. Further, a local leader of the Klan, James W. Cole, was disgusted by the Supreme Court's 1954 *Brown v. Board of Education* ruling. He sought to ensure that Black and Lumbee people alike remained in their place. In 1958, white vigilantes, led by Cole, came together and began a series of cross burnings intended to intimidate the Black and Indigenous residents of Robeson County. When those acts went mostly unnoticed, Cole called for a Klan rally in Maxton, North Carolina, and bragged to reporters that he expected more than five hundred hooded men to show up.

On the actual night of the rally, Cole and fewer than a hundred Klansmen gathered at the site near a flagpole to discuss the need for segregation and to terrorize local community members. There, in the midst of a wide field lit up by cars and lights that the Klan had brought with them, were white men, women, and children—some having crossed the state line from South Carolina. In what became known as the Battle of Hayes Pond, Lumbee men surrounded the Klansmen, outnumbering them at least five to one, though some accounts claim almost a thousand Native Americans were present that evening. Most, if not all, of the Lumbee men were armed. As one of the Klansmen spoke into a microphone, a single bullet ominously pierced one of the lightbulbs and Lumbee men began firing guns into the air, ululating and shouting, "God damn the KKK." With the sound of war whoops fading behind him, Cole ran for the nearby swamps, leaving behind his wife, Carolyn, and the white men he was supposed to be leading. It wasn't long before the white families also fled.

Victorious, the Lumbee people paraded through the streets with confiscated paraphernalia, posing for photos and even giving interviews to reporters. A few months later, Cole and his second-in-command were convicted by an all-white jury and sentenced to prison by Judge Lacey Maynor, the second Native American judge in Robeson County history.

Lumbee men,
Charlie Warriax
(left) and Simeon
Oxendine (right),
hold a captured
KKK banner
(MPI/STRINGER).

Black Robeson County residents had not overtly participated in the standoff but were instrumental to the Lumbee success that night. Many Black people were employed by various Klansmen and thus in close proximity to key leadership who didn't have the sense to be discreet with their plans. According to Malinda Lowery's book *Lumbee Indians in the Jim Crow South,* several Black community members operated almost like spies, passing on information to Lumbee leaders that allowed them to anticipate the Klan's numbers and thwart them.

But these sorts of wins were few and far between. Most attempts at self-defense were met with even more brutality. The Great Migration is often portrayed as mostly an economically motivated shift of Black people to the North Atlantic, Midwest, and West Coast, when the reality was much more traumatizing. In her critically acclaimed book *The Warmth of Other Suns,* Isabel Wilkerson illuminates the ways Black Americans were turned into domestic refugees fleeing violence. Wilkerson quotes a 1917 article from *The Cleveland Advocate:* "There is no mistaking what is going on; it is a regular exodus. It is without head, tail, or leadership. Its greatest factor is momentum . . . people are leaving their homes and everything about them

under cover of night, as though they were going on a day's journey—
leaving forever."

Over time, massacres with survivors weren't cutting it and the goal became the violent expulsion of *all* Black people. Entire towns and counties
were ethnically cleansed through the violent and de facto creation of "sundown towns" and all-white counties throughout the South. Sundown
towns got their nickname based on a mostly unspoken rule that a Black
person shouldn't be found in said town after dark. In some cases, this rule
was made incredibly explicit with signage.

Road sign along U.S. Highway 70 just outside of Smithfield,
Johnston County, North Carolina (GETTY IMAGES).

To help guide unsuspecting travelers, Victor H. Green created *The
Negro Motorist Green Book,* announcing which towns and counties were
safe for stops and which should be driven through as fast as possible, if at
all. The story of the *Green Book* focuses so much on the presence of white
violence, we often don't even remember that parts of the country that had
been predominantly Black for well over a century were suddenly devoid of
Black people or businesses.

The creation of sundown towns was intentional and hyper-localized,
with white residents deciding for themselves how they wanted to get rid of
their Black, and occasionally Asian or Latine, neighbors. Property was
central to the efficacy of these regional campaigns. Sometimes, purposeful

Newspaper articles from the Arkansas Gazette *showing the beginnings of Cotter, Braxter County, Arkansas, and Bonanza, Sebastian County, Arkansas, becoming sundown towns.*

neglect was used to push Black residents out, requiring the complicity of government officials. For example, much-needed levees would fall into disrepair, flooding Black farms and pushing people out, as we saw with the aftermath of Hurricane Katrina. In other instances, outright violence was used as the primary tactic toward racial cleansing. In these instances, the brutality was so severe that survivors coped by never speaking of what happened. But in all cases the Land remembers. And so do the ghosts.

———

Lake Lanier is a reservoir in northern Georgia notorious for suspicious deaths and spooky experiences. Most Black people I know won't go anywhere near the lake, though it remains a prime attraction for families looking to enjoy a day on the water, boating and riding Jet Skis. In my lifetime up until the point of writing this book, more than two hundred people drowned in Lake Lanier or died in boating accidents. While the legend has made daredevils even more excited to dance with death, few lake-goers know the story of 1912, and later 1956, that may be the foundation of why the area feels so haunted to this day.

In the early twentieth century, the Forsyth County section of the 38,000 acres that now make up Lake Lanier was known as Oscarville. The community was predominantly white, though Black people made up about 10 percent of the population. In 1912, several Black teenage boys and men were accused and convicted of raping local white women. In one instance, the trial lasted a single day before the defendants were sentenced to death by hanging. In the months that followed, white community members refused to settle for the justice meted out by judges and juries. Instead, groups of white men calling themselves Night Riders rode all around Forsyth County with explicit warnings to all Black residents. They were to leave town in twenty-four hours or be killed.

Few people waited around to call the Night Riders' bluff. Some families used their twenty-four hours to sell land, businesses, and homes at a loss while others ran immediately and without looking back. Approximately 98 percent of Black residents countywide were gone in a few months' time, and by 1920 the Black population of Forsyth County had dwindled to zero. According to journalist Elliot Jaspin's research, these pushed-out residents had collectively owned almost two thousand acres of farmland, which was either abandoned or sold for pennies on the dollar. All of the Black churches in the county were torched and not a single Black person remained. An article in *The Atlanta Constitution* headlined "Negroes Flee from Forsyth: Enraged White People Are Driving Blacks from County" documented what was deemed "one of the largest racial cleanings in America." It would be decades before any Black families would return, and even then, the numbers were dismal at best. According to 1990 census records, only fourteen Black people lived in Forsyth County, which had a population of just over 44,000 people.

In the 1950s, the U.S. Army Corps of Engineers decided to construct a lake providing nearby communities with water. Local residents—almost all white—were offered sums of money to purchase their land, and approximately seven hundred families sold 56,000 acres to the government that were flooded in 1956. Wooden structures and tall buildings built by the previous Black residents were destroyed to prevent liabilities and later complications but a lot remained, including old chicken coops, forests with towering trees almost sixty feet tall, and cemeteries. While Canada geese, great blue and green-backed herons, and kingfishers now call the lake home, so do the remains of Black families and businesses that were forced out to make space for white comfort.

While I'd love to tell you that Lake Lanier is the only horrific example, the sad and traumatic reality is that there are hundreds, if not thousands, of "Forsyth Counties" across America. While strategic banishment was notorious in states like Georgia, Texas, Illinois, Kentucky, Arkansas, Louisiana, Alabama, and Missouri, all forty-eight mainland states in this nation have had at least one.

There are likely other towns and communities whose names have never been spoken precisely because there were no survivors or direct descendants to tell their stories. Though we may never speak their names, a great debt is owed.

THE GREAT MIGRATION
AND THE GREAT LOSS

═══

**It occurred to me that no matter where I lived,
geography could not save me.**

—ISABEL WILKERSON

My grandfather Alfred has always been a humble man with a strong internal moral compass. Or, as my Auntie Deanna says, "He could live in a white man's world but was always aware of racism." On the surface, he is straightforward yet unlikely to raise his voice—though I'm sure his children, who knew him as "the Disciplinarian," would disagree with me. Beneath my grandfather's calm exterior has always been someone deeply perturbed by unfairness. Once, Grandpa was driving three of his six kids on Route 20 in New Jersey when a white man with bad road rage yelled "Nigger" out of his window at them. Grandpa was stoic, with little visible anger, yet he accelerated and stayed behind the car until the man was forced to pull over. My aunt, uncle, and father were young then and seated in the backseat, watching as their pastor father refused to turn the other cheek. Grandpa got all in the white man's face until he acquiesced with a simple "You got it, partner." Alfred Baker has always refused to be treated like a boy.

Despite being one of the youngest of more than seventeen children that Martha and Frank L. Baker shared together, Alfred operated like a big brother or young man of the house. Whether on an interpersonal level or systemically, Grandpa believed that some things weren't as difficult as others made them out to be. It's no wonder, then, that he never had a great relationship with his father. Frank L. was often rigid with his children and grandkids, yet more gracious with himself. In many ways we can consider him a product of the times where Black elders and parents didn't accept backtalk from anyone their junior, let alone children. "Grown folks' business." The rigidity was a protective cloak in a world where Black people couldn't afford too many slip-ups. It also ensured every Black child had some "home training." What began as a method of maintaining respect for and deference to those who came before you became a double-edged sword when someone older than you refused to accept accountability. A cloak of silence often drowned out harm that should have been addressed. Not with Alfred.

From a very young age until the day she "passed on home," as we say, Grandpa saw it as his mission to ensure Martha wanted for nothing. So it's no wonder that when Alfred discovered his father cheating on his mother, there was nothing that could or would stop him from speaking up. Not even the fact that he was just a teen at the time. When Alfred confronted his father, Frank L. exploded. He was furious that his son—a child, at that—had the nerve to level an accusation at him. His rage grew until Martha realized that her husband was angry and crazy enough to kill his own son for what he saw as an unforgivable act of disrespect. Martha did what any loving mother with a gladiator for a son would do: She siphoned what money she could from their earnings and put Alfred on the next train north.

Alfred was one of the first of his siblings to leave North Carolina. With but a few dollars in cash and a hastily packed duffel bag, he sat on the train headed into a deep unknown. As the train barreled down the tracks, sprawling farmland gave way to smog-covered urban centers. When he arrived in Paterson, New Jersey, Alfred knew only one person there. After staying with his sister and finding employment, he hit his stride and soon became a host to other Southerners—like his siblings and cousins—also making their way north. From his perch in Paterson, New Jersey, Alfred never lost touch with his Carolina roots or his parents.

Prior to this research, I rarely heard Grandpa speak of his father except to call him the weak link who squandered the family's most prized possession: our land. Distance certainly made the heart grow fonder, but also caused certain beliefs to cement and blur his vision. As the years, and soon decades, passed, the several hundred acres the Bakers had tended to since just after Emancipation became fewer than two hundred. Many of my grandfather's other siblings also migrated north, diminishing the free labor pool that previously made such a monumental family venture somewhat manageable. Without them, Frank L. needed to hire field hands, cutting into the family's profits. Not to mention all the other barriers standing in Frank's way as a Black landowner.

It's said that Frank L. always enjoyed a stiff drink, but over time this casual practice developed into an insatiable case of alcoholism. Maybe it was a predilection for addiction, maybe he was self-medicating to cope with the consequences of remaining in the South while so many others fled. Owning land *and* growing on said land was no easy feat in the twentieth century for a Black person, but some of Frank's children felt their father was more focused on his next glass of brown liquor than on being a savvy steward and businessman. My Uncle Ernest, the knee-baby of the family, had a more level perspective: "My dad did a lot of bad things. So did a lot of white people, and they still have their land."

When I sit with my grandfather's older siblings, many of whom never left the South and were privy to the day-to-day challenges their father endured, they speak of him as a complicated man who tried his best despite warring with demons both within and outside of himself. Those closest in age to my grandfather echo a less forgiving refrain: Frank L. *let* white men take what was theirs. I've let the question of what-could-have-been marinate. Do I think my own grandpa was better suited than his father to resist the violence of the time—both explicit and implicit? Perhaps! But is it ever productive to blame a victim for how quickly their oppressor succeeds?

I don't blame Frank L. for what was taken from him. Nor do I blame his children, who wanted more from their patriarch—and from the South as a whole. The North offered Alfred a life away from his father and also the chance to finish school without fieldwork getting in the way. He could follow a non-agricultural career. As the Great Migration swept through the South, bringing millions to the North, Midwest, and West Coast, it became easier to lose sight of what this mass migration meant for those who stayed.

Industrial booms and new migration patterns meant that people didn't feel the same sense of responsibility to land as they once would have. In Northern ghettos where development and redevelopment became a way of life, land wasn't treated as a living thing—it wasn't being *tended to*—anymore. Slow Southern ways that prioritized connection were replaced by a faster pace. Once land was transformed by capitalism from a living thing into an inanimate plot on which to erect structures, Black Southerners-turned-Northerners became accustomed to that new way of relating to the world around us. They made new cities their home.

As people fled and never looked back, Black Southerners lost some of the strength in numbers that helped to serve as a buffer between Black communities and the white supremacy that threatened their very existence. Much is said of the way the Great Migration transformed urban centers whose Black populations ballooned, but what of the South?

———

By the 1940s, tall tales of uninhibited affluence and opportunity began to lure people out of the "Black Belt." Owning land and businesses in the South had proven to be a death sentence. Maybe in other parts of the country a Black person could thrive without threat. Swarms of people stepped out on faith, boarding trains and buses for cities whose names they could barely pronounce.

Six million Black Americans fled the South and the land they'd given so much to—often with little notice, under the cover of night. Knowing that three steps forward would always be followed by theft and bloodshed, what were Black folks supposed to do? It was a mass exodus that was organic without being happenstance. Those who traveled west and north during the first waves of the Great Migration entered an abyss with so many variables and unknowns.

Many Black migrants left behind small, rural communities where interconnectedness was a social norm, food was fresh, and life was slower. Former Texans began to call Minneapolis and Los Angeles home. Mississippians and Alabamans traveled all the way to Chicago and St. Louis. Georgians headed to Detroit and New York, where they met Black Americans from the Carolinas.

It's difficult to track whether most migrants were landless to begin with, or had sold and transferred their holdings before they set out for their new homes. What we do know is that the lucrative landholdings Black people had accrued over the last half century were mostly in the South, and this wealth had to be left behind. They were running toward something—anything—less stifling, less violent, than what they'd known.

The South had symbolized repression, exploitation, and cyclical loss for the Black Americans who were born into the Jim Crow era. Many were also leaving the South emotionally. While some cultural practices remained, many Black migrants began to turn their noses up to the agricultural world they'd once known. The original dream for many newly liberated Black people had included a home, land for growing and grazing, and the ability to spread one's lineage across the acreage. Land that could provide for a whole community or extended family, if need be. It wasn't long before the dream quickly shifted from land ownership to home ownership. The subsistence and agricultural component was lost.

Renard "Azibo" Turner calls this an *anti-agricultural blacklash,* where Black people subconsciously associate agricultural work with slavery. Leah Penniman remarked that "there is so much land-based trauma. For us, land was the scene of the crime, as six million people would flee the rural agrarian South . . . people were raised thinking that the way to succeed was to get as far away from the land as possible." There are definitely internalized elements, and most often Black Southerners were bullied for being "backward" and "unskilled." Shirking off those labels meant assimilating to Northern industrial culture with the hopes of becoming a welcomed and respected member of society. Aspiring to a homestead was a Southern thing; here, one was lucky to have a clean apartment to rent and a bustling social calendar to distract from the homesickness.

Some Great Migration domestic refugees found the prosperity and safety they'd craved. Many others found that the trade-offs didn't work in their favor. Verdant, sweeping fields were traded for Northern ghettos and tight spaces. Active lifestyles built around the agricultural economy of the South were replaced by monotonous factory jobs. Unfortunately, those domestic refugees, who sought a life untethered by Ku Klux Klan intimidation, found racist police forces with billy clubs and water hoses. White supremacist violence wasn't left behind at all. The grass wasn't much greener on the other side of the Mason-Dixon.

In terms of economic opportunity, ownership was as rare for Black people in the North as it had been in the South. Redlining, a set of codified, discriminatory housing practices, blocked Blacks from safe, healthy, and equitable access to housing. Some of the more notorious and commonly used tactics included disproportionate denial of loans, insurance, and other financial services needed to purchase or maintain a home. But of course, intimidation still had its role to play.

Many white civic leaders of Northern cities sought to drop Black home ownership rates and house values, and one of the more effective strategies used was outright violence. In *Warmth of Other Suns,* Isabel Wilkerson writes briefly about the series of riots that erupted in Great Migration destinations. "These were the riots in East St. Louis, Illinois, in the summer of 1917 . . . 'Black skin was a death warrant on the streets of this Illinois city,' wrote an observer shortly afterward . . . All told, 39 Blacks and 8 whites were killed, more than a hundred Blacks were shot or maimed, and 5,000 Blacks were driven from their homes." Those who survived the riots and rampant police brutality were prey to the meticulously designed deprivation made easier by white flight. For all of the romanticization of the North in juxtaposition to the South, the American dream proved just as difficult to attain regardless of where one lived. The utopia that seemed positioned to offer a softer landing turned out to be a nightmare continued.

Dr. Ellora Derenoncourt's research at Princeton University shows that this was even more true a few generations removed from migration. In her article "Can You Move to Opportunity? Evidence from the Great Migration," Dr. Derenoncourt argues that "from the vantage point of 1940, there was every reason to believe future generations of Black children would continue to reap the benefits of their parents and grandparents having migrated. The results from the empirical analysis in this paper suggest otherwise."

Drawing on census records, municipal spending reports, and her own empirical research, Dr. Derenoncourt explores how the children and grandchildren of Black migrants were impacted by leaving the South. "Those growing up in former Great Migration commuting zones (CZs) today have lower adult income than those from similarly resourced families, but in locations less affected by the Migration . . . Today, roughly 27 percent of the gap in upward mobility between Black and White families in the urban North can be attributed to changes induced by the Great Migration." She further notes, "Black men face the largest reductions in individual income rank from having grown up in Great Migration CZs, and this is true for those with both low- and high-income parents." Ultimately, Derenoncourt concluded that "millions of Black migrants moved North to improve their economic outcomes, and in response, northern cities changed in ways that eventually shuttered Black economic progress."

And these weren't the only concessions Black emigrants made. Predatory systems and practices proliferated like wildfire, consuming communities of Black people in urban centers across the nation. This was by design. Orchestrated by those who hoard land the most, the modern engineers of gentrification and power-building are following the blueprints left behind by this nation's first thieves.

Even before she met my grandfather Alfred, my grandmother Jenail knew she wanted to move back South. The choice to move North wasn't one she made for herself, and the longer she remained in New Jersey, the more she yearned for the South. As the daughter of sharecroppers, she had never known equity for herself, but she *had* known—and *loved*—the land. The trauma of the South hadn't turned my grandmother away from her dream of securing a sliver of safety, family, and love right there in the South.

It's unsurprising, then, that she met and married another North Carolinian who felt that same pull to his motherland. "I met [Alfred] at Bethel Church, where he was attending with his sister, Ardell," she tells me as we sit in the living room they built together. "The young people all hung out together from the different churches and traveled to one another's homes for dinner after service, so we became close."

The two were married when Jenail was just eighteen years old, right before Alfred's twenty-first birthday. Their marital bliss was cut short when Alfred's Uncle Eustis was murdered down south, just miles from our inherited family land. Mystery surrounds his death to this day. His official death certificate lists "accidentally ran [*sic*] over by car" as the cause of his death. The unofficial story, passed down for generations, is that Ulysses "Eustis" Brown had done something to attract the ire of a white person. Eustis's loved ones cautioned him to leave town and not return. One morning, an unsuspecting driver pulled to the side of the road to determine whether he'd hit a small animal or branch in the road. After hopping out of the vehicle, this driver found parts of a human body. "They found his body throwed on the road," my grandmother said with downturned eyes. When authorities were called, they found Eustis cut up into pieces that were strewn near the shoulder of the road and nearby wooded areas. "They think that the Ku Klux Klan got him," my grandma murmured, without much emotion, as though she had accepted the truth of what happened long ago.

Jenail accompanied her new husband as they drove to North Carolina for the closed-casket funeral. It was a despondent way to meet her new in-laws, but the home-going allowed for the many branches of the Spruill and Baker families to return to North Carolina. Alfred took his bride to the house where his family still lived, teaching her all about the acres they collectively owned. "That was the first time that I knew a lot more about Alfred's family, the land. There was a white house. Up on the hill a little bit. Alfred and I went walking and he told me that all that back there was their property and that he was born in the house in back of that house." At the time of this visit, the Baker-Spruill land owned by Alfred's parents, Frank L. and Martha, had dwindled to about two hundred acres from the close to five-hundred-acre farm they'd once owned. "From a kid that grew up with sharecroppers who worked and worked to be able to buy back even an acre, that concept of five hundred acres, I was like whooo."

Alfred wasn't as impressed with his family's landholdings. He was upset, he told her at the time, that Frank L. "done sold some more of that land and Continental Can bought that land from them." After a beat, my grandfather had added, "I wish I had the money, I would buy that land back." Knowing the scale of the systems designed to take land from Black people, I was acutely aware of the word choice used. I asked my grandmother whether Grandpa Alfred had specifically used the word "sold" as opposed to "lost" or even "stolen." She confirmed that this was how he saw the shrinking farm. "[Frank L.] would use the land as collateral to buy the crops, and if he wanted another piece of equipment or something like that he would, you know, go and borrow money on the land."

Archival government documents confirm some elements of the stories passed down about the Baker-Spruill family's land loss, but there's much more still to be revealed about how corporations like the Continental Can Company strategically benefited from the debts of Black farmers. A manufacturing and packaging company, Continental Can produced metal containers and occasionally military aircraft parts and bombs. Headquartered in Connecticut, the company owned land and facilities across America and Canada. In 1958, Continental Can somehow ended up with 238 acres of Baker land in North Carolina. The official notice of the transfer, which is available at the Warren County Register of Deeds, declares that Frank L.'s 238 acres were exchanged "in consideration of Ten Dollars and other valuable considerations." Adjusted for inflation, my great-grandparents lost 238 acres of land for what would be about $106 in 2023.

Reading the deeded records, there is an air of "business as usual" that adds insult to injury. While the formal and emotionless language is standard for a deed transfer, I felt the transaction deserved more explanation. The land that was taken was part of a 348-acre tract full of red oak trees and bordered a bridge that ran over Shocco Creek. The land had been in our family for generations and was passed down to Frank L. by his father, Frank W. I don't know what I hoped to see . . . maybe an explanation of why ten dollars was sufficient, or an apology for disrupting a generations-long legacy.

Frank L. may have been an alcoholic and fallen on hard times, but he and the farmland he'd cultivated were targeted by predatory lenders and businessmen. Between 1941 and 1958, Frank L. and Martha (Spruill) Baker lost, regained, and lost land again countless times, as did his father before him. From 1912 to 1934, Frank W. and his wife, Annie B. (Jones) Baker, also existed in a violent cycle of losing land through indentures. The terms of Frank W.'s debts weren't as flagrantly offensive as the 1958 theft by Continental Can, but in the end, 174 acres (and two mules) were taken in response to a default on a $1,177.49 bill. Considering that pre–World War II farmland fluctuated between $20 and $70 per acre at the time (according to the U.S. Department of Agriculture), the land and other assets, covered in red and white oak trees as well as small willows, was likely worth at least seven times that amount.

By the 1970s, Black families across North Carolina (like mine) were rendered landless while the Continental Can Company was reaching $2 billion in annual sales. We weren't the only ones being manipulated by sneaky corporations and legal representatives. Black communities around the nation fell prey to corporate hoarding and industrialization efforts. On a road trip through Robeson County, North Carolina, I stopped to visit a small museum of local Indigenous history. While purchasing books in the museum bookstore, I struck up a conversation with Benjamin, the young man behind the cash register.

Benjamin and his co-worker, Tyler, speculated that most land in the region was privately owned and used by industrial farmers. This was a fair guess, considering much of the state now profits off of soybeans, tobacco, feed corn, and cotton. Tyler mentioned that the private land ownership was spurring more incessant flooding, even outside of hurricane season, which was rare for the area.

Benjamin and Tyler have spent most of their lives in North Carolina, and I was curious about their regional understandings of land ownership. I didn't need them to do the actual data-pulling for me; I was much more interested in what local perspective they had on landholdings, if any at all. Could the average person name the largest landowners in the area? And, whether those guesses were correct or not, what informed their perception?

When I asked them about some of the biggest landowners in Robeson County, Benjamin answered quickly—not bothering to even look up from ringing me up. "I know back in the day here in Pembroke, Pates owned tons of land," he said casually. Tyler added more context. The Pates were a wealthy, white family who owned a series of supply and grocery stores in southern North Carolina. "They would take anything as collateral for your groceries," Tyler said. "They would start with your animals, then take your farm equipment, and then they would move to your land and then they would lease you back your land."

Benjamin came over to chat with me. "Somebody told me that Pates actually owned so much land in North Carolina that they can't even buy anymore," he told me while I fumbled to write down as many facts as possible. We crossed the room talking more about local Indigenous legends, like Henry Berry Lowry and the Lowry Gang, who operated like Robin Hoods of Robeson County. Made up of a few fugitive Black people, some Scottish men, and mostly Lumbee tribal members, the Lowry Gang were notorious for guerilla attacks on Confederate soldiers, and robberies. "They would literally go into banks and steal twenty thousand dollars. They would go to a general store and steal a bunch of food. They would go to rich white landowners' homes to raid all their meats out of their smokehouses," Benjamin told me. The Lowry Gang never took unnecessarily and were known to distribute their spoils among poor people, and to return stolen horses and wagons.

Though Lowry and his gang were outlaws with large bounties on their heads, no one ever turned them in. I'd like to think that the recipients of their aid understood their frustration with the violent theft they and their loved ones had been victims of before. Though almost a century separates the legend of Henry Berry Lowry and twentieth-century land theft, they both speak to a legacy of exploitation and resistance. Benjamin and Tyler knew of these stories through word of mouth. I attempted to corroborate the rumors about the Pates that had passed through the community but my research ran dry. This doesn't mean the theft didn't take place.

What we know is that the Great Migration is an era where Black wealth was stolen and siphoned away. Black families across the South were preyed upon and regularly fell victim to racist strategies, which almost always ended with the family's eviction from their land.

WHAT DOESN'T KILL YOU

A long leash is still a leash.

—OCTAVIA BUTLER

Beginning in 1916 and continuing until 1970, the mass exodus of Black people out of the South transformed the entire country and its agriculture—especially in the rural South. Against the odds, in the early twentieth century, Black farmers had turned large profits and even sharecroppers had managed to negotiate better wages and working conditions, thanks to their formal and familial systems of economic cooperation. But with less strength in numbers for bargaining and a huge demand, planters and large landowners scrambled to develop a new vision for the South that wasn't so dependent upon human labor.

Almost overnight, the agricultural industry that brought prosperity to the South was getting a facelift. Land soon became consolidated by larger corporations seeking a more mechanized style of growing and harvesting. These production methods depended on harmful chemicals, expensive machinery, and the erasure of small farmers—most of whom were Black and Native.

Further, many ancestral practices that had been co-developed by Black and Indigenous land stewards were labeled unscientific. These time-proven methods of caring for land were pushed to near obsoletion by wealthy white landowners whose pockets were lined by more extractive planting and harvesting strategies. The image most Americans have of farmland—neat rows of one or two lucrative crops like tobacco, cotton, and corn—is a rather recent invention. Cash crops have overtaken North Carolina, a state that boasts land fully capable of growing a wide range of fruits, vegetables, grains, and nuts. Muscadine grapes so dark, they look black until you squint your eyes. Fig trees bearing fruit as sweet as honey. Bright red strawberries and pecan trees. But diversified growing and the use of cover crops (like peas and oats) to protect soil from erosion didn't fit the modern vision being pushed by "industry leaders" of the time. The desire for a pristine growing process outweighed the utility of more long-standing and time-tested methods.

Small, sustainable, and communally owned ventures were replaced by massive industrial productions. Families like mine, who had previously been able to work and live off of their own land, faced a new normal that threatened their entire way of being. The older Baker siblings who still lived in the South were starting their own families and had less and less time to help Frank L. Meanwhile, in 1952, Frank L. purchased his first tractor; prior to that he had depended on horses, mules, and his children to divide the labor. But now his younger children were headed to New Jersey and nearby cities where they sought less backbreaking work. By the time my grandfather traveled north, there weren't many Bakers remaining at home to help on the family land.

Faced with an aging body and an empty nest, Frank L. looked around at the legacy he'd been gifted by his father, as well as by Martha's parents, and counted more burdens than blessings. Keeping up with the Joneses—or in this case, with large corporations—was becoming increasingly difficult. To worsen the odds for marginalized farmers, the few federal and local agencies designed to mitigate the struggles that farmers like Frank L. faced were behind the entire exploitative operation.

The U.S. Department of Agriculture (USDA) develops and implements national policies and legislation around natural resources, food, forestry, and rural land development. At the time of this writing, the USDA has "a vision to provide economic opportunity through innovation, helping rural America to thrive; to promote agriculture production that better nourishes Americans while also helping feed others throughout the world; and to preserve our Nation's natural resources through conservation, restored forests, improved watersheds, and healthy private working lands." In service of these aims, the USDA oversees all national forests, the regulation of grains and oilseeds, and even the Supplemental Nutrition Assistance Program (SNAP) providing food assistance to low-income families. The USDA is also the key federal liaison with America's farmworkers, growers, and landowners.

This department was established during a time when the need for national leadership on agriculture was high, and when the U.S. agrarian economy reigned supreme. Half of all Americans at the time lived on farms, and most people were tied to agriculture in some way. The business behind growing, harvesting, and shipping crops was the most lucrative industry in America for much of the nineteenth century, as well as the first few decades of the twentieth. In 1862, about eight months before signing the Emancipation Proclamation, President Abraham Lincoln established the Department of Agriculture, which he intended to be "the People's Department."

The USDA was created through the passage of the notorious Morrill Act, which put the final nail in the coffin of Indigenous land sovereignty. At the same time President Lincoln was making it easier than ever to seize and redistribute Native land to white homesteaders, a bureaucratic entity was deputized as the largest regulator of land—and the food, water, and biodiversity that comes from it. Further, due to slavery and the segregation that followed, many of the USDA's programs were inaccessible to non-white people in its first few decades of existence. It's clear in Lincoln's actions—even when not explicitly stated through his words—that the federal government's primary concern was, in fact, white people.

By the 1930s, a quarter of all Americans were involved in farmwork and the USDA was expanding its footprint across rural America. When the Great Depression hit, agriculture was in disarray. Overworked land, spiking unemployment, and global economic upheavals created dangerous conditions for farmers and the people who depended on them for food. Initial plans to stabilize crop prices and relocate farmworkers to other parts of the country with more arable land were quickly shot down. Many

feared the plan was too similar to socialism and would lead to a more drastic redistribution of land. Out of the ashes, the Farm Service Agency (FSA)
was born to revamp America's agrarian economy.

The Farm Service Agency—which later became the Farmers Home
Administration (FmHA)—occupies a unique space as a national entity
that implements agricultural policy on a hyper-local level, through a massive network of offices located around the country. These offices lead programs around cultivation and conservation, as well as disseminate credit
and loans. This organizational structure positioned local FSA offices and
the USDA as a whole to be primary gatekeepers for agricultural workers
and rural landowners. Overwhelmingly, these USDA administrators and
FSA/FmHA officers have been white men. Based on this fact alone, it's no
wonder the USDA has not only hindered equitable agriculture but outright upholds white supremacy when it relates to land ownership and
farming. They did it by:

> The discrediting and disincentivizing of Black and Indigenous
>   cultivation methods in favor of strategies that regularly
>   bankrupted family-owned productions
> Intentional bureaucratic neglect, such as withholding loans,
>   grants, and aid to Black farmers while funneling those
>   resources to white farmers and landowners
> Limited access to federal programs and conservation initiatives

Professor and public historian Pete Daniel has published one of the
most thorough analyses and explorations of USDA discrimination in his
book *Dispossession: Discrimination Against African American Farmers in
the Age of Civil Rights*. According to his research, some 600,000 Black
Americans were pushed off of their land between 1940 and 1969. Daniel
goes on to say that "historians have rarely glanced offstage at the vast
USDA federal, state, and county apparatus that generated research, distributed information, assigned allotments, made loans, and controlled
funding that dictated the direction and pace of this rural transformation."
USDA personnel, many of whom were educated at the same land-grant

schools created through the Morrill Act, dubbed themselves the foremost thinkers and leaders on agricultural knowledge. Farmers who refused to comply with USDA-approved expertise were considered outdated and ignorant, despite grounding their practices in time-tested methods. "Knowledge handed down or gained by trial and error was devalued and forgotten while formulaic methodology and machines grew in importance," Daniel asserts. "Federal agricultural policy and laborsaving science and technology became weapons that ruthlessly eliminated sharecroppers, tenants, and small farmers."

"It's basically redlining," offers Leah Penniman, a farmer and author known for her work as the co–executive director of Soul Fire Farm, an Afro-Indigenous community farm that facilitates food sovereignty programs. Soul Fire Farm has been blessed through a series of public and private investments and is able to operate without federal aid, yet even Leah has seen the way the USDA keeps non-wealthy, non-white farmers from owning and operating successful agricultural projects.

"They rank the soil from best to worst, and if your soil is at the bottom, you get no loans." I wasn't sure I heard her correctly. The USDA, which has access to all of the latest technology and science, labels swaths of land as too desolate to even bother *trying* to rehabilitate. That in itself feels like a shocking waste of resources, platform, and stature. When you compound this with the fact that Black farmers have been disproportionately pushed onto "bad" land—which the USDA can undoubtedly track—this becomes less of a coincidence and far more calculated. Even if one could make it past that discriminatory screening process, the loan applications regularly have difficult-to-meet criteria and are incredibly cumbersome. "Sometimes requests for proposals are released July first and are due a month later, despite this being prime time for harvesting." Even the smaller, more accessible programs like the Environmental Quality Incentives Program (EQIP) and the Conservation Stewardship Program (CSP) are out of reach for the average Black farmer.

When Penniman and the Soul Fire Farm team were told their soil was too heavy and uncultivable for investment, they didn't just give up on the Land the way they were advised to. Instead, they did what Black and Indigenous people have always done—they rolled up their sleeves to listen to

*Leah Penniman holding dark, fertile soil in her left hand
and the previous heavy soil in her right.*

the Land's needs. "We move at the speed of trust," said Leah. Over a decade later, and thanks in no part to the USDA, the soil at Soul Fire Farm is
flourishing.

In an Instagram post, Penniman holds the old, dry soil in her right
hand and the revitalized soil in her left, with a caption that reads:

Soil before—left. Soil after—right. 15 years of mulching, compost,
low/no till, cover crops, inoculant drench, raised beds, and polycul-
ture brought our soil from gray to deep brown, rich in humates,
capturing carbon, cradling life. I am soooo in love with soil and
endlessly fascinated by how she can heal when we lean on Afro-
Indigenous farming wisdom and technology.

The team at Soul Fire Farm aren't the only ones who've experienced the USDA's neglect. From the very beginning, programs administered by the USDA and the FSA were skewed in favor of larger farms that were incredibly expensive to maintain, relying on machinery and chemicals instead of human labor and intuition. These standards were extremely difficult to maintain without access to large sums of money—especially pre-harvest and during seasons with unexpected weather. Driven by greed and a belief that white and Western techniques were inherently better, the USDA routinely withheld aid and resources from Black farmers while funneling billions of dollars into the hands of white landowners.

No doubt, moves like this were intended to make agribusiness a rich man's game. Larger operations run by wealthy white men and major corporations built agricultural monopolies in place of family-owned farms. Smaller farms were more accessible for a working-class Black person, especially when one considers the reality that so many hurdles blocked Black farmers' path to ownership. Daniel makes this clear in his book: "White men both formulated and executed agricultural policy . . . and agrigovernment cooperated, some might argue conspired, to replace labor-intensive with capital-intensive farming operations."

By prioritizing the whims and preferences of politically connected white farmers, the USDA and FSA/FmHA also disproportionately denied Black loan applications and pushed Black people into bankruptcy through predatory lending. Data shows that the chance of the USDA foreclosing on a Black farmer was six times as likely as the department doing the same to a white farmer. Further, a Civil Rights Commission report in the 1980s found the following:

> . . . complaints claim that they are often denied the opportunity to submit loan applications; that the amounts of loans awarded are always less than requested; that often they do not even receive the full amount awarded; that loan repayment schedules are accelerated without explanation; that loan payments are applied to the wrong accounts . . . and that creditors and other business are routinely contacted by the county FmHA Office and informed that no loans will be made to these [B]lack farmers, thereby preventing

them from obtaining other credit, goods, and services needed to continue their farm operations.

Inequitable access to loans and funding can prove stunningly detrimental. It's important to remember this was an agency that awarded millions of dollars to farmers—just not Black or Indigenous ones. In fact, a 1982 report by Pamela Browning of the U.S. Commission on Civil Rights found that more than 90 percent of all FmHA funding went to white farmers, while less than 3 percent went to Black farmers and just over 1 percent went to Native Americans. An investigation into Gates and Hertford counties in North Carolina found that while a Black community made up almost 55 percent of their local area, they received less than 30 percent of farm loans awarded in 1979. On several occasions, seasoned Black landowners were told no aid existed and were advised to seek off-farm employment. Meanwhile, a twenty-one-year-old white man with no land could receive a six-figure loan to purchase a farm, followed by another six-figure economic emergency loan a year later.

On top of the many external pressures facing Black farmers, such as climate change, a disappearing workforce, and a centuries-long disadvantage, they were also competing against white peers with access to millions in federal funding. As a result, Black farms disproportionately faced foreclosure, or were liquidated after no warnings to Black landowners that their loans were delinquent or that procedures needed to be followed to prevent the sale of their land. Few were offered the grace of refinancing processes or loan forgiveness; asset forfeiture was almost always the course of action when it came to Black families.

According to Browning's investigation, some Black farmers later found out that the USDA officials assigned to their case were conspiring with the white landowners who later ended up with their land. Lost property and land, which was supposed to go to public sale, often ended up in the hands of the same timber conglomerates and wealthy white people. "The frequent pattern," the report reads, "is for land to remain in minority hands only as long as it is economically marginal, and then to be acquired by whites when its value begins to increase."

In more extreme instances, local USDA officials were known to use outright intimidation tactics to keep Black farmers from attempting to access aid and programs. The 1982 Civil Rights Commission cited a North Carolina complaint that Black farmers were "subjected to disrespect, embarrassment, and humiliation" by the agents paid to serve them and their land. Protestors at an Atlanta march in 2000 told stories of a white employee who was found guilty of carrying a loaded gun into the office and threatening Black farmers and constituents with it. The man was suspended for only one day, with pay.

Various USDA reports have acknowledged culpability—to a degree—in maintaining racial divides in agriculture and have admitted to a "well-documented" record of systemic racism within the department and its satellite locations. A 1965 report conducted by the U.S. Commission on Civil Rights found that "for decades the general economic, social, and cultural position of the southern Negro farmer and rural resident in relation to his white neighbor has steadily worsened" and that "most of the 4.7 million Negroes living in southern rural areas are seriously disadvantaged when compared with rural white southerners."

The report goes on to express that the burden for meeting Black farmers' needs fell to the handful of Black staff employed by the USDA and Farmers Home Administration, resulting in gains for white farmers who were overrepresented. "Negroes have been consistently denied access to many services, provided with inferior services when served, and segregated in federally financed agricultural programs whose very task was to raise their standard of living . . . the prevailing practice has been to follow local patterns of racial segregation and discrimination in providing assistance paid for by Federal funds." A series of recommendations were made to correct this racist pattern, including "the abolition of racially segregated administrative structures," increased Black participation in local committee elections, and training all USDA staff to adequately serve "Negro clientele." Unsurprisingly, few of them were implemented.

By 1982, not much had changed for the better. The U.S. Commission on Civil Rights again conducted a study of the USDA's relationship with Black farmers, titled "The Decline of Black Farming in America." At the time, approximately 57,271 Black-operated farms remained, down from almost one million Black-owned and/or -operated farms in 1920. In other words, Black people had gone from owning almost 15 percent of all farmland to less than 1 percent. The report opens with an introduction that states, "While displacement from the land looms as a threat to all small farmers, land loss has occurred most severely among [B]lack farm operators." Later report findings profess that "the Farmers Home Administration [FmHA] of the U.S. Department of Agriculture is in a unique position to provide assistance that could prevent the loss of [B]lack farms. However, only 2.5 percent of the total amount loaned through FmHA's farm credit programs in FY 1981 was awarded to [B]lack farmers."

New recommendations called for congressional oversight hearings, revised FmHA regulations that better favored Black farmers, and more intentional outreach to marginalized farmers. If implemented, these policies might have slowed the impact of the land loss. Black farmers were becom-

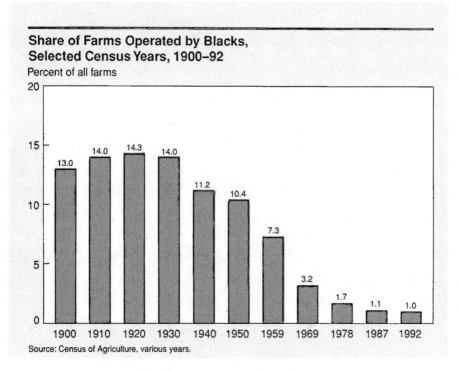

1995 USDA/Economic Research Service report
revealing shrinking Black landholdings.

ing near-extinct and the federal agency designed to do something about it continued to prioritize white landowners. A 1998 report by the USDA National Commission on Small Farms expressed that "discrimination has been a contributing factor in the dramatic decline of Black farmers over the last several decades," as seen in the chart on the previous page.

Rife with hidden agendas of devaluing Black farmers, the USDA systemically acted as an arm of white capitalistic expansion. It's no wonder that Black rural land stewards consider it to be the "The Last Plantation."

WEAPONIZING
THE LAW

**Where massive profit was concerned, loopholes were
found, exceptions granted, blind eyes turned.**

—ANNA-LISA COX

"They were selling the family land to outsiders because what a lot of
people don't realize is that land is power." I sat across from my computer
where my Uncle David's face gazed at me from a Zoom window. We were
discussing the historic family land and what remains of it today. After the
passing of their parents, Frank L. and Martha, the Baker siblings became
more and more divided. Some siblings carried a deep sense of responsibility to the land that had been passed down across three to four generations
of Black farmers. It's not that others weren't as aware of that rich history;
rather, living paycheck to paycheck had made them more economically
vulnerable and fast cash became harder to turn down.

My grandma asked me once, "How much do you think this house is
worth?" Bewildered, I replied, "This house?" She responded by adding
"and the land." The land she was referencing encompasses over eighty-six
acres, including two large ponds, some farming land, some wooded land
perfect for hunting or clearing. I answered her as best I could: $250,000 to
$300,000 for the house; together with the land, I estimate, over a million.
She tells me she gets these letters through the mail offering to buy this land
all the time. "How much are they offering?" I almost regret that I've asked.
"Eight thousand dollars."

When received by someone who knows the full value of the land, these sorts of letters in the mail are regularly ignored and treated as the insults that they are. For someone who doesn't even know they are an active heir to land down south at all, a surprise letter offering $8,000 in exchange for a quick signature might be difficult to turn down.

Heirs' property laws were developed to govern situations where a will isn't present or where there are multiple named beneficiaries to property. For Black people who have always been wary of (and had limited access to) the U.S. legal system, heirs' property laws have been overwhelmingly applied to the settlement and distribution of Black assets. In these scenarios, heirs cannot make major decisions regarding the property (such as selling it or profiting from industries like timber) without the agreement of all heirs—but heirs may transfer their stake in the property.

Heirs' property seems straightforward enough to be nonthreatening, right? When only a handful of people are owners, maybe that is the case. If an heir receives land from someone else—take, for instance, Robert Freeman Sr., who first developed the 5,000-acre Freeman Beach property after receiving a stake in land from his parents, Alexander and Charity Freeman—they are co-owners alongside a small group of people whom they know and trust. But in such situations, when the heir later dies, whether without a will or with multiple heirs—such as Robert Freeman Sr.'s eleven children and dozens of grandchildren—the parcel becomes further fractured.

Now each of Robert Freeman's eleven children has a stake in the land, alongside their second cousins; depending on how many children they each have, Alex and Charity Freeman's great-grandchildren may be just a few of hundreds of heirs. This was not uncommon in Black Southern families. In a family like mine, where land passed to seventeen children and the many grandchildren who came from them, this can mean that hundreds of people, regardless of whether they live on it or are even aware of their property rights, have a stake in family land. Anytime an heir wants to propose selling or mortgaging the land, they'll need to consult each of the other heirs. And if at any point an heir decides they no longer want the responsibility associated with their share, that heir has the power to transfer their stake to a non–family member. Once named an official stakeholder, this person (or business entity) would have a path to blocking (or forcing) decisions on family land.

With great incentive to acquire shares in heirs' properties, real estate companies and private developers concocted a stealthy strategy of identifying properties with as many claims in the land as possible and locating at least one relative willing to sell their share. Preferably, this relative would also be someone with little emotional attachment to the land. Andrew Kahrl reiterated this dynamic in *The Land Was Ours:* "Often the persons who sold their share did not even know they possessed it beforehand, had little knowledge of the land's true value, and failed to appreciate the disastrous implications of the transaction for the persons still living on the land. Even if they did, such considerations were often overshadowed by the prospect of a onetime windfall. Indeed, it was no coincidence that 'share hunters' targeted the most distant and destitute shareholders."

The Freemans of Wilmington's Freeman Beach learned the dangers of heirs' property laws as the number of stakeholders swelled and exploded. Initially, the expansive acreage presented seemingly endless opportunities from which each of the heirs could hope to profit. Several of Alex and Charity's children opened banquet halls adjacent to hotels operated by neighbors and, by mid-century, the family businesses were expanded by the Freeman grandchildren and great-grandchildren to include restaurants and juke joints. The state-imposed limitations on collective ownership means that heirs' property presents more challenges than benefits.

In 1940, one of Alex and Charity Freeman's sons, Ellis Freeman, was between a rock and a hard place. He faced personal bankruptcy due to a defaulted loan. In a moment of desperation, Ellis sold his shares in the family land to a non-Freeman-owned realty company composed mostly of white developers. Unsurprisingly, one of the first moves this company made was filing for a partition of the land in alignment with the shares available to them. In doing so, these white developers were handed the rights to a prime piece of real estate, which they began building upon almost immediately.

This land sale signaled the beginning of the end for the Freemans. To this day, the land that formerly made up Freeman Beach doesn't legally belong to Freeman family descendants. One of the living heirs, Bill Freeman, has spoken openly about the family's ongoing struggles. In 2019, he told representatives and WWAY News, "[Freeman Beach LLC] is NOT a group of Freeman Family members. Much of that land has long since been removed from our hands, but we are about to place a monument on Freeman Beach in honor of all that our ancestors owned, all that they did to add to the lives of the people of the area. We want to help ensure that our children remember that if we did it before, they can do it now."

Legal professionals regularly preyed upon Black heirs' property owners, taking advantage of the hefty fees they could demand—but only from property sales! In other words, preserving landholdings was less lucrative, as far as white lawyers were concerned. And as Kahrl reiterated, "Given the dearth of [B]lack lawyers who specialized in real estate law in the South—a legacy of the Jim Crow era—[B]lack landowners often had little choice but to turn to lawyers who were, more often than not, working in collusion with developers and public officials." With tainted legal representation came tainted advice, which almost always recommended forced-partition sales that snowballed into total land-acquisition efforts.

The feigned saviorism of Southern lawyers regularly separated Black families from their land under the guise of clearing titles or turning a profit. Shiny promises marketed to bring Black Americans into coastal and farming industries almost always ended up with Black land going to the highest and whitest bidder. Keeping land in the family was a priority for Black people, but the lawyers representing them and the white corporations that hoped to acquire their land were all working against Black interests. Kahrl put it plainly: "As family properties became high-end hotels, private gated resorts, and golf courses, and savvy speculators and developers became millionaires, low-country [Black people] steadily became landless and dependent on the party wages of the service economy."

Beyond the threats to family dynamics, the legal classification designated to heirs' property is often incredibly limiting and leaves owners to fend for themselves. Being an heirs' property owner automatically blocks individuals and families from accessing loan modification and financing programs designed specifically for heirs, making most of them susceptible to foreclosure and eviction. Many grants offered through the USDA, the

Department of Housing and Urban Development (HUD), and the Federal Emergency Management Agency (FEMA) aren't available to heirs' property owners because of the heirs' "cloudy" or easily contested titles. White developers have exploited this legal loophole, taking advantage of the Black landowners who are especially vulnerable in moments of crisis.

The term *disaster capitalism,* coined by Naomi Klein, describes "orchestrated raids on the public sphere in the wake of catastrophic events," allowing powerful people to profit from moments of precarity and vulnerability for marginalized people. Much of the disparity stems from inequitable access to disaster recovery. In the case of heirs' property owners during times of natural disaster, working-class Black people are typically displaced as the money that could have rebuilt their homes goes to already-wealthy developers in the form of loans, grants, and tax incentives.

In 1954, when Hurricane Hazel passed Florida and began moving more inland, it was already on target to become the deadliest hurricane of the season. Eleven-foot tides hit all along the coast of the Carolinas, killing nineteen people in North Carolina alone and damaging tens of thousands of homes. Freeman Beach was devastated by the hurricane, but most Freemans—like Frank and Lula—had no access to disaster aid for rebuilding their property.

For many Black families, one or two setbacks like this regularly lead to land loss. The USDA has called heirs' property laws, and their disproportionately negative impact on Black landowners, "the leading cause of Black involuntary land loss." Over fourteen million acres of Black-owned land in the early twentieth century were siphoned away from communal landholdings to white-led corporations. Black people were able to accrue land in their own lifetimes, but passing that to the next generation was proving to be a more difficult story.

———

"In that place, where they tore the nightshade and blackberry patches from their roots to make room for the Medallion City Golf Course, there was once a neighborhood." This is how Toni Morrison introduces readers to the fictional town of Medallion, Ohio, and the Black neighborhood there known as "the Bottom," where one of the most archetypal examples of land theft takes place. (Please make *Sula* the next book you read if you haven't already.)

The story goes that a Black laborer was exploited by his white employer, who took the laborer's backbreaking work in exchange for what was supposed to be fertile land. Instead, the laborer's white boss gifted him land atop a hill that overlooked Medallion with a duplicitous promise that this parcel was some of the best land around. Over the next few years, the Bottom proved to be too hilly and vulnerable to erosion for planting. The Black people who came to call the Bottom home had no choice but to fight with the rocky terrain and make do.

Toni Morrison threads throughout the book the idea that, as she writes, "sometimes good looks like evil and evil looks like good." The undesirable land that Black people were tricked onto became prime real estate for white suburban families. The beech and pear trees that offered shade to children, along with the buildings that lined the road, were all set to be razed as the hill land became suddenly valuable.

The underlying trend that shows up throughout *Sula* is the reality that whenever white people decide they don't want land, they are able to manipulate Black people onto those scraps; and when white people decide they want land that Black people are on, they use the legal system to make those whims a reality.

Jordan Lake, west of downtown Raleigh, North Carolina, is a massive reservoir created in the early 1970s. On any given weekend, families drive out of their respective city centers and meet along the shores for camping, boating, swimming, and great fishing. The almost 14,000-acre reservoir, with the most breathtaking sunrises, once belonged to many Black farming families who fought valiantly but ultimately lacked the political capital to hold on to their land. Holding land and property in community with others has been one of the most quintessential aspects of egalitarian societies, and yet most of the wealthiest nations in the world uphold individualism as a constitutional prerogative.

Historically in the United States, the complicity of the federal government and legal system as a whole in land theft began with the emphasis of states' and property rights. The bicameral Congress we are still governed by was formed through the myth that "states" would lose representation if we organized federal representation by population. State governments are not people, yet our Senate, to this day, grants power to centuries-old border declarations diminishing the voting power of citizens in more densely populated parts of the nation where people own less land. From the meeting of the first dual-branch Congress, and with each amendment added to the Constitution likening property to liberty, nails were beaten into the coffin of collectivist political economies. First you make the landowners white. Then you make America a country by and for landowners. With this codependency in place, white supremacy props up the hoarding of land and natural resources, and vice versa.

As the wealth of this nation bloomed, the consolidation of power in white landowners' hands was baked into the DNA of American property law and in legislation governing political participation. The "Founding Fathers" built a federal government where only property-owning white men could vote, and the land ownership prerequisite was retracted on a state-by-state basis. In states like Rhode Island, poor white men fought back against their political exclusion in what became known as the Dorr Rebellion. Still, it would be more than fifteen years after the Dorr Rebellion before North Carolina became the last state to eliminate property restrictions to civic engagement.

But as abolitionists have always pointed out, systems of oppression evolve when not dismantled from the roots. Throughout the twentieth century, white property owners became more and more powerful and legal traps were set to ensnare Black farmers and landowners. One of the most frustrating aspects of the way legal systems have historically worked against Black landowners is how community-centered mindsets were actively threatened to ensure that wealthy Black people remained on islands of their own. The more isolated, the easier to control. Black land ownership patterns pre-colonization were always more anti-capitalist in nature, in that extended families and tribes were known to own and cultivate land together. From maroon communities to family homesteads, Black collectivist economic and environmental independence stood in the way of white land-grabbing.

In pursuit of the American dream, Black landowners who prioritized sustainability and heritage over profit were mostly eradicated through whitelashing, USDA discrimination, and a predatory legal system. From heirs' property limitations to skyrocketing property taxes, the law made it difficult for Black people to avoid foreclosure and having their land turned over to white families and their businesses. Unpaid property taxes—no matter how negligible the amount—could be cause for one's land to go up for auction.

Worse than vultures, developers wait for any slipup to pounce on vulnerable tracts of land. Even Black landowners who own their homes and acreage outright can be ensnared in unfair property tax burdens. Property taxes are calculated based on tax rates determined by district and assessed values that vary from owner to owner.

Wrongful property tax assessments nationally have resulted in disproportionately higher property taxes for the lowest-valued homes. In their 2022 report "The Assessment Gap: Racial Inequalities in Property Taxation," Carlos Avenancio-León and Troup Howard found that Black property owners face an almost 13 percent assessment gap that results in lost liquid capital. Even worse, a missed payment here and there quickly snowballs into unpaid bills leading to property seizures, as many generations of Bakers learned firsthand.

———

A shaky Wi-Fi connection and a mix of both anger and love filled the space between myself and the Jones siblings: JT, Michael, and Brenda. Seated in two staggered rows, both JT and Michael wore button-up shirts and Brenda wore a light-colored blouse. As we spoke, the gravity of their loss, coupled with the reality that the chance to tell their story meant so much to them, made me sit up straighter in my chair. I wanted to feel as official as the Jones family needed me to be. The stakes for them couldn't have been higher.

When their father, Willie Faye Jones, was born, he became part of the fourth generation of Joneses set to inherit access to the family plot in Huntsville, Alabama. Willie inherited a ten-acre plot from his father, Tommy Lee Jones, who had inherited the land (along with some that went to Willie's other siblings) from his mother, Lizzie Jones, who'd inherited the land from her father, Columbus Jones, who purchased a plot of land on January 4, 1870.

That ten-acre purchase almost a century before was still bearing fruit in the twentieth century. The Jones family may not have seemed wealthy by more limited standards: Willie, for example, read at a third-grade level well into adulthood and never lived a lavish life, but he was one of the largest Black landowners in the area and able to provide a home and source of employment through that land. Black folks for miles in each direction knew about the Jones family; they were talk of the county! Willie, his wife Lola Mae, and their family regularly hosted fish fries with their famous cakes and the freshest water, straight from the Jones family well. Willie Jones was known for his benevolence, and he took every chance to share that giving spirit with his eight children, as had each generation of Joneses before him. By keeping the land in the family, a deep sense of responsibility was passed on to care for themselves and others.

Around 1954, the local city government discovered that the Jones family land featured a well and wanted access to its water source. According to research done by Where Is My Land—which works closely with families to acquire as much proof of ownership and/or theft as possible—the City of Huntsville offered Willie Jones the obscenely low amount of nine hundred dollars for the portion of land containing the well, which he didn't accept. The same year that local Alabama officials first began eyeing the Jones family land, a landmark Supreme Court decision was being handed down that would change their lives forever.

The right to own private property is constitutionally protected by two amendments. The Fifth Amendment states (among other things) that "no person shall be . . . deprived of life, liberty, or property." Section one of the Fourteenth Amendment similarly offers equal protection under the law for American citizens, including one's right to property. While I consider it very dangerous to protect property rights alongside human ones, it's important to note this constitutional precedent because it becomes conveniently misapplied when Black people are concerned. The intention was always to prevent mass redistribution of property, even though that is precisely what the federal government accomplished for white settlers.

Eminent domain is the exception to the rule. In cases where property (whether land or buildings) is needed for public use, the government can seize that property. Eminent domain is expected to take place only in exchange for "just compensation" as calculated through appraisals of market value. Typically this will include condemning land for the creation of highways, or destroying abandoned buildings that are blights on the community, in order to build something more useful to the community. However, as Derecka Purnell wrote in *Becoming Abolitionists* when reflecting on the impact of eminent domain in her native St. Louis, even "highways are not neutral passageways and the violence . . . reverberates . . . for generations to come."

Halfway through the twentieth century, the blurry lines of eminent domain were called to the carpet. A city planning proposal in Washington, D.C., was developed to revitalize a 76-acre section of the southwest quadrant of the city. Through eminent domain, a city agency intended to seize an area full of single-family homes, apartment complexes, and private buildings and replace it with schools and parks while selling the remainder to private developers. One business owner contested the plan on the grounds that his private business was well maintained and not a threat to the community, and yet it was being taken, destroyed, and gifted to wealthier businessmen with fewer ties to the community. Where was the "public use" in that? In the end, the Supreme Court unanimously agreed to allow the use of eminent domain, which pushed thousands of low-income, mostly Black families out of their homes with few, if any, options. This case, *Berman v. Parker,* made it exponentially easier for local, state, and federal government officials to take land from Black landowners and farmers.

Back in Huntsville, four years after the Supreme Court ruled that the collateral damage of a few small landowners was a necessary expense in spite of any future public-interest land use, the city began the eminent domain process for condemning the Jones family well. The Joneses are one of countless Black families who have been subject to what has been dubbed eminent domain abuse. A 2014 briefing report called "The Civil Rights Implications of Eminent Domain Abuse" found that "private to private condemnations are often used for the benefit of the politically powerful at the expense of the politically weak . . . In most cases, those displaced by blight condemnations ended up worse off than they were before, and were not fully compensated for their losses." According to the Where Is My Land team, the Jones family contends they did not receive any notice of the condemnation of their land, so they could not prevent the condemnation or receive any compensation.

Dr. Mindy Fullilove's "Eminent Domain and African Americans" quantifies how, of the more than one million Americans who have been displaced through eminent domain, two-thirds of those people were Black. According to Fullilove, Black Americans were five times more likely to be displaced when compared to our proportion of the population. "What the government takes from people is not a home, with a small 'h,' but Home in the largest sense of the word: a place in the world, a community, neighbors and services, a social and cultural milieu, an economic anchor that provides security during the ups and downs of life, a commons that sustains the group by offering shared goods and services."

JT needed very few words to describe the devastating impacts of this land theft on the Jones family: "There were no good times." Overnight, the Jones family became sharecroppers living on isolated farmland in filthy, rodent-infested housing. Whereas the family had formerly never wanted for clean water and fresh produce, the Jones children were now forced to walk miles for water and to scrounge the nearby forests for almonds and vegetables. Prior to the legal troubles with the City of Huntsville, Willie's wife, Lola Mae, was occasionally sickly, but in this newfound isolation, her illness worsened. Things went from bad to worse; Lola Mae died with each of her eight children circled around to bear witness to her last breath.

In a matter of months, Willie Jones went from being a beloved patriarch and community leader to a landless single father of eight. Their eldest children became de facto sibling-parents to the youngest of the Jones children, taking on the burden of watching and feeding those who came behind them. "They were robbed of their childhoods and the right to get an education," spoke Michael with indignation.

Then, in 1971, Willie Jones dropped from two hundred pounds to less than eighty, and the two eldest brothers prepared to assume the role of formal guardian for their preteen siblings. "My father," spoke Michael solemnly, "is the greatest father we ever had. To see and to know that he was robbed of his inheritance, and died without anything in his pocket. It's horrible just to fathom that."

An entire family's trajectory was derailed so that the City of Huntsville, Alabama, could do . . . what exactly? In 1995, decades after initially being pushed off of their father's land, JT and Michael began to do some digging. The condemnation of their father's land was predicated on a claim that the water coming from the Jones family well was unfit for human consumption. The brothers' research uncovered that, post–eminent domain, a pump house was erected on the former Jones family plot. Later, that pump serviced a nearby pub and many other businesses. Other areas of the land, outside of the well, were transitioned into a university parking lot. Anyone attending an artistic performance at the University of Alabama in Huntsville may find themselves parking just outside of Wilson Hall, a theater that seats eighty people. Those cars and trucks currently reside on the family's stolen land.

The Where Is My Land research team is constantly poring over records, meeting with local officials, and interviewing family members to reveal how the legal system becomes an active player in pushing Black people off their land. "People can be pushed off of the land even long before any work is initiated," one of the researchers explained. "Once eminent domain is declared, any claims to the land are time-barred, even if the land

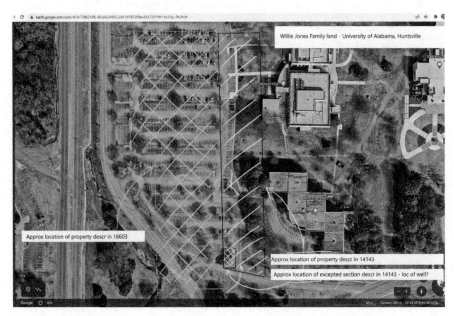

The Jones family land (COURTESY OF WHERE IS MY LAND).

wasn't ever developed for those initial purposes or was later sold to some-one else." The Jones siblings know this well.

Where Is My Land connected me to Beverly Moore and her daughter, Kadija, whose story echoes those of dozens of other Black families. There was an eerie familiarity in how she shared being unjustly targeted for con-demnation and how her family's lives have been irreparably disrupted. Beverly was four years old when she and her mother, Juanita Diane Moore, moved to a half-acre plot of land situated at 502 Enterprise Avenue. "The lot was big! We had a big side yard and my mother had a woodpile for the fireplace. All our blackberry bushes and fig trees and pear trees, my mother grew everything. She would hang the garlic and onions and stuff upside down to dry it out."

Everyone knew the Moores, mostly because everyone in the Black community of Richmond knew one another. But the Moores were uniquely active in the community, and their home at 502 Enterprise Avenue became a physical symbol of their community advocacy. In addition to the pro-duce, which was shared with neighbors near and far, Juanita Moore also ran a community library. Her open-door policy was what initially embed-ded them in the community, but it would be her children's advocacy that would start attracting more attention.

As Beverly entered her teen years, she became very outspoken about injustice. As a young girl, she was instrumental in pushing the city council to eradicate an antiquated and sexist rule that girls must wear skirts to school. "I never forgot the winter when we were still in high school and still had to wear skirts even when it was storming." Then, the Black Pan-ther Party for Self-Defense was exploding on the political scene. When the Black Panthers became nationally recognized, it was for their insistence upon using their Second Amendment rights to protect Black people against racist violence. But long before the rest of America even knew they existed, Black Panthers were running survival programs all throughout California in cities like Oakland and Richmond. The first-ever issue of the Black Panther Community News Service featured a cover story of a young Black man from North Richmond who was shot and killed by police.

Enterprise Avenue is a short dead-end street off of Sixth Street, where Huey Newton and the Black Panthers were setting up one of their first physical offices and meeting places. "The Black Panthers were across the street so everybody joined and were helping people with WIC, passing out information, and giving out food." The Panthers' Free Breakfast Program was a widely impactful initiative that fed tens of thousands of children each week across dozens of cities. By 1969, every city with a Black Panther Party chapter was operating a Breakfast Program and many others also leveraged community and urban gardens toward feeding community members. Beverly was young then and not quite sure what this work would amount to, but she had been raised to live a life of service.

From the mid-1950s through the 1970s, Juanita Moore and her children were renters. Then, in 1980, Beverly Moore purchased the only home she'd ever known. Thirteen years later, the City of Richmond seized her land. The proposed use: drainage for a highway project. "They 'needed' our land," Beverly said sarcastically while motioning air quotes, "but apparently they didn't need any of the land around ours." Five-oh-two Enterprise Avenue was the only land seized on the block and the only home torn down by the city.

Throughout our conversation, Beverly spoke confidently but in a reserved way. Her daughter Kadija had a bit more bass in her throat and resolve in her eyes. She often chimed in to hammer home a point that she needed me to understand or to fill in details that she felt her mother had left out. "My mom and her siblings were radicals . . . they were associated with the Black Panthers and making change within the community and going to college . . . I feel like if there was a way to stop a family that was making a very huge impact in the community, [eminent domain] was the tactic they used." Kadija clearly sees her family as an intergenerational group of activists who were targeted for what they meant to Black people in Richmond. And after looking at the records and hearing their story, so do I.

Eminent domain abuse is well documented. Hilary O. Shelton has worked on the front lines of civil rights and has been instrumental to the passing of several groundbreaking pieces of civil rights legislation, including the Native American Free Exercise of Religion Act, the Reauthorization of the Voting Rights Act, and the Civil Rights Act of 1991. In a 2014 briefing report compiled by the U.S. Commission on Civil Rights, Shelton testified that elected officials disproportionately misuse eminent domain against non-white people and the economically disadvantaged. Shelton cited two studies proving that eminent domain use displaced African Americans five times more often than their representation in the nation's population.

Asset forfeiture has become normalized in a twenty-first-century world where law enforcement can seize one's car, property, and other belongings for the purpose of keeping or selling it—all prior to a conviction. Most justification for the practice includes claims that civil asset forfeiture allows police to "cripple" organized crime rings, yet it's most often low-income people of color who pay the price. To take it a step further, the use of asset forfeiture to retaliate against and make an example of Black political leaders is prevalent. Many don't bother to report the theft of their land, homes, vehicles, and other possessions due to fear of law enforcement involvement.

The Moore family was never the same after being displaced from their home. "Our history was gone and there was a lot of addiction in our family after that," Beverly admitted. First Juanita Moore suffered with alcoholism and then Beverly's sister (and Kadija's aunt) began to struggle. Beverly's sister also grew up at 502 Enterprise Avenue and had been an accountant with a master's degree before addiction pushed her into homelessness. "She never left the community," said Beverly through what sounded like a lump in her throat. "She would have rather been on the streets in Richmond than go anywhere else."

Most recently, Beverly's brother was released from prison after serving seventeen years for a nonviolent offense—yet another abuse of a system of power that disenfranchised a member of the Moore family. After his release, Beverly's brother had few places to go while rebuilding his life. "Richmond is family. Richmond is connectedness." Long after their family home was taken and torn down, the family has been scrounging for a slice of what they once had. Beverly has held on to their once-blossoming garden through a 2' x 2' urban plot, and many of her siblings roam the streets craving what once was.

Beverly added in an almost-whisper, "And we had no choice. It was supposed to be for the betterment of the city and they talked about bringing in more jobs to do this and that." The city never used the land for drainage and it has sat as a vacant lot for several decades. In 2022, the City of Richmond designated the lot as "surplus land" and planned to put it up for sale rather than returning it to Beverly Moore. When asked if she had any demands, Beverly spoke up: "I want my land back."

PART FOUR

THE
OUTCOME

The elders were wise. They knew that
man's heart, away from nature,
becomes hard; they knew that lack of
respect for growing, living things, soon led
to lack of respect for humans, too.

—CHIEF LUTHER STANDING BEAR,
SICANGU AND OGLALA LAKOTA

THE RACIAL
WEALTH GAP AS
WE KNOW IT

**The five largest landowners in America, all white, own
more rural land than all of Black America combined.**

—ANTONIO MOORE (2016)

In a country where land and its resources are commodities, the exclusion
and expulsion of Black and Indigenous people from the land economy has
been an act of financial warfare. Take the fact that Black Americans own
less than 1 percent of U.S. farmland, or that Indigenous households have
approximately eight cents of wealth for every white household's dollar.
White supremacy's campaign to exclude communities of color from land
for financial gain is a war not yet ceased.

The mainstream conversation on the racial wealth gap is nearly devoid
of how much money was amassed, passed down, and repurposed through
land theft and hoarding. There is of course the evidence: testaments of
sacred, ancestral land being vandalized; Black family farms becoming university parking garages, vacant lots, military forts, and corporate cam-
puses; and gentrification raging on, further displacing working-class
(mostly Black and brown) people. However, the national dialogue leaves
most of this out. It's why economists and sociologists like Charles C.
Geisler have worked so tirelessly to bring landholdings back into the national framing of poverty. In his 1995 paper titled "Land and Poverty in the
United States," Geisler claims that "land influences wealth and poverty in

a variety of important ways" and that "indirect ownership of property of all kinds increases with wealth." Geisler's more explicit plea to the reader is that connections between land, power, and wealth be "dragged out of the closet, carefully examined, and used to forge more direct and more effective national, state, and local policy."

There is a mountain of quantitative and qualitative evidence to back up the claim that the wealthy landowners of the past developed trusts and endowments for future generations. The wealth they hoarded has since funded and birthed the CEOs, politicians, and corporations who control our food, media, and housing into the twenty-first century. Further, the children and grandchildren of the sharecroppers, farmers, and landowners who had their labor and acreage snatched from under them are just as poor and in debt—if not more so—than their foreparents were decades and centuries ago. Land and property were not by-products of this dynamic; they were critical tools used to create systematic barriers.

Cross-generational asset hoarding by white families and corporations has led to new heights of wealth accrual, and attempts to address them by working twice as hard have been sending Black people to early graves. For all the fearmongering around taxing the rich, fairly little is said of the ways white families have redistributed Black and Indigenous wealth for themselves. And for all of the advocacy around pay equity and wage equality, few are acknowledging trust funds and estates that can't be outworked. The cards that are stacked against us have been compounding interest, and it's time to follow the money.

Dedrick Asante-Muhammad is one of the leading subject-matter experts on racial economic inequality. In a conversation I had with him about the role of land ownership and passed-down assets in building wealth, he stated, "Wealth is the clearest indicator of socioeconomic stability and inequality." It's a fuller metric and highlights that the country isn't on the path to bridging inequality but widening it. Further wealth is broader than immediate financial returns. Having access to money is important for immediate survival, but the ability to stow money away for the future is how wealth accumulates for the benefit of future generations. "You can't be as long-term or strategic when you're in asset poverty," he remarked. "You make decisions about the immediate future."

Dedrick continued, "Asset poverty is not the condition of an individual or a household. It's when the whole community is asset poor." Assets can be leveraged for wealth-building through liquidation of assets or leveraging them as collateral. Yet at almost every critical juncture and economic shift in American history, Black Americans have had less capital to engage in those moments of great prosperity for white America. "Whether individual household wealth or community wealth was more about land in the early twentieth century, home ownership in the late twentieth century, or finance in the twenty-first century," Dedrick stressed, "Black people have less and we generally get less in returns."

Black land theft has not only reduced Black economic opportunities, but it has also often been used for the direct benefit of white peers. When touching on the double-edged sword in these persistent inequities, Dedrick called attention to the ways white public benefit has always superseded Black autonomy. "Oftentimes, Black land has been taken to develop public space like highways or parks. These projects created white public benefit by confiscating Black land or by using Black land as a dumping ground. So it's two things: It's appropriating Black land, and putting negative externalities that further drive down the value of the land as well as Black lives themselves."

In a 2018 Brookings Institution report, Andre M. Perry, a commentator on structural inequality and the devaluation of Black assets and author of *Know Your Price: Valuing Black Lives and Property in America's Black Cities,* posed the critical question *What is the cost of racial bias?* "Homes of similar quality in neighborhoods with similar amenities are worth 23 percent less ($48,000 per home on average, amounting to $156 billion in cumulative losses) in majority Black neighborhoods." Further, the report states, "the devaluing of Black lives led to segregation and racist federal housing policy through redlining that shut out chances for Black people to purchase homes and build wealth, making it more difficult to start and invest in businesses and afford college tuition."

According to a 2019 report by McKinsey & Company, Black families are more than three times less likely to receive an inheritance, and when we do it's at about a third of the value of white families. This report highlights that "Black families begin with lower levels of wealth: only 8 percent of black families receive an inheritance, compared with 26 percent of white families. When an inheritance is distributed, it is 35 percent of the value of that of a white family." Across history, Black Americans have worked tirelessly to invest in their families, in order to be able to pass on wealth, and we know that it is not lack of financial literacy or business acumen, but systematic inequity beginning with land and wealth hoarding, that prevents this.

In 1901, Rep. George Henry White, a Black congressman from North Carolina, delivered a speech to the House of Representatives where he listed the economic achievements of Black Americans nationwide:

> We have accumulated over $12,000,000 worth of school property and about $40,000,000 worth of church property. We have about 140,000 farms and homes, valued at in the neighborhood of $750,000,000, and personal property valued at about $170,000,000. We have raised about $11,000,000 for educational purposes, and the property per capita for every colored man, woman, and child in the United States is estimated at $75 . . . We have over 600,000 acres of land in the South alone. The cotton produced, mainly by black labor, has increased from 4,669,770 bales in 1860 to 11,235,000 in 1899. All this we have done under the most adverse circumstances.

Based on Congressman White's words and access to research, Black America owned and controlled what today would be worth more than $30 trillion in land and property, with the majority of that land being communally owned and evenly distributed among Black families and community institutions. For all of the sociopolitical gains that we have made, most Black Americans are worse off financially now than they were a hundred years ago.

By 1910, multiple records show that 16 to 19 million acres of land were owned by about 210,000 Black people. But with the Wilmington Massacre, Congressman White had seen the carnage in his home state as a foreshadowing of the theft to come. His term came to an end as Wilmington marked a temporary halting of multiracial organizing and Black wealth-building across North Carolina. In that same 1901 speech, he said, "This, Mr. Chairman, is perhaps the negroes' temporary farewell to the American Congress; but let me say, Phoenix-like he will rise up some day and come again." Over the next seventy years after White's term in office, no Black people were elected to Congress (Congresswoman Barbara Jordan would be the one to break this streak!), and Black wealth was slashed until only crumbs remained.

When talking about Black wealth, it's necessary to focus on Black farmers in particular. Because of historic exclusion from most other industries, Black Americans were pigeonholed into the agrarian economy, so any wealth we could have passed down likely would have been tied to land or farming. Further, most Black Americans have genealogical roots in the South, and Black families presently remain concentrated in Southern and Midwestern states like Louisiana, Arkansas, Mississippi, Alabama, Tennessee, Florida, Georgia, the Carolinas, Illinois, and Michigan, where farming and agriculture more generally dominate the economy. A November 2021 McKinsey Institute for Black Economic Mobility report highlighted that the median income and net worth of Black farmers are significantly higher than those of all Black Americans. Ownership and participation in the agricultural economy present some of the greatest opportunities for Black wealth-building.

According to that 2021 McKinsey study, if Black farms were to achieve parity on a per-farm revenue basis, they stand to generate $5 billion in economic value. The reality is, year after year, Black farmers have been blocked from their rightful place in the larger rural land, agricultural, and mineral economy. Dr. Darrick Hamilton, an economics and urban policy professor who has shaped progressive federal racial justice proposals and announced a first-of-its-kind study to quantify the land stolen from Black farmers, hasn't been shy about reminding people that Black land loss isn't a hypothesis or one-off experience. "This is empirical," he says, and if you ask him, lead author Dr. Dania Francis, or any of the other economists who worked on the study, they'll tell you that Black American farmers lost more than $326 billion's worth of land throughout the 1900s.

According to the Historical Survey of Consumer Finances, by 1968, the median white household had ten times as much wealth as the average

Black household. Notably, their research also found that while income grew at comparable rates, though still substantially uneven, most wealth inequality stemmed from persistent pre–civil rights era disparities. The report, "Income and Wealth Inequality in America, 1949–2016," explicitly states, "The wealth gap [between 1950 and 2010] is much larger than the income gap. The median Black household disposes of 12% of the wealth of a median white household." The report goes on to describe one of the only periods when racial wealth gaps temporarily narrowed: the housing boom of the 1990s and early 2000s. When Black households were disproportionately impacted by the 2008 financial crisis and subsequent housing price collapse and recession, racial wealth gaps widened once again.

The late twentieth century showed no signs of slowing down the wealth loss and theft. A thirty-year assessment of Federal Reserve data titled "The Road to Zero Wealth: How the Racial Wealth Divide Is Hollowing Out America's Middle Class" found that between 1983 and 2013, median Black household wealth decreased by 75 percent, from $6,800 to $1,700. The Winter 2002 edition of *Rural America,* titled "Who Owns the Land? Agricultural Land Ownership by Race/Ethnicity," cites census data which finds that, by the late 1990s, Black farmers and landowners were still highly concentrated in the South and owned less than two million acres of land. Whereas before, almost one million Black farmers owned and tended to land, an investigation by *The Counter* discovered that by 1997 this number had declined by 98 percent, to fewer than 19,000 Black farmers. By 2002, the USDA reported that Black people owned less than 1 percent of rural land in the United States, valued at about $14 billion combined. Of all private U.S. agricultural land, the report explains, white Americans make up 96 percent of landowners and control 97 percent of all land value, which means that, in addition to owning more land, white Americans also tend to possess more *lucrative* land. America's total land value in 2023 is more than $23 trillion for 2.4 billion acres of land, water, and biodiversity, 98 percent of which is still owned by white Americans. Thirty years after abusing policies, violently seizing land, or deceiving and manipulating Black folks into selling, Black farmers and landowners have still not recovered.

Beyond farmland and rural acreage, Black people are less likely to own assets in general—unsurprising when you consider how much disposable income would be needed to do so. According to the National Community Reinvestment Coalition, while 72 percent of white Americans own a home, only 42 percent of Black Americans do. This gap has remained fairly consistent over the last one hundred years. Similarly, statistics available from a 2019 Board of Governors survey of the Federal Reserve System express that less than 6 percent of Black Americans own stake in a business and that Black households have about one-fourth the liquid assets of white households.

Visual representation of racial wealth gaps based on data from the Center for American Progress's 2021 study "Wealth Matters," which reveals that white American households have double the home equity and quadruple the liquid assets as Black American families (ART BY @CHI.SOULART).

As of 2021, Black Americans held 4 percent of America's household wealth despite making up about 13 percent of the U.S. population. Millions of Black American families—approximately 19 percent of us—have a negative net worth, and millions more have a net worth less than $10,000. We're overrepresented in jails, prisons, and debt metrics and underrepresented in areas that could holistically nourish our people, like: being business owners, pursuing higher education, investing in new crafts, or otherwise developing regenerative and independent communities. Generations of Black people who were forced to weather storms without so much as a raincoat have vanished safety nets.

Our economic precarity as a people has only been compounded by ongoing racial discrimination. Black people are more vulnerable to predatory lending, financial fraud, and housing insecurity. Living in zip codes accessible to working-class Black people has also typically meant surrendering to a lifetime of bad schools, crumbling infrastructure, limited healthcare, and weak public safety—all of which are expensive in both the short and long run.

The violence of chronic poverty and racial capitalism has been incessant, and the hoarded spoils have built modern empires. Unfortunately—and irresponsibly—many of the reports I've cited throughout this chapter have not named white supremacy, land theft, or capitalism as the culprit behind the statistics. It's important that we remember and reiterate that racial wealth gaps are not accidental, nor to be blamed on an alleged lack of ambition or work ethic. Poor and/or racially marginalized people cannot outwork a centuries-long head start, and certainly not if our opponent continues to cheat.

THE LAND WANTS
US BACK

═══

**I was raised with the belief (through Islam and culture)
that the land holds a memory, that it is a living being.
Many of the tribal, Indigenous people, and
sharecroppers who have been forced to flee are not
only hurting for the loss of their homes, they are aching
for their land which connects them to generations of
family members behind them . . . It is beyond material
loss, it's spiritual and emotional. The land is in pain,
we feel it too . . . This is not to diminish the very serious
economic effects of losing crops and homes and
businesses, but to also share what is not easily visible.**

—AYISHA SIDDIQA

Our family's land is inland, but not too far from the coast. North Carolina's barrier islands have historically protected the rest of the state from natural disasters and the Atlantic Ocean. Increasingly, as the utility of those wetlands and small islands has been ignored in favor of resorts and golf courses, floods swallow up streets, destroy dams, and make gainful farming even more precarious than it already was. After Hurricane Matthew ravaged most of the state, the dam on our family land cracked and the lake that once teemed with beavers and fish is now more mud than anything else. Water from nearby creeks and brooks flows through the area with nothing keeping the water in place. The flooding is insistent.

Working-class Black people and other marginalized people across the country are forced to live in areas where no one else wants to live: places with infertile soil that flood easily; areas categorized as food deserts; crowded apartments with lead poison in the paint, toxins in the play-

*Photos of the dried-up lake juxtaposed with images
of the lake from less than a decade ago.*

ground soil, and pollutants in the air. This is not accidental or naturally occurring; often Black and Indigenous people are pushed onto depleted land and forced to bear the weight of problems created and exacerbated by wealthy white people, primarily because the powerful get to decide who pays their consequences. Land theft, then, is a centuries-long public health crisis.

Sometimes, especially throughout the nineteenth century, environmental degradation was a purposeful act of warfare against an already disenfranchised people. Unfortunately, the generals who ordered the destruction of land, animals, and natural resources were too shortsighted to see how those choices would ripple out and impact their own descendants as well. In his piece "A Rational Agriculture Is Incompatible with Capitalism," Fred Magdoff argues that the strategies which "make eminent sense for the individual capitalist or company . . . end up being a problem not only for workers, but the capitalist system itself . . . Many practices and side effects of the way the system functions degrade the ecosystem and its processes on which we depend and may also directly harm humans."

The same violent methods used to push Black and Indigenous people off of land have had dire consequences for the planet, too. Public health and environmental health are inextricably linked; what hurts soil, water, animals, and air almost always hurts us as well. By separating ourselves from the natural world, we are dooming the planet to apocalyptic nightmares, and Black and Indigenous people to early graves. With each species of animal that goes extinct, every site of natural beauty that is desecrated, all of the trees that are torn down, and every body of water that turns sour from oil, trash, chemicals, or a combination of the three, we all suffer.

The American bison once roamed in large herds estimated at tens of millions across the Great Plains and in American river valleys. However, due to a concerted effort by the U.S. military to deprive Indigenous peoples of their key food source, the bison was nearly made extinct. In just a few years, more than four million bison were killed, making wild bison rare to this day. Beavers, too, were driven to near extinction due to excessive fur trapping, but twentieth-century conservation efforts revived American beaver populations. An unprecedented study by the American Economic Association quantified the long-term effects of the mass slaughters. Physiologically speaking, the near extinction of bison led to a significant decrease in bison-dependent peoples. The financial damages are even more severe:

We compile historical, anthropological, ecological, geographic, and modern economic data to show that the elimination of the bison affected the well-being of the Indigenous peoples who relied on them, both immediately after the bison's decline, and up to 130 years later. We argue that the loss of the bison resulted in a dramatic reversal of fortunes: historically, bison-reliant societies were among the richest in the world and now they are among the poorest . . . Nations that lost the bison slowly had approximately 20% less income on average, whereas those that lost the bison rapidly had approximately 40% less income.

This coordinated attack pushed various Native nations, who were previously able to sustain their families with the plentiful bison meat and hides, into intergenerational poverty. With these nations struggling to evade starvation, the U.S. military was able to easily displace these tribes and snatch up the natural resources they had access to. Plenty Coups, chief of the Crow Nation, mourned the loss deeply: "When the buffalo went away the hearts of my people fell to the ground, and they could not lift them up again."

Railroad tycoons have also been notoriously callous in disrupting natural habitats and ancestral land whenever profit calls. Throughout the 1800s, treaties were regularly forced onto Indigenous nations under threat of violence if they resisted. All of this was done to permit railway construction, though those developments rarely benefited Native American people and almost always resulted in harm to animals and plants that the tribes had depended on and lived in harmony with for generations. The introduction of high-speed trains without sufficient fencing regularly led to animals being struck. The railroad stops demanded for land and businesses to be cleared. In *I've Been Here All the While,* Alaina E. Roberts details the ways that railroad companies ignored treaties and Indigenous land sovereignty at the expense of both people and planet: "Even though railroads had to pay for the Indian land they built on through stock exchanges, per the Treaties of 1866, this initial purchase meant they then had the built-in ability to also purchase the six miles on either side of the railroad track. This quickly wore away at tribal land holdings." In other words, letting a railroad company take an inch would surely lead to them taking several hundred thousand acres of pristine land.

About a half century later, into the 1900s, encroachment upon Indigenous land was proving to be deadly as land's resilience to natural disasters waned and the severity of storms increased. Thanks to white industry leaders and federal USDA experts who preached the gospel of mechanization and cash crops, farmers across the central United States began to plow the grassy plains in hopes of introducing new non-native plants that would be more lucrative. During the 1930s dry season, which coincided with the Great Depression, drought-resistant grasses were nowhere to be found and loose topsoil took to the sky once high winds kicked in. From South Dakota all the way down to Tennessee and even further to Texas, dust clouds blocked out the sun and stifled the air in what became known as "Black Sunday blizzards."

Hundreds of thousands of Americans were left homeless, with countless family homesteads leveled to the ground. Thousands more died from Dust Bowl–related illnesses, including heatstroke, starvation, and dust pneumonia. (These storms occurred during a summer when temperatures regularly exceeded 100 degrees, leaving people stuck in their homes during unbearable heat.) These folks became climate migrants.

Public educator and self-described eco-communicator Leah Thomas has heavily explored the relationship between social justice and environmentalism. In *The Intersectional Environmentalist*, a book named after both a term she coined and the platform she founded, Thomas introduces readers to Black environmental activists who have been sounding the alarm on the extractive practices of engaging with the planet for decades, as well as naming and amplifying the dire consequences for biodiversity, wildlife, and natural resources. Those outcomes in turn are deadly, and the people doing the most harm—those who hire private firefighters in the face of incessant wildfires, for instance—move around the globe freely, even search for new planets to hide on, while the rest of us shoulder the burden.

One of the advocates who Thomas profiles in her book is Hazel M. Johnson, a Black woman from the South Side of Chicago who became a researcher and community activist after watching her husband and neighbors die from lung cancer at alarming rates. Johnson's research revealed that Altgeld Gardens Homes, the housing project where she lived, was constructed upon a plot of land known to have abnormally high asbestos levels, and that their neighborhood was surrounded by landfills and toxic waste sites. Having abruptly become a single mother of seven, Johnson began investigating the respiratory, carcinogenic, and skin conditions that her loved ones were facing after extended exposure to the fumes and water of the Altgeld Gardens area. Johnson later coined the term "toxic doughnut" to describe the phenomenon experienced nationwide but especially in urban centers, as well as throughout the South, where you are exposed to high concentrations of hazardous waste.

The ominously known "Cancer Alley," which some residents feel is more apt to be called "Death Row," is a less-than-100-acre stretch of land in southern Louisiana with the ninth-highest cancer death rate in the nation (as of 2020) and is responsible for more than a quarter of all petrochemical production. According to the 2021 Toxics Release Inventory Factsheet, which tracks the management of chemicals that threaten human health and the environment, Louisiana has the second-highest amount of toxic releases per square mile in the country. Along the Mississippi River, industrial headquarters and towering metal forts have been stationed as great return on investment to shareholders, but the greatest cost being paid is by the Black residents along the riverbanks and nearby parishes.

In one parish that falls within Cancer Alley, St. Gabriel residents are surrounded by more than two dozen chemical plants within ten to fifteen miles of their homes. Further south, in Wallace of St. John the Baptist Parish, where 90 percent of the population is Black and has spent the majority of their lives just miles from where their ancestors were enslaved, petrochemical plant emissions have created abnormally and astronomically high cancer rates. Clint Smith quoted civil rights leader Rev. Dr. William J. Barber II, who said this of Cancer Alley: "The same land that held people captive through slavery is now holding people captive through this environmental injustice and devastation."

The density of chemical plants in such a small area has compounded risks for many Louisianans who call the St. James Parish area home. Despite decades of protests, plans to build new chemical plants continue to be introduced and approved by local officials while more Black people die or lose the only land they've ever known. In 2018, the St. James Parish Council approved a private development initiative led by one of the largest plastics facilities in the world. The "Sunshine Project" would build fourteen new facilities in Cancer Alley atop 2,400 acres, thanks to more than $1 billion in government subsidies and tax breaks. If successful, the project would allegedly bring in $9 billion and countless jobs in exchange for more than double the risk of being diagnosed with cancer for St. James Parish residents. Representatives of the United Nations have resisted the proposed expansion, claiming that the emissions of a single parish would exceed the emissions of 113 countries.

The hazy smoke-filled air, full of mysterious chemicals that simultaneously flow into the river, affect the almost one million people who live in what has been dubbed a "sacrifice zone." Just as it sounds, these zones have been deemed irreparably damaged for both people and land. The term first popped up to describe the ghost mine sites and the long-term effects of extracting so much from the land that there is little else to do with said land. That's not to say that sacrifice zones are uninhabited, but that the damage will be felt by anyone deciding—or forced—to remain post-designation. As Naomi Klein divulged in her book *This Changes Everything: Capitalism vs. the Climate,* "Extractivism is also directly connected to the notion of sacrifice zones—places that, to their extractors, somehow don't count and therefore can be poisoned, drained, or otherwise destroyed for the supposed greater good." One Brooklyn high school teacher, Rosemarie Frascella, explored the concept with her eleventh-grade students, breaking down the idea that the sacrifice came without choice: "Someone else is sacrificing people and their community or land without their permission."

The same year that Hazel Johnson founded a nonprofit organization, People for Community Recovery, solidifying her place as the "mother of environmental justice," Dr. Robert Bullard was publishing his findings on toxic waste and its effects on Houston's Black community. A son of Alabama who has studied, taught, and lived across the South, Bullard is an expert on eco-racism. Through his research, he uncovered the fact that all of Houston's publicly owned landfills, and the majority of the private ones too, were in predominantly Black neighborhoods despite the city being only 25 percent Black. Bullard published his first book, *Dumping in Dixie,* which established the research-backed conclusion that Black communities in the southern United States had been targeted for the placement of landfills and incinerators, lead smelters, petrochemical plants, and other toxic facilities.

Even in more middle- to upper-class areas where Black home ownership rates were higher, many residents found themselves with few options when it came to their ecological safety. "It was a form of apartheid," Leah Thomas writes in her book *The Intersectional Environmentalist.* "According to a 2008 study by J. Andrew Horner and Nia Robinson, 71 percent of Black Americans live in places that violate federal air pollution standards, and 78 percent of us live within thirty miles of a coal-fired power plant. Further, just under one in two Black Americans lives in what are called heat islands, neighborhoods that retain heat due to a void of green spaces and an oversaturation of pavement. Indigenous people are least likely to have access to safe running water, which becomes even more threatened with each new oil pipeline project. These statistics are more than just figures; they have shaped every part of our lives, including the food we have access to, whether public spaces are sites of joy or conflict, and quite literally whether we can survive at all.

———

I do my best meditating when floating in water. Maybe it's the way floating requires you to trust nature and your body to do what they do best. Surrendering to your own buoyancy with the water muting all sounds is a freeing reminder that we overcomplicate life to our own detriment. We are born with everything we need to float, and so the only thing left to do is be. Only when we doubt nature does our body begin to panic and sink.

I've begun to think that our relationship to the environment around us operates in the same way. Capitalists have tried everything under the sun to make farming—and everything associated with it—faster, cheaper, bigger, better. Call it the God complex in them. Time and time again we find out that these human interventions are disrupting an age-old process. Instead of deferring to Indigenous expertise, the pursuit of money will always lead greedy people to believe they know better than anyone else.

Capitalists' hubris is not-so-slowly killing us all, including this planet we call home.

Only when we release the need to be subduers of all else will we return ourselves and this land to its rightful equilibrium. Indigenous people across the world have always centered reciprocity with all living things and the refusal to mind that wisdom has proven fatal. History has shown us repeatedly that Indigenous and Black people must lead the charge to re-membering and restoring. We crave a return to the land, yes, but the land wants—needs—us back too. Reparation is a racial and economic justice policy as well as a climate necessity. The future of this planet depends on our collective willingness to deliver that justice.

Throughout the twentieth century, a series of man-made issues have plagued the coastal Wilmington area, much of which was once beaches be-longing to the Freeman family. In the early 1930s, coastal land was appropri-ated from Freeman landholdings to create an artificial canal called Snow's Cut. This canal, connecting Myrtle Grove Sound to Cape Fear River, was initially intended for commercial fishing and turned nearby Carolina Beach into its own barrier island. In the process, the water of Myrtle Grove Sound became deep enough for large vessels to enter into the waters.

Patrons who had grown accustomed to their short walk or swim to the beach now had to drive through segregated Carolina Beach or book the newly added ferry. As the maritime industry boomed and wealthy white people got richer, the once-accessible Freeman Beach, which welcomed Black people when few other waterfront properties did, was becoming more out of reach.

The Freemans had already lost some land to eminent domain, but with the changing tides and water patterns, soon erosion took hundreds more acres. The man-made canal, which was only ever intended to be about a hundred feet wide, has widened over the last half century to a whopping seven hundred feet. As a result, much of the land lining Snow's Cut still regularly floods, creating contaminated water that pollutes Myrtle Grove Sound and kills immeasurable amounts of marine life. A good portion of the damage caused by Hurricane Hazel in the mid-1950s was irreparable without governmental aid, leaving businesses along Freeman Beach with-out the once-lively hub they'd come to know and love.

No one was willing to take accountability for the land loss created by the man-made Snow's Cut or the harsh natural disasters that followed. The land loss created from the construction of this inlet is indisputable and well documented (thanks to the tireless advocacy of Frank Freeman's daughter Evelyn Williams), but the Freeman family has received no restitution. By the mid-1950s, local government was using strategies like eminent domain to gather hundreds more acres of Freeman land—until Supreme Court–mandated desegregation in the '60s put the final nail in the coffin of Seabreeze Resort and the many businesses Freeman Beach was home to. By 1975, Bop City was devoid of all Black businesses.

The impact of Black and Indigenous land loss, as well as the extractive methods typically used by the capitalists who orchestrate that loss/theft, has devastating impacts on the Land and Her resources. In 1877, Chief Sitting Bull gave a speech to the Powder River Council in which he said, "They claim this mother of ours, the Earth, for their own use, and fence their neighbors away from her, and deface her with their buildings and their refuse. They compel her to produce out of season, and when sterile she is made to take medicine in order to produce again. All this is sacrilege."

To reverse this desecration, we must follow the lead of those who had the foresight to resist the eco-violence when it was happening. According to the Indigenous Environmental Network, "Indigenous resistance has curbed 12% of US and Canada's annual emissions over the last decade . . . Indigenous people have always been our planet's greatest protectors." Further, a 2022 study by Jocelyne S. Sze (et al.) found that "Indigenous lands—covering a quarter of Earth's surface and overlapping with a third of intact forests—often have reduced deforestation, degradation, and carbon emissions, compared with non-protected areas and protected areas." If this is possible in the face of continued broken treaties, underinvestment, and erasure, imagine what could be achieved if the most powerful and wealthy people in the country claiming to care about the future of the planet directed their resources to Black and Indigenous people. Imagine what we could achieve through the restoration of healthy ecosystems by natural processes, where wildlife re-consumes swaths of land, also known as "rewilding."

While the Land is resilient, Her memory is extensive. At every turn in American history, wealthy white Americans have had the option to build a society that works for all of us, and instead opted to care for themselves and their immediate relatives at the expense of everyone else. The children, grandchildren, nieces and nephews, and other heirs to those legacies must choose between being hoarders or helpers. Neutrality isn't possible when some of us can't breathe.

PART FIVE

THE
TAKEBACK

**We didn't come all the way up
here to compromise for no more than
we'd gotten here.**

—FANNIE LOU HAMER

**And I will plant them upon their land,
and they shall no more be pulled up out
of their land which I have given them,
saith the LORD thy God.**

—AMOS 9:15

A LABOR OF LOVE

═══

I'm goin' back to the South . . .
Where my roots ain't watered down . . .
Of life on fertile ground,
ancestors put me on game.

—BEYONCÉ, "BLACK PARADE"

Throughout the late twentieth century, Black farmers and landowners waged a war on any institution standing in between the Black community and the wealth and sovereignty we are owed. In this battle over birthrights, land was the first frontier, and reparations one of the most consistent demands. Working the land had been a labor of love, and so would owning the means of production. It always came down to love.

During the research process for this book, I attempted to retrace those acts of love. Written records were a priority, and I found myself driving one-lane roads to county registrar, clerk, and deeds offices across the state of North Carolina. Most of these buildings stood out in their colonial architecture and slow foot traffic. Redbrick courthouses trimmed in white became recurring site visits. Walking around the side of the building, up the ramp, and through the metal detector was a pilgrimage of sorts.

Stepping into quiet country offices and thumbing through anything with the name "Baker" on it brought me closer to my not-so-distant family history. I was often the only non-employee there, playing with microfilms, sifting through old archives, and making photocopies. I was slowly piecing together a story of great loss, love, and redemption within my family. Each visit, I silently prayed for the answers I sought and often left with more questions. There isn't a day that passes when I don't regret not being able to interview my paternal grandfather.

Alfred made it his life's mission to ensure his children and grandchildren understood why we must fight for land, and that in order to fight for it, his children had to first learn to love it. "He never stopped talking about moving back to North Carolina. It was almost like he knew something about North Carolina that the rest of us didn't," my Uncle David said of his father's fixation. "He used all his vacation days taking us kids to North Carolina, and bought another plot of land when I was about twelve or thirteen."

When my Auntie Deanna looks at photos from back then, it triggers smells from her girlhood—the earthy smells of dirt and animals rolled into one. She hugs her belly while remembering the animals, the horses, mules, and pigs, especially Big Lucy, "the biggest, ugliest, fattest pig." Auntie Deanna remembers a childhood full of joy and feet pounding the springy grass during summers spent on the land. "I always felt the land and family there and a sense of belonging. Even though I grew up in Paterson, New Jersey, I also felt like a North Carolinian."

My father, Steven, is the oldest of Alfred and Jenail's children, and he recalls the thick clay dirt, smell of pine, and sputterings of an old tractor.

My grandfather Alfred Baker on the front steps of Grandma Martha's home (left) and my Auntie Deanna as a child on the side of that home (right).

"He never allowed the country to leave us," he says of my grandfather, of his resolve to keep them connected. "I remember driving down in the station wagon. It had three rows of seats and the last row faced backwards, looking out of the trunk and towards traffic." I laughed incredulously at the lack of passenger safety measures for such small children. "We knew we were close because the ride would get rougher as half the roads weren't paved," my dad remembers before describing the blackberry bushes that lined the driveway and wrapped around the mailbox of the old home in which his Grandpa Frank and Grandma Martha raised their children.

Like my Auntie Deanna's memories of down south, my dad's center around family. "Every time we went to North Carolina, other family members went. We were never there by ourselves. As if the original seventeen siblings would call one another and coordinate." Both my grandfather and great-uncle William found themselves up north in adulthood, but they always yearned for the South. Every chance they got, Grandpa and Uncle William piled their families into station wagons and vans and headed to North Carolina.

The Baker family with my Uncle David, smiling in the front row,
and my grandfather Alfred Baker in the back row, second from the left.

It was like there was always one foot in the South and another far outside of it. Despite their having been raised in and near cities, North Carolina brought out the rolling-in-grass, swimming-in-lakes, and playing-in-hay versions of themselves.

My grandmother Jenail Baker and Bishop Yancy with two children (above). My father, Steven; Auntie Karen; and Uncle Brian with their cousin Tyrone on the shore of the lake they swam in every summer (right).

Even though I was born in New York, North Carolina feels like my birthright and is part of the reason I feel the South is a homeland for Black Americans. A brilliant young activist and creative, Michael David Desir, commented on a social media post of mine when I asked for opinions on the matter: "No deeper are many of our seeds down than in this place. I hope people come to heal their relationship with the land we have, the places and spaces our mind inhabits . . . We're here now, why not do something beautiful with that? Joy, not rich from freedom of escape, but from freedoms claimed and reclaimed?"

My father and his siblings got to fall in love with the land the way Alfred and Jenail had: firsthand and, as Desir says, *from freedoms claimed.* "One day," my dad began with a smile already curled up on his face before he could get the memory out, "Uncle Ed and my dad called me over to the pig pit with Big Lucy." It's clear Big Lucy was part of many core memories on the land and a family favorite. "She was on her side giving birth and I remembered thinking, 'That's where pigs come from?' It felt cool to witness," he says, and I can almost see the twinkle in his eye. It's the same look my Uncle David makes when talking about his childhood memories: "Only Bakers lived on the land, and they had cows and grew crops like corn, tobacco, and cotton. I'd walk through the cornfield to get to my aunts' and uncles' homes."

I imagine a smaller, younger version of my Uncle David running through fields with his older brothers and sisters chasing after him, knowing that everything around him belongs to someone he knows. "It felt more like a 'compound' where the 'job' was to live off the land," Uncle David said, in an effort to help me understand how work and harvests were shared and what that felt like as a young boy. To know ownership up close and not as some glamorous thing passed down with ease, but as an asset that needed to be maintained, was monumental to him. The Baker kids felt powerful; a beautiful and strange feeling for Black children and teenagers who are often told they are anything but. Land can do that to you—it can make you feel bigger than you really are, just by being in close proximity to nature's wonders.

"The old land," my Auntie Deanna says to me, distinguishing the inherited family land from the latest plot that my grandfather bought, "is hallowed. Land is forever." My Auntie Karen recalls regular trips to the family plot to visit deceased family members: "It was his connection to never forgetting. His way of proving that he and all of us were from 'good stock' and a people to be proud of." I probed a bit to understand what she meant by good stock. "During a time when Black people in general could

*Baker cousins—my Uncle Brian; my father, Steven; and their cousins
Millard Jr. and Eric—with makeshift fishing poles they made out of bamboo
stalks (left). My Auntie Karen and Uncle David, posing near the lake (right).*

not have, my father [Alfred] took pride in being able to say [his ancestors]
were [more]. They were teachers, landowners, and founded things. They
fed people and were independent. Greatness in the sense that they contributed and had voices in a time when we were voiceless."

"Daddy would take us to the county courthouse so he could look at
records," Auntie Karen recalls. "There weren't great records kept inter-
nally except through oral history, so he was acting as the family historian
doing that. It helped him remember things and confirm his memory of
where family members had lived and who owned that land now." After
picking up records, they'd visit the tax commissioner's office next, to see
which family members had outstanding property taxes, covering any over-
due payments on the spot. "He'd tell them about it later, though, like 'I
paid your taxes! Keep up with that!'" Alfred was always watching, always
understanding how easily it can all be taken away.

My father similarly recollects that the documenting and archiving process became so intense that it consumed not only their North Carolina
trips but also life back home in New Jersey. "Eventually we had a copy
machine at home in Jersey and he would print and copy any and every-

thing," he says. I imagined him parking his car in front of one of the few meters on the street, walking through the metal detector as I had, and hunched over the same records books that I'd pored over. I wonder if he had spoken to the same government employees that I had, and if, when looking at my identification, they remembered the last name and quietly smiled to see a new generation just as curious as the last.

By the time I was born, Grandpa's stacks of papers—the culmination of decades of independent research—consumed his New Jersey home. "It all mattered to him to have physical representation." For him, paper, like land, was a tangible reminder of heritage and legacy. "If Alfred's father [Frank L.] called and said that he needed to buy back some of the land that had been taken, the kids would buy it back to ensure it stayed in the family. Eva has bought back quite a bit of the land, as did Edmond and William. And Alfred bought back a huge chunk of land, put that trailer on the land," my Grandma Jenail says. This trailer is where Grandma Martha lived out the remainder of her life.

Frank L. had supposedly asked Alfred for a house in a conversation that caused the unspoken tension in their relationship to boil over. "Alfred said, 'I'm not gonna put a house there. You gon' sell it and you gon' lose the house and the land.'" Frank was furious at being told what to do by his now-adult son. "Him and Alfred used to get into it all the time," Grandma said casually. Alfred was frustrated at the cavalier nature with which some family members seemed to approach the family land. His motto was "What we got, let's keep" but he felt as though the family wasn't always working in concert on that mission.

In some ways, it's a lot to ask of such a large group of people with different motivations, personalities, and outlooks. Half the family didn't even agree on which denomination of Christianity to follow or where to be buried when they died, so expecting a smooth business-partner relationship was always going to be a stretch. For years, Martha and Frank Baker, despite being the same denomination of Christianity, worshiped at separate Baptist churches where their ancestors had worshiped before them.

Martha and Frank Baker had four sets of twins, but the kids who acted most alike were the two who weren't: Uncle William and my grandfather Alfred. "Their relationship was special," my father recalls. Growing up as children in North Carolina, William and Alfred were thick as thieves going to school and working the family farm together. When Alfred moved up north as a teenager, William soon followed him. In New Jersey, the two lived minutes away from each other, going to school, finding employment, and eventually raising their children together. My father and his siblings spent countless weekends at their Uncle William's barbershop, and at church services together with their cousins Cedina and Nicey.

The two moved as one. One night, William had a dream that woke him out of his sleep. According to him, God came to him and showed him a church that he was supposed to build in North Carolina. The dream was so vivid and realistic that William drew a blueprint for the church from memory. (His long-held carpenter skills came in handy!) When William showed Alfred the blueprint, there was no question of what to do next.

My father was a young teenager when his dad and uncle began funding the reconstruction of their other brother Millard Baker's church. The brothers joined forces with some North Carolina deacons and purchased the acres where the new church building would go. Not only did those Baker men pay for the land and materials, they also laid most of the bricks. "I always saw Uncle Millard with a construction helmet, as if he was the foreman," my dad remembered. Building out the large sanctuary and side rooms for communing and meeting, everyone leveraged the skills they had toward establishing that new church.

Martha died before she saw the final version, but the church site also housed a new family cemetery for many of her children, grandchildren, and even great-grandchildren. Every time a loved one passes away, we make the trek to North Carolina, to that church; I've been there many times, but I didn't know until researching for this book that Baker hands made all of it possible. There is a spiritual relationship, yes, but the church is an extension of us as a family.

No matter how old he got, my grandfather never stopped hungering for a better understanding of our family and community history. As my father and his siblings grew to be adults with children, nieces, and nephews of their own, the tradition continued on with my generation. Grandpa took us with him to the courthouse, clerk's office, and register of deeds. I believe his goal was to normalize archiving and maintaining our family his-

My maternal grandfather, Ronald H. Carter (left),
Uncle William (middle), and paternal grandfather, Alfred Baker (right).

tory. Knowing how hard former generations fought for the land was half the battle to ensuring future generations preserved and expanded that legacy.

By the time I was in high school, my grandparents had accrued a sizable retirement fund and there was no question how they intended to use it. In 2012, they purchased eighty-six acres. There were two edifices on the land when my grandparents became the newest owners and stewards there: an old gristmill and a barn atop a hill. Other than that, the land was a lush, green slate covered in hundred-foot-tall loblolly pine trees and ponds fed by a winding brook. My Uncle William and Aunt Linda similarly purchased new acreage of their own, while still maintaining the family land they were stakeholders in. But having a clear deed was an untethered start for these land-owning couples who had seen the limitations of owning heirs' property.

Alfred and Jenail took their time. William moved back to North Carolina and, for the first few years, Alfred continued living in New Jersey, with frequent road trips to visit the land. On those trips, Alfred and Jenail walked the land hand in hand, dreaming aloud about the home they'd erect and the gatherings they'd host. My grandfather spoke of getting back

*My cousins—Linnaye, BJ, and Ashley—and me (top). My cousins BJ
and Joshua, my sister Brooke, and me (bottom).*

The land purchased by Alfred and Jenail Baker in 2012, now affectionately known as Bakers' Acres.

to hunting while my grandmother only cared about a large bathtub and a back porch to sit on, marveling at the life they'd made. Not bad for the daughter of sharecroppers and the son of working-class farmers.

"What's your favorite part about living on the land?" I once asked my grandmother.

"Knowing it's mine."

ʾIʾVE GOT INDIAN
IN MY FAMILYʾ

**One of the longest unwritten chapters in the
history of the United States is . . . of the relations
of the Negroes and the Indians.**

—CARTER G. WOODSON

Black Americans—and many across the African diaspora—have been a displaced people for centuries. That fact affirms our shared history with and responsibility to Indigenous Americans, because we know that displacement doesn't erase one's birthright or cultural heritage. Black liberation is bound with Indigenous liberation; if our collective subjugation has always been central to the project of land theft, our unity must be the antidote. A haunted land can only be saved through our leadership and autonomy. It's why the Black reparations movement and the Indigenous LANDBACK movement can and should coexist; they necessitate each other.

Indigenous Americans and Black Americans have historic relationships as land stewards, regardless of continent, which has made us massive threats to settler colonialism and environmental destruction. Take the Gullah people, who have lived in the Lowcountry Sea Islands and have retained their Indigenous cultural identity after they were forcibly transported to the Americas. Similar climates allowed many of their practices to remain the same.

As bell hooks said, "From the moment of their first meeting, Native American and African people shared with one another a respect for the life-giving forces of nature, of the earth." Indigenous Americans, like en-slaved African people and their descendants around the world, view wealth and assets far differently than the European settlers, by whom they were exploited. A study on women of color and wealth accumulation called "Lifting as We Climb," by the Insight Center for Community Economic Development, found that "[Native people] are more likely to identify edu-cation and family as assets and also to identify communal assets such as natural resources and the environment. Land—all that nature provides—is 'wealth,' it is communally owned, and the goal is stewardship."

This form of land ownership was de-incentivized by the federal gov-ernment and white private owners to make way for more selfish forms of hoarding. In order to maximize profits off of the land, white people pushed Native people off it and forced Black people to work that land. Land theft, then, was made possible through the exploitation of Black and Indigenous communalism and stewardship where we opted for mutually beneficial re-lationships with the planet, over capitalism.

———

Strong relationships are not devoid of conflict or tension. On the contrary, the most sustainable bonds are those that have proven the ability to navi-gate difficult histories and harm to arrive at a loving conclusion. Authentic relationships, then, need courageous conversations so that painful feelings are excavated and addressed and resolved. In the pursuit of justice, we cannot get in the habit of flattening important truths in favor of conve-nience.

Black and Indigenous relations are no different. Interdependency and accountability go hand in hand. To truly live out the belief that what we do affects each other, we have to be willing to name the times when our ances-tors and elders fell short of that promise. Holding multiple truths at once doesn't invalidate our demands for reparations but deepens our resolve to be in right relationship with both the Land and Her first stewards.

Black people are not responsible for Indigenous land theft but, at dif-ferent points, some Black people have been participants in white America's violence, such as in the boastful stories of Buffalo Soldiers "conquering" the West. Indigenous nations did not create and expand the institution of chattel slavery, but some tribes did engage in and profit from it when doing so served them. Some might say the actions of the formerly enslaved and their descendants are acts of survival not to be held against them. Some might say the same about the actions of the consistently displaced Indigenous Americans. Contrary to what scarcity-minded folks would like us to believe, both of these perspectives can exist, because there's enough space for all of us and our nuance.

It's easy to dwell and harp on the contentious points in our pasts at the risk of getting distracted from our individual and collective pursuits of justice. "These fissures and divisions [between Black and Native American people] are very intentional," Amber Starks once told LANDBACK University webinar attendees. Starks is a Black and Muscogee scholar and activist who is also known as Melanin Mvskoke. If Black and Indigenous Americans united around redistributing this nation's wealth, they would flip this country upside down and replace it with something far more equitable. "My life is a personification of Black and Indigenous solidarity," Starks later shared. Black-Indigenous relations go far beyond the nineteenth-century enslavement of Black people or recent tensions. We have more in common than our shared oppressor would like us to believe.

The "Five Civilized Tribes" may have been involved in chattel slavery; however, hundreds of autonomous Indigenous nations were never involved. Further, the role of Indigenous people in the abolitionist movement has been invisibilized. Many Indigenous tribes weren't just neutral, but they actively took up arms against enslavers. There are many abolitionist Indigenous nations who refused to partake in chattel slavery at all. "Bleeding Kansas" was the name given to the more-than-five-year-long violent battle over the legality of slavery in the soon-to-be-admitted state.

In nineteenth-century Kansas, the displaced Shawnee people were fractured from their forced removal and resettlement—as had been designed by the U.S. federal government. In this weakened economic state, and living on reservations, Shawnee leaders were forced into a dependency upon both federal agents and white missionaries. Introducing the institution of slavery was one of the first orders of business.

"Some tribal leaders of both the Shawnees and Wyandots, most of whom were mixed blood, acquired slaves as they attempted to assimilate into white

society and enhance their status," Diane E. Miller wrote. Indigenous spiritu-
ality and respect for people and planet went against extractive and violent
chattel slavery. The handful of white and biracial Shawnee and Wyandot
leaders who were happy to profit from the enslavement of Black people were
outnumbered by tribal members who disagreed vehemently. "This set the
stage for sometimes bitter conflicts within the tribes," Miller notes.

Wyandot and Shawnee tribal members began refusing to patronize
businesses that depended on slavery and orchestrating physical attacks
on pro-slavery churches. Many were known to hide Black fugitives in
their homes and operated several stops along the Underground Railroad,
to the chagrin of nearby white slavers. "Tribal members," Miller later
wrote, "expressed that the idea of slavery was contrary to their beliefs and
they did not support a religion that made it acceptable." In addition to
guerilla warfare tactics against the encroaching threat, Wyandot tribal
members petitioned Congress, leading a series of ideological fights and
treaty renegotiations. These conflicts coincided with white American
struggles over the institution of slavery, and years of violence ensued.

In the end, Kansas was admitted as a free state just three months before
the Civil War officially broke out. Miller's research acknowledges that this
moment in history didn't exist in a vacuum and was the natural manifesta-
tion of Indigenous approaches to relating to other living things, as well as
Black and Native solidarity networks. "From the colonial period, enslaved
Africans escaped bondage," she notes. "Colonial records and treaties reveal that they often sought refuge with Indian tribes." In *Black Indians,*
William Loren Katz chronicles this as well when sharing more about the
Afro-Indigenous maroon communities and Black Seminoles of Florida, as
previously touched on in Chapter Two. "Ease only came when people escaped to the forests and swamps . . . [M]aroons saw their settlements as
the fulfillment of an American dream—a sheltered home in freedom."

While the first half of the twentieth century consumed Black and Indigenous people in onslaughts of violence, broken treaties, and land theft, the
latter half presented new opportunities for multiracial coalition building.
In the 1950s, as Dr. Martin Luther King Jr. was working with Birmingham
ministers to desegregate the city, the Poarch Creek Nation sought support
in fighting rampant colorism against Indigenous youth within southern

Alabama schools. Racist local officials barred darker-skinned Native young people from riding school buses despite being part of the same tribe and even the same household as others allowed to ride. Dr. King stepped in and worked with Poarch Creek leaders to resist the unfair policy and successfully desegregate the school bus system.

King's awareness of the plight of Native American people regularly showed up in interviews, speeches, and books. In *Why We Can't Wait,* King wrote, "Our nation was born in genocide when it embraced the doctrine that the original American, the Indian, was an inferior race. Even before there were large numbers of Negroes on our shores, the scar of racial hatred had already disfigured colonial society." August 1964, the month and year that book was released, Dr. King assumed one of his largest platforms yet, onstage at the March on Washington for Jobs and Freedom. In the sea of people before him was a massive Native American contingent, with some traveling from as far as South Dakota. Many Indigenous leaders, inspired by Black-led organizing, went on to model organizations and movements in their likeness, such as the Native American Rights Fund, which provides legal and advocacy support to Indigenous tribes.

In the 1960s, after a series of arrests where Indigenous people were criminalized for fishing with nets or out of season, various Native fishermen and tribes initiated what became known as Fish-ins or the Fish Wars. Under the guise of conservation, the federal government has regularly policed Indigenous people whose right to engage in ancestral fishing practices like net-fishing, as well as to access public land, are protected under treaties. Non-Native commercial fishers notoriously overfish the Washington rivers, depleting salmon populations, yet Indigenous people—who have always been stewards of the land, rivers, and animals—were regularly blamed and punished.

Indigenous activists began engaging in acts of civil disobedience, such as fishing without licenses, in defiance of the federal government, which had broken its promises yet again. The government labeled these activists "poachers" and "criminals." In 1966, comedian and activist Dick Gregory, as well as his wife, Lillian, joined activists along the Nisqually River in Washington state, where they were arrested and found guilty of aiding in illegal net-fishing.

Dick Gregory as he and a member of the Nisqually Tribe staged a fish-in on the Nisqually River in Olympia on February 15, 1966 (ASSOCIATED PRESS).

Their act of solidarity brought much-needed attention to the larger issue of sovereignty, an issue that the Gregorys, as Black Americans, understood intimately. Congressman Lloyd Meeds said of that time: "The fishing issue was to Washington state what busing was to the East." After years of advocacy, U.S. district court judge George Hugo Boldt upheld Indigenous treaty rights and affirmed that Native fishermen should have decision-making power, and that conservation efforts should curb non-Native overfishing first.

In the last years of his life, Dr. Martin Luther King Jr. planned a multiracial "nonviolent army of the poor," called the Poor People's Campaign, with the Southern Christian Leadership Conference. Though he was assassinated in April 1968, colleagues and coalition members continued on and staged marches, sit-ins, and demonstrations looking to achieve economic justice through a significant investment in working-class people and people of color. While the campaign was Black-led, Indigenous Americans were instrumental to its development and ensuring Native people were included in the fight for civil and human rights. Many of the community leaders involved were particularly outraged by Native unemployment rates ten times the national average and more than half of Indigenous people living in poverty.

When a committee of one hundred spokespeople delivered demands to Congress, about ten Native American activists were present. At the launch event on May Day 1968, Melvin D. Thom of the National Indian Youth Council spoke:

> We have joined the Poor People's Campaign because most of us know that our families, tribes and communities number among those suffering most in this country. We are not begging, we are demanding what is rightfully ours . . . The Interior Department began failing because it was built and operates under a racist and immoral and paternalistic and colonialistic system. There is no way to improve racism, immorality, and colonialism. It can be only done away with.

That Juneteenth, at a Washington, D.C., Solidarity Day rally of more than 100,000 people, Indigenous activist Martha Grass spoke about Native American poverty rates, stolen land, and lack of economic opportunities. The next day, Indigenous community leaders protested outside the Bureau of Indian Affairs for hours, sharing demands around food, jobs, and education. Less than a month after the Poor People's Campaign launch, the American Indian Movement was founded.

In the late 1960s and throughout the '70s, Black and Indigenous people shared similar calls for land and self-determination. In 1972, when Native American activists launched the Trail of Broken Treaties caravan, Black leaders lent their support. Kwame Ture, the man to first popularize the phrase "Black power," joined as protestors seized the Bureau of Indian Affairs. "The question of Native Americans is not just a question of civil rights," he notably said. "This land is their land . . . there can be no settlement until their land is returned to them." In a later speech, Ture expressed his criticism of Indigenous erasure and land theft:

> South Africa is a settler colony. Rhodesia, which is really named Zimbabwe, is a settler colony . . . The settlers' aim is to make the

colony an extension of their original country. Mozambique is a settler colony. Angola is a settler colony. Portuguese Guinea is a settler
colony. Australia is a settler colony. My brothers and sisters, Israel
is a settler colony . . . But, my brothers and sisters, more impor-
tantly for you and for me, we must come to understand that America and Canada are settler colonies.

In 1973, Angela Davis joined national advocate Oren Lyons of the Red
Power Movement at the site of Wounded Knee, remembering the massacre
of Lakota people. The following year, Davis joined forces with Rev. Ben
Chavis of Wilmington, North Carolina, and Clyde Bellecourt, co-founder
of the American Indian Movement, at a Chicago press conference. Together, the three announced the creation of a multiracial anti-racist organization with Black and Indigenous leadership, focused on ending police
brutality and political repression.

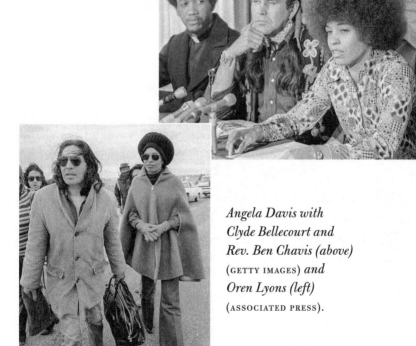

*Angela Davis with
Clyde Bellecourt and
Rev. Ben Chavis (above)*
(GETTY IMAGES) *and
Oren Lyons (left)*
(ASSOCIATED PRESS).

These relationships have continued on well into the twenty-first century with strong ties between the Movement for Black Lives, founded in response to calls to end mass incarceration and racist policing, and NDN Collective, an Indigenous-led organization dedicated to building collective power among Indigenous peoples. What does it look like for us to fight for land together? The aforementioned models are our teachers, and we won't find quick and easy steps to liberation. There is no shortcut to building solidarity; Black and Native American people deserve real institutional and interpersonal relationships. We need political education and emotional reminders that, at the end of the day, we are family and there is an abundance of land and natural resources to go around.

The LANDBACK Manifesto, developed by NDN Collective, reads:

> It is a relationship with Mother Earth that is symbiotic and just, where we have reclaimed stewardship.
>
> It is bringing our People with us as we move towards liberation and embodied sovereignty through an organizing, political and narrative framework.
>
> It is a long legacy of warriors and leaders who sacrificed freedom and life.
>
> It is a catalyst for current generation organizers and centers the voices of those who represent our future.
>
> It is recognizing that our struggle is interconnected with the struggles of all oppressed Peoples.
>
> It is a future where Black reparations and Indigenous LANDBACK co-exist. Where BIPOC collective liberation is at the core.
>
> It is acknowledging that only when Mother Earth is well, can we, her children, be well. It is our belonging to the land—because—we are the land.
>
> We are LANDBACK!

During a webinar on Black Indigeneity, Nadya Tannous of the NDN Collective opened by stating that "LANDBACK is a people-centered movement. When we talk about the return of land, we're also talking about the return of everything stolen with the land, so the return of life, the return of kinship systems, and also the return of people to land." After a brief introduction, Tannous passed the figurative mic over to Amber Starks and Kyle T. Mays, who held an incredible conversation about historical perspectives on Black and Native peoples. They both masterfully held the tension and opportunity in Afro-Indigenous solidarity. That begins with a nuanced look at the past, present, and future.

Starks invited Black Americans seeking to honor the forced contributions of our ancestors to this country never to lose sight of the original stewards, who were also violated by white supremacy and settler colonialism when they were dispossessed. "The settler state owes us something, but if this is Indigenous land, the settler state also doesn't have the right to offer this up," Starks poignantly suggested to and seeded with webinar attendees. It made me reflect on how I want to relate to another displaced and disrespected people with care and reciprocity instead of domination. Or, to reiterate a question that Mays posed: "How could we talk about reparations for Black folks without also talking about returning land to Indigenous peoples?" And vice versa.

Through dialogue and intentional awareness, we have the chance to develop a shared understanding that prevents us from replicating the harm done to us. When non-elite Europeans fled across the Atlantic, they claimed to be pursuing freedom on new lands but they re-created serfdom with themselves at the top of the pyramid. This is the curse that capitalism presents as a gift. But in the aftermath of settler colonialism and white supremacy, Mays gives us permission to dream of the life we want to build and the reparations that would make that possible.

"We are more than capable," Amber Starks reiterated during the LANDBACK webinar, "of having dialogue with one another to figure out what works for all of us."

In an article by PennElys Droz for *Yes!* magazine, Kyle Mays names how "the unsteady relationship to place and land remains unresolved for Black Americans in search of home." In the same article, Leah Penniman shared a poignant reflection: "Land was the scene of the crime, but land was not the criminal. Now, some are returning to the land, and their souls, heritage, and wisdom." For these and so many other reasons, Black and Indigenous claims to land are complementary, not competitive.

Leah Penniman introduced me to the concept of "cultural respect easements": a new way of relating to land and one another. "The Cultural Respect Easement welcomes indigenous people to regain access to lands they have been separated from for, in most cases, centuries," explained Ramona Peters, founder and president of the Native Land Conservancy, in part one of a multipart blog post on conservation and Indigenous relations. "Access may be desired to exercise spiritual and cultural practices including recitation of historic information in the form of oral tradition, a legacy for future generations." Black-led land trusts, cooperatives, and other private owners have already begun to explore cultural respect easements, also known as cultural use agreements. Soul Fire Farm, for example, works with the Mohican Nation to extend perpetual access of their farmland to Mohican citizens.

"The ideas of place, home, and land," Mays said in that *Yes!* magazine piece, "are an unresolved trauma at the core of Black belonging." Resolving that trauma and reconnecting with this American homeland need not come at the expense of Indigenous peoples. There can be no justice in this country economically, environmentally, or otherwise so long as either of our groups remains landless. A nation where Indigenous people don't have access to their ancestral lands will never respect Black life. A country where Black people receive no redress for chattel slavery or racist violence will never adhere to treaties or honor tribal sovereignty. We need one another, and we can reclaim far more land together than divided.

RETURNING FOR
OUR BIRTHRIGHT

═══

I am the debt collector for my ancestors.

—TRICIA HERSEY OF THE NAP MINISTRY

The first Supreme Court decision that ruled in favor of justice for Black Americans came in 1923, when unionizing sharecroppers from Arkansas appealed death sentences and won. That moment triggered a series of legal, cultural, and narrative wars. The mid-twentieth-century civil rights movement pushed back against white violence and segregation while farmers waged all-out resistance against developers and debtors. Land was top of mind for everyone. Most mainstream understanding of the civil rights movement is centered around uprisings in Southern cities like Birmingham, Montgomery, and Selma in Alabama and Jackson in Mississippi, as well as the specific struggle over voting rights. While that advocacy was critical to Black people's access to power, a missing arc is the way the South served as an incubator for radical Black activism that was mostly driven by farmers, sharecroppers, and landowners.

The most vocal and consistent proponent of reparations throughout the twentieth century was Queen Mother Audley Moore, a daughter of Louisiana, born in 1898. Queen Mother's grandfather was lynched long before her birth, leaving her grandmother a widow and her mother fatherless. Surviving the violence of the racist South, Queen Mother was drawn to organizing opportunities that emphasized dignity and self-determination for Black people and prioritized land and cash reparations as primary demands.

In the 1950s, Moore presented two petitions before the United Nations, calling for $200 billion as redress for centuries of chattel slavery as well as additional compensation for any Black Americans who wish to return to the African continent. Moore was greatly influenced by Marcus Garvey's repatriation and repayment work. Over the next several decades, Queen Mother Moore continued to advocate for reparations as the primary step to achieving racial justice. "No matter what we are going to do, unless we have reparations we will never be able to do anything," she famously proclaimed.

In his 1963 "Message to the Grass Roots" at a conference in Detroit, Malcolm X called on audiences to understand what a revolution entails and why we fight in the first place. "Look at the American Revolution in 1776. That revolution was for what? For land. Why did they want land? Independence." He went on to mention the French, Russian, and Chinese revolutions as examples of battles waged over land. "Revolution is based on land. Land is the basis for all independence. Land is the basis of freedom, justice, and equality."

In a May 1967 interview, Dr. Martin Luther King Jr. discussed structural issues in American society that "cannot be solved without costing the nation billions of dollars." King went on to detail the ways that the U.S. government excluded Black people from land ownership while flooding white farmers with aid:

> Not only did they give the land, they built land grant colleges with government money to teach them how to farm; not only that, they provided county agents to further their expertise in farming; not only that, they provided low interest rates in order that they could mechanize their farms; not only that, today, many of these people are receiving millions of dollars in federal subsidies not to farm and they are the very people telling the Black man that he ought to lift himself by his own bootstraps. And this is what we are faced with, and this is the reality.

That same month, the Black Panther Party distributed the second issue of their newspaper, unveiling its official ten-point program titled "What We Want Now!" The tenth demand opens with: "We want land."

Two years later, in 1969, on a cloudy yet warm spring day, James Forman, a key organizer with the Student Nonviolent Coordinating Committee (SNCC), strolled into Riverside Church in New York City with the "Black Manifesto," which called out white churches and synagogues participant in slavery and segregation, as well as the wealth they amassed and profited from. The manifesto included a petition for an establishment of a $200 million Southern land bank. "We have seen too many farmers evicted from their homes because they have dared to defy the white racism of this country. We need money for land. We must fight for massive sums of money for this Southern Land Bank."

Angela Davis, a daughter of Birmingham and friend to the four little girls bombed in a church there, recalls growing up in "the most segregated city in the country, and in a sense learning how to oppose the status quo was a question of survival." Davis has decried land theft globally, from the Deep South to Palestine to South Africa. "The idea of freedom is inspiring," she once said. "But what does it mean? If you are free in a political sense but have no food, what's that? The freedom to starve?"

In November 1969, Kwame Ture, who previously went by Stokely Carmichael, wrote the essay "Pan-Africanist—Land and Power." Born in Trinidad and Tobago before migrating to Harlem as a boy, Carmichael had a different relationship to the Deep South than some of his comrades, but the diasporic urge to fight for one's birthright resonated deeply with him. Carmichael knew that Black sharecroppers in the South were in the most unique position to "alter the course of American history," and said as much any chance he got. In 1971, while speaking in California, the activist identified what he saw as one of the major problems facing Black people globally:

We are people who have no land. We do not own any land. We do not control any land . . . Even on our own continent the resources of our continent are built for the benefit of Europeans, not for the benefit of Africans. Landless, victims of capitalism, the victims of racism.

After quoting Malcolm X's words from several years prior, Carmichael rallied the audience with a singular call to action:

> We have to take land because it's from the land that we get every-thing. The clothes that we wear comes from the land in the form of cotton. What we eat comes from the land in the form of agricultural food stuff. All of the elements and materials necessary to build this building, and to build big machinery in an industrialized society, comes from the land in the form of raw resources: peroxide, copper, zinc, etc., etc. Thus, it is he who controls the land that will control the people who live on the land. And because we do not control any land, we are dependent upon the white man who controls the land. Land, then, is what we're talking about.

At one point, Carmichael began chanting the word "land" with many audience members joining him, their voices merging together in a boom-ing, rallying cry.

"Land!"

With the country's most respected and visible Black leaders calling for reparations and equitable access to land, various organizations and coali-tions sprung up to fight with and for Black farmers and landowners. Just as was the case in the early twentieth century, Black faith spaces—including churches and mosques, and schools such as historically Black colleges and universities—became a lifeline and safety net for rebuilding Black land-holdings and maintaining Black agricultural connections. Many of these economic cooperatives and initiatives popped up organically, led by Black people with access to land who used it to care for community.

"Land is the key," Fannie Lou Hamer said. "It's tied to voter registra-tion." Having grown up in a large family of sharecroppers in the Missis-sippi Delta, Hamer was not speaking in theory. She had worked in fields since she was six years old and was known for her intellect and her ability to pick hundreds of pounds of cotton each day. In a county where Black illiteracy was expected and encouraged as a form of political disenfranchisement, Hamer worked her mind just as much as her hands, as a records keeper on the plantation her family sharecropped. Hamer had hoped that her ability to read, write, and do math would serve her well when she began volunteering with SNCC as a field organizer.

For one of her first campaigns, Hamer guided local Black Mississippians to register to vote. In 1962, hers and seventeen other Black citizens' voter registration applications were rejected under the claim that every single one of them had failed the literacy test. Over the next few months, Hamer was fired, evicted, and shot at for her attempts at political participation. "They kicked me off the plantation," Hamer said, "they set me free. It's the best thing that could happen. Now I can work for my people." This changed the trajectory of Hamer's life and led to the creation of one of the most imaginative and visionary campaigns at the intersection of land, food, and racial justice: the Freedom Farm Cooperative.

Seven years after facing retaliation for registering to vote, Hamer was a globally recognized civil rights leader and political strategist. Leveraging her platform, new celebrity relationships, and a $10,000 donation, she purchased forty acres of prime Mississippi Delta real estate, not far from where she was raised. In her explosive book *Freedom Farmers,* Monica M. White offers an in-depth look at how Hamer's life changed: "There was also dire need there. If Mississippi sought to starve [B]lack residents into compliance with the racial hierarchy, it was succeeding in Sunflower County." Hamer herself decried that "down in Mississippi, they are killing Negroes of all ages, on the installment plan, through starvation." Public health outcomes in the region were disproportionately negative for the county's Black residents, and a 1967 community clinic found that many residents were suffering from malnutrition. According to White, "most of the prescriptions were for food." Hamer saw this unmet need and resolved to be the change she wished to see.

Hamer's objective was to run a farm that housed and fed its members, without the economic burden of the farm falling on any one person or family. Membership at the farm was open to all who needed it and included mostly poor Black families and a few white ones, too. Members were able to live on the farm in exchange for their labor to keep the cooperative going. Freedom Farm operations included significant acreage for member housing as well as thirteen acres for growing subsistence crops that fed thousands of members each year, as well as non-co-op families in need. "Co-op members planted greens, kale, rape, turnips, corn, sweet potatoes, okra, tomatoes, string, and butter beans," recounts White.

As the farm expanded, hundreds more acres were purchased to plant cash crops (crops grown for profit, i.e., tobacco, cotton, soybeans, and wheat) to raise revenue for the farm. Livestock and fish were also introduced to feed even more of the community while diversifying income streams for paying down the mortgage. A major Freedom Farm funder, the National Council of Negro Women, reported that "the plan was not to provide instant food by butchering the livestock, but to breed them, thus establishing a 'pig bank,' which would be self-sustaining." The Freedom Farm pig bank produced thousands of pounds of meat and became a signature program of the farm, with pigs becoming widely known as "Sunflower Pigs." Education, too, became one of many investments by the farm. "Hundreds of participating families," says White, "received health and dental care, early educational experiences, and supplemental nutrition." Noting that education was critical to self-sufficiency in America, Hamer arranged for the Freedom Farm to become one of the first locations for the newest government pilot program: Head Start. Hamer had been part of the program's development since 1965 and was instrumental in ensuring Mississippi youth were served by the anti-poverty initiative, which has since become a widespread staple in early childhood education.

The Freedom Farm's work was holistic and put the federal government to shame by doing it all without tax dollars. With more consistent funding and government support, we can only imagine what could have been achieved. Unfortunately, in the mid-1970s, a series of damaging floods and droughts created a financial hole that the Freedom Farm could not escape. Hamer fought tooth and nail to the end, donating speaking engagement fees and any other income to prop up the organization. After being diagnosed with breast cancer, she could no longer afford to be the farm's de facto fundraiser and operations manager. In 1976, the Freedom Farm Cooperative closed for good, and the following year, Fannie Lou Hamer died at the age of fifty-nine.

Often the civil rights movement is thought of as the work of a few exceptional people, when in reality many everyday people took great risks to ensure justice wouldn't be denied to working-class Black Americans throughout the South. Take west Tennessee, for example, where white land-owning families controlled the local political landscape for decades. When Black residents began registering to vote in 1959, Fayette County's white citizens retaliated with violence and economic embargoes.

"Most people were sharecroppers who didn't own anything," Barry Glenn Towles tells me. He was born and raised in Tennessee in a large family of farmers. I went to college with Towles's daughter, Ashtan, who first shared about her family's legacy of land ownership and advocacy on social media. "When [Black people] decided to protest and vote, the white farmers conspired to kick them off their land." More than 1,400 Black people registered to vote in Fayette County that year, and 257 Black sharecroppers were being made an example of. White grocery store owners and other service providers began refusing to sell food, medicine, or gasoline to blacklisted residents. Undoubtedly, the intention was to starve these Black activists out.

Barry Towles's father, William Shepherd Towles, owned approximately two hundred acres of land in Fayette County and was a well-respected and well-known community member. When Black voters began getting fired and evicted from some of the few housing and employment opportunities countywide, in the dead of winter 1960, Shepherd stepped in. "My dad got together with the local civic league to do something about it," Barry Towles said. After a bit of strategizing, Shepherd and another landowner, Gertrude Beasley, decided to use their own land to both house and employ any and all of Fayette County's Black residents—as well as those from neighboring Haywood County. Shepherd was by no means carefree. Then a married father of twenty children, Shepherd had his own mouths to feed and safety to be concerned with. Yet none of that would keep him from lending his resources and access to support his fellow brothers and sisters. Consciously or otherwise, Shepherd was participating in the radical, ancestral tradition of communalism. Not too long after, Shepherd reportedly commented, "These people had nowhere to go. I decided to let them come in free, let them use the water from my deep well—as long as it lasts."

Families in Tent City (left)
(COURTESY SPECIAL COLLECTIONS,
UNIVERSITY OF MEMPHIS LIBRARIES)
*and a landscape shot of the
tents themselves (below)*
(ASSOCIATED PRESS).

With about a dozen donated tents and food donations, Shepherd welcomed the first few families while saying goodbye to his own. "My mother took us younger kids to Memphis, where we could be safe until things quieted down," Barry remembered. Quiet wouldn't come for another four years, as Shepherd's encampment expanded and became known regionally and nationally as "Tent City."

Mary Williams and her husband, Early B., were one of many Black families evicted by their white employer and landowner. "There wasn't any place to go," she recalled. That is, until the Williamses were directed to Shepherd Towles. After a local church donated a tent, the Williams family set up shop for what they thought would be only a few days. "Me and [Mary] and the four kids, we lived in that tent, we cooked in that tent, and we slept in that tent," Early B. remembered. "In the wintertime, the tent would get like a deep freezer."

At several points, the Ku Klux Klan antagonized Tent City activists by shooting at the tents and stalking the site. In one instance, Early B. was shot while holding his child in his arms. "The next time they came by to shoot, his uncles were waiting in the ditch for them and fought back," said Mary.

For years, Shepherd had been using his family business as a nonprofit organization, and it was beginning to take a toll on him. "There came a point when my dad almost lost the land because he didn't produce a lot of crops or make any money," Barry admitted. "My oldest brother stepped in and purchased about a hundred acres of the land to help Dad keep the land."

In 1961, the federal government "intervened," donating wood so that the tents would have proper flooring. They also issued decrees—which went ignored for years—prohibiting housing and employment discrimination in Fayette County. But that's where their intervention stopped—the National Guard was not deployed to stop the violence, the Department of Justice did not investigate and charge white residents for their crimes, there was no recognition of the way law-abiding citizens were being mercilessly terrorized. Labor unions and Baptist churches did more for these protesting sharecroppers than their own government, shipping truckloads of food, clothes, and tents to Shepherd.

Eventually, as more national legislation was passed, Tent City residents were able to find work and housing elsewhere, and the makeshift refugee camp dissipated by 1965. Many former sharecroppers later purchased their own farms, including Early B. and Mary Williams. Others fled in the last waves of the Great Migration to bigger cities where Black people were less isolated. Most Black families received no restitution for the years of blackballing and disenfranchisement that they faced for simply exercising the right to vote. Shepherd's work was not done in vain. His family keeps his memory alive and the land remains Towles land.

———

Throughout the late 1960s and beyond, nonprofit and advocacy organizations were established to support Black people directly in retaining and purchasing land. Whether offering legal support, grants and funding, or skills-building opportunities, these collectives held the laser-focused goal of getting more land into the hands of Black people, families, and institutions. A mutual aid network of sorts had developed to support Black landowners and, in 1967, almost two dozen such economic cooperatives joined forces and became what is now the Federation of Southern Cooperatives (FSC).

Through economic programs like credit unions and worker-owned cooperatives, as well as vocational training and policy development, the federation lives out the "collective agency and community resilience" framework developed by Monica M. White. According to White, collective agency and community resilience are enacted through a series of strategies that include communalism, economic autonomy, and the practice of envisioning utopias that don't yet exist.

According to White, communalism is where we contest "dominant practices of ownership, consumerism, and individualism" in order to emphasize "community well-being and wellness for the benefit of all."

Economic autonomy is where we develop new systems of resource sharing that subvert exploitative dynamics and ensure "funds and resources have direct benefits for all of its members."

Finally, we have what White calls *prefigurative politics,* or space and opportunity for people to interrogate the way things are and "think creatively about the current political situation and how they would reconceptualize those arrangements." Whether helping its members—most of whom are Black but also Chicanos and working-class white people—purchase thousands of acres of land or access capital, the federation is committed to the proletariat.

Robert S. Browne, founder of the Black Economic Research Center, which established the Emergency Land Fund (ELF), was already a seasoned strategist and mentor to many civil rights legends by the early '70s. What Browne had seen while advocating against the Vietnam War and working with leading Black economists rattled and radicalized him. In every facet of U.S. society, it seemed to Browne that Black people were expected to be nothing more than pawns. Over time, his commitment to economic reparations as the "*sine qua non* for genuine development," as he wrote in his article "The Economic Basis for Reparations to Black America," led Browne to take more material steps toward a "major capital transfer."

The ELF's first executive director, Joseph Brooks, recalls that Browne recruited him for the role by first sharing "his thinking on creating a [B]lack institution that would have as its mission the retention, acquisition and development of [B]lack owned land." Prior to their conversation, Joseph Brooks had recently published an article about the need to own and control land across the Black Belt in order to build a long-lasting racial justice movement. Together, Browne and Brooks set out to offer direct aid to Black landowners, conduct studies that made the case for reparations more compelling, and keep Black land in Black hands.

In 1973, Robert Browne published "Only Six Million Acres: The Decline of Black Owned Land in the Rural South," a groundbreaking study outlining the endangered species that is Black landowners and the very real threat that Black Americans could become completely landless if immediate interventions weren't made. The study wasn't an exclusively pessimistic one; Browne illustrated what he saw as the opportunity in Black land ownership and how through educational programming, as well as legal, technical, and financial assistance, the ELF could help regenerate Black land ownership. By 1982, the ELF had a national office based in Atlanta, a team of more than one hundred staff and volunteers across the South, as well as a proven track record for spurring other organizations and coalitions dedicated to Black rural land cultivation.

A *Chicago Tribune* article from approximately one decade after the ELF's founding, said of the fund's work:

> For the past 12 years, ELF has been helping poor black families in the Deep South hold onto their farm land by giving legal, technical and financial counseling assistance. In most cases, the blacks were elderly and illiterate. When they weren't losing their land because they couldn't pay the mortgage, they were losing it by means just short of fraud or theft—through tax sales schemes, partition sale ploys, resulting from the lack of estate planning and wills, and outright foreclosure . . . Many times the landowners had migrated up North. Five out of eight, or about 740,000 of the 1.2 million black Americans who own rural land in the South, were living in the North—Up-South . . . Black Chicagoans are sitting on a gold mine and don't know it, Joe Brooks says. "We're talking about a billion dollars in real wealth. That's why it's so important for urban blacks to pay more attention." To fight this problem, ELF decided to concentrate some of its efforts "Up South" where the majority of the black landowners are.

As ELF sought to expand its reach beyond the South to include all Black landowners nationwide, a strategic merger was taking shape. In 1986, the Emergency Land Fund and the Federation of Southern Cooperatives decided to work smarter, not harder, and united under one banner: the Land Assistance Fund.

By the 1990s, decades of pooling resources and making a dollar out of fifteen cents had allowed a deep resentment to fester and take root among Black farmers. All of the data and community organizing had ensured land loss hadn't worsened; however, little had been done to *reverse* land theft. They needed to come together as a people, but, more than that, they needed a reckoning. Black people shouldn't be depending on the kindness of one another when the federal government was the one who should be footing the bill. They needed reparations and restitution.

In 1997, on the heels of a damning report on USDA discrimination by the Black-led firm D. J. Miller & Associates, Timothy Pigford was one of many Black farmers who were sick and tired of being sick and tired. The corn and soybean farmer from North Carolina accused the USDA, then under the leadership of Secretary of Agriculture Dan Glickman, of denying his loan application solely because of his race. When Pigford's case was filed, more than four hundred Black farmers joined him and requested class-action status that would allow for a speedier and less expensive legal fight than if the farmers had decided to individually pursue restitution. Uniting allowed Black farmers a shot at justice after decades of harm.

Less than four months after the filing, the U.S. government agreed to mediation and a settlement was reached in the spring of 1999. In his official opinion, Judge Paul L. Friedman wrote, "As the Department of Agriculture has grown, the number of African American farmers has declined dramatically . . . the Court finds that the settlement is a fair resolution of the claims brought in this case and a good first step towards assuring that the kind of discrimination that has been visited on African American farmers since Reconstruction will not continue into the next century." Finally, a true admission of a guilt that was supposed to be followed by material redress. Any Black American who attempted to farm between 1981 and 1996 and believed themselves to have been discriminated against when pursuing USDA program benefits (including farm credit) now had a so-called path to repair.

To many in white America, the Pigford settlement was misrepresented as an unprecedented handout to Black agricultural workers, and not a thought was given to the countless handouts to white farmers dating as far back as the Homestead Act. Congresspeople like Steve King of Iowa were quick to decry what they saw as "pure fraud" and an attempt to secure reparations for slavery. Sharon LaFraniere, a *New York Times* reporter, alleged that "an examination by *The New York Times* shows that it became a runaway train, driven by racial politics, pressure from influential members of Congress and law firms that stand to gain more than $130 million in fees." LaFraniere went on to claim that "from the start, the claims process prompted allegations of widespread fraud and criticism that its very design encouraged people to lie . . . Even now people who say they were unfairly denied loans can collect up to $50,000 with little documentation." LaFraniere quoted many former and (at the time) current USDA employees—many of whom had likely contributed to the racist culture that predated the Pigford settlement—who called the settlement a waste of taxpayer dollars, among other things.

In the end, most of the Black landowners who were most affected by the USDA discrimination had already lost their land, and a $50,000 maximum settlement was nowhere near enough for them to buy back that land. Many more hadn't bothered to file a complaint against the USDA because they didn't believe it would amount to much. Other applicants either missed the cutoff for applying for settlement funding or were denied for not having enough proof of discrimination. None of the USDA policies that led to Black land loss and disproportionate foreclosures of Black land were changed. But with the settlement on public record, mainstream society considered the issue of Black land loss handled, and therefore expected calls for justice to halt.

The narrative around the USDA—and its sub-agencies—being a department "for the people" is something the agency has leaned into heavily in the twenty-first century, despite the continued power hoarding. There has been a coordinated effort to sanitize the USDA's legacy and brush its racism under the rug as a thing of the past, despite ongoing discrimination. Notwithstanding their Diversity, Equity, Inclusion, and Accessibility journey, the USDA's current website makes little mention of accountability to Black Americans or the ongoing work to be done to restore Black land to Black people. Even less is said about the Indigenous nations whose land was stolen, redistributed, and stripped of organic matter.

In 2017, Secretary of Agriculture Tom Vilsack reflected on the past 150 years of the department's work: "As the United States has changed and evolved over the years, at USDA we have not lost sight of Lincoln's vision . . . Today, USDA truly remains a 'People's Department' that touches the life of every American. Folks depend on us." Nathan Rosenberg and Bryce Stucki, reporters at *The Counter,* conducted a two-year investigation to see where the USDA measured up against its own claims of progress:

> As his eight-year term as secretary of agriculture drew to a close, Tom Vilsack claimed to have ushered in a "new era for civil rights" at the United States Department of Agriculture (USDA) . . . Under Vilsack, USDA employees foreclosed on Black farmers with outstanding discrimination complaints, many of which were never resolved. At the same time, USDA staff threw out new complaints and misrepresented their frequency, while continuing to discriminate against farmers. The department sent a lower share of loan dollars to Black farmers than it had under President Bush, then used census data in misleading ways to burnish its record on civil rights. And although numerous media outlets portrayed the Pigford settlement payments as lavish handouts—a narrative that originated with right-wing publisher Andrew Breitbart—USDA actually failed to adequately compensate Black farmers, and many of them lost their farms.

Rosenberg and Stucki's report busts several myths about USDA discrimination and efforts to address that sordid past, including the myth that the federal agency had resolved its backlog of civil rights complaints, and that disparities had been significantly reduced since the Pigford settlement—neither would end up being true. Further, discrimination continued unfettered well into the twenty-first century.

[A] 2016 report from USDA shows that 86 percent of all microloans issued between 2013 and 2015 went to white farmers, and demonstrates that at least two-thirds went to white men. Around 7 percent went to Black farmers, according to the report, which does not include the total dollar amount of loans that went to Black farmers . . . Far from "raining money," it is likely that the majority of Black farmers—and often-forgotten aspiring farmers—between 1981 and 1996 never received settlements.

Visual representation of Black generational wealth being siphoned away by white America (ART BY @CHI.SOULART).

Ultimately, the investigation concluded that misperceptions about the Pigford settlement hurt Black farmers a great deal—and this hurt is what continues to widen the disparities that the settlement was designed to address.

ANOTHER CASE
FOR REPARATIONS

===

r/evolution means protecting the people. the plants.
the animals. the air. the water. r/evolution means
saving this planet. r/evolution is love.

—ASSATA SHAKUR

I need some real nigga reparations.

—NIPSEY HUSSLE

This is a book in service and defense of reparations as a foundational racial, economic, and environmental justice policy to address the rampant inequity in this country. There are many innovative proposals being positioned—public apologies, baby bonds, free higher education, debt cancellation, individual checks—and they are all important and should be implemented. But in order for natural disasters to be less catastrophic, for food insecurity to be eradicated, and for wealth gaps to be narrowed to obsoletion, we must repair the harm created and compounded by land theft. In a robust policy platform for reparations, the Movement for Black Lives called for the following (among other things):

> Reparations for the wealth extracted from our communities through environmental racism, slavery, food apartheid, housing discrimination and racialized capitalism in the form of corporate and government reparations focused on healing ongoing physical and mental trauma, and ensuring our access and control of food sources, housing and land.

An accompanying toolkit opens with a Ta-Nehisi Coates quote as grounding for the content to follow: "Virtually every institution with some degree of history in America, be it public, be it private, has a history of extracting wealth and resources out of the African-American community . . . Behind all of that oppression was actually theft." If we know this to be true, especially when it comes to land and property, then in the words of Dr. Martin Luther King Jr., "We are coming to get our check."

On May 14, 2022, an eighteen-year-old white man drove hours away from his own home to one of the only grocery stores in a predominantly Black community of upstate New York and killed ten people. The shooter used an XM-15 assault rifle that he had written white supremacist messages on, to unequivocally state his intentions. One of the phrases written on the stock of the rifle read, "Here's your reparations!"

This act of domestic terrorism, like all forms of whitelashing, came just a few years after increased calls for reckoning and repair. Nikole Hannah-Jones's The 1619 Project had swept the nation, exposing how pervasive white supremacy is, and the most influential Black people in the nation had been testifying before Congress on the need for a real reparations process. Those necessary conversations about justice and redemption have instilled fear in the hearts and minds of vigilantes and white nationalists who believe themselves to be outnumbered by an invading people. (The irony is not lost on me.)

Resistance is strongest when we're on the brink of real impact. When that teenager opened fire on Black community members in Buffalo, he was rejecting truth and reconciliation. Those—the beneficiaries of history— who remain so violently opposed to repair are fearful of what will be done to their power by being honest about this country's failures, de-radicalizing those who have believed the myth of Great Replacement or the Lost Cause, and addressing inequity through economic redistribution. As the National African American Reparations Commission states, "The fulfillment of a 'more perfect Union' is not possible without an unequivocal acknowledgment of and unqualified apology for the 'original sins' committed by the European colonialists in brutally dispossessing the Native people of their lands and the horrific enslavement of Africans to be the economic life-blood of the 'American nation.'"

The first Black American on record to develop a campaign for reparations was Callie Guy House, a Black woman born into slavery during the

Civil War who spent most of her life fighting for Black Union soldiers' pensions and reparations for other survivors of slavery like herself. In her book *My Face Is Black Is True: Callie House and the Struggle for Ex-Slave Reparations,* Mary Frances Berry lovingly wrote about Callie as a racial outlaw who refused to "stay out of 'white folks' things.'" Callie House's work developing mutual aid networks through Black churches attracted the disdain of federal officials, who commented that her advocacy was "setting the negroes wild."

"Old and disabled by so many years of manual work, bad diet, and no medical care," Berry wrote, "these people understood and supported the association's demand for pensions to compensate for years of unpaid labor." House specifically demanded that taxes on Southern cotton production go to the Black people whose labor made it possible. Despite being accused of fraud, banned from using the post office to distribute materials, and surveilled by federal agents, House continued to charter new chapters of formerly enslaved Black people, demanding their just due. Though even Black newspapers of the time joined the chorus of people who believed her work to be outlandish, House continued spreading the message that Black Americans deserved retribution.

N'COBRA (the National Coalition of Blacks for Reparations in America) defines reparations loosely as: "material forms of reparations includ[ing] cash payments, land, economic development, and repatriation resources particularly to those who are descendants of enslaved Africans." In a 1963 pamphlet titled *Why Reparations?,* Queen Mother Audley Moore wrote, "Without preferential treatment the Negro will never be on equal terms with white America. The white American has a 344 year start on the descendants of American slaves."

Queen Mother Moore continued:

Slaves and their descendants have contributed to the wealth of the United States and at the same time remained impoverished economically, weakened culturally, and demeaning socially. Referring to the fact that the United States is a signatory to the International Organization of United Nations, which charter and conventions prohibit cruel and oppressive treatment of any racial or ethnic

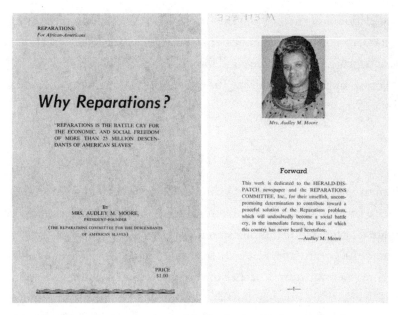

The Why Reparations? *pamphlet by Queen Mother Audley Moore*
(SCHOMBURG CENTER FOR RESEARCH IN BLACK CULTURE
AT THE NEW YORK PUBLIC LIBRARY).

group, the claim sets forth that various states within the domain and under the central power control of the United States Government, since the Emancipation Proclamation, have violated and continue to violate the express provisions of the Federal Constitution and supreme laws of the land including the charter of the United Nations which is otherwise known and recognized as the crime of GENOCIDE.

In 2005, the United Nations General Assembly adopted a resolution outlining basic principles and guidelines on the right to reparations. The resolution states that in cases of gross violation of international human rights law, there is an obligation to redress with no statute of limitations. "Restitution should, whenever possible, restore the victim to the original situation before the gross violations of international human rights law or serious violations of international humanitarian law occurred," the resolution reads. Further, "Compensation should be provided for any economically assessable damage, as appropriate and proportional to the gravity of the violation and the circumstances of each case, including physical or mental harm, lost opportunities, material damages and loss of earnings, moral damage, and costs required for legal or expert assistance."

For us reparations believers, the question is not if, but when and how, we start.

Philanthropic and Community Efforts

The movement for reparations is shrouded in mystery and myth. The false belief that only the federal government can issue reparations has kept private citizens and institutions from doing everything in their power to address the wealth and resource hoarding of white America. While researching innovative approaches to reclaiming land, I happened upon an article by Christina Cooke for Civil Eats called "Youth Are Flipping an Abandoned North Carolina Prison into a Sustainable Farm." The article described a group of high school men transforming an abandoned North Carolina prison into a sustainable farm and education center through a nonprofit called GrowingChange, led by Noran Sanford. "In his prison-flip work," Cooke's article reads, "Sanford has his sights set on a number of problems at once: the high number of young people entering the criminal justice system; the absence of job opportunities for veterans; the decline in small, independent farmers in the area; residents' lack of access to local, sustainable food; and the health disparities between urban and rural areas." As an abolitionist, it felt to me like serendipity to see an initiative at the intersection of all of my passions.

Hundreds of deserted prisons exist across the United States, including more than sixty in North Carolina alone. Deserted spaces where no humans live, work, or play serve as the biggest opportunities for reclamation. Cooke's article explores the way Sanford's work not only supports the young men he serves, but also the Robeson County community—which is predominantly Black and Indigenous—as a whole, where most people live in poverty and food insecurity. Youth participants gardening on the former prison grounds regularly prepare boxes of fresh produce for community members. During the COVID-19 pandemic, when many in the region's rural and suburban areas were left to fend for themselves, GrowingChange distributed food and flowers to people in need, including restaurant workers and furloughed hospital staff. "GrowingChange serves three counties near the southern border of North Carolina in the eastern part of the state," Cooke writes. "The area is extremely diverse, home to equal parts Native American (primarily members of the Lumbee Tribe), Black, and white residents." In addition to pursuing food justice, Sanford is bridging racial divides in an area that is divided.

Because the prison is abandoned, the North Carolina Department of Public Safety allows Sanford and his organization to lease the property at no cost. In turn, youth at GrowingChange cultivate about sixty-seven acres; their activities include beekeeping, herding sheep for both wool and meat, reducing non-recycled waste, and growing food for the community. Plans for aquaponic tanks and mushroom foraging, as well as more educational opportunities for the public, are also in the works. "GrowingChange engages in a constant give-and-take with those around them," the article states. "They receive around 600 pounds of discarded produce from the University of North Carolina at Pembroke (UNCP) each week; they redistribute the edible portions of that food to food banks, feed other scraps to the chickens, and give the spoiled pieces to either the compost pile or the soldier flies, whose larvae they're raising to help feed the animals."

The GrowingChange cooperative, supported by local land-grant colleges and agricultural experts, has a mission to reclaim, attain, and sustain. They also engage in profit-making practices such as selling eggs and vegetables at makeshift farmer's markets that allow young people to remain tapped into ancestral roots: "Though the garden they're tending this spring will supply free food to the community, they eventually plan to grow the ingredients for chowchow—a recipe that honors the various backgrounds of program participants: collards for the Black youth, tomatoes for the Native Americans, cabbage for the Scotch-Irish, and jalapeños for the Latinxs—and offer the product for sale." Sanford's benevolence doesn't end with the young people he mentors; he has documented his prison-flipping model for others to re-create in their own communities, and hopes to see others "convert spaces meant to confine and punish into spaces that nourish and rehabilitate."

"I don't know what it is about soil, but it changes you—it humbles you, and it brings a sense of calm that the youth need," board member Davon Goodwin shared with Christina Cooke. "When you're growing food, there's fellowship that happens that doesn't happen anywhere else." I'm sure Ron Finley of South Central Los Angeles would agree. In 2010, Finley looked out at the community that made him and saw a problem: neglected dirt patches that were being underutilized. After being cited for planting vegetables without a permit from the property owner—the City of Los Angeles—Finley began what he calls a "horticulture revolution." There are enough vacant lots in Los Angeles to make twenty Central Parks, Finley reminded people.

After successfully resisting the criminalization of his land stewardship, Finley expanded his scope with the hopes of making it easier to garden and grow food in L.A.'s "food prison," as he described it. "We did it in L.A. and we can do it all over the world," Finley expressed in a 2015 documentary interview after starting Green Grounds and the Ron Finley Project. "A garden can change people's lives, it can change the destruction of a community." Finley's TED Talk on guerilla gardening has been watched by more than four million people. "Just like 26.5 million other Americans, I live in a food desert, South Central Los Angeles, home of the drive-thru and the drive-by," he said. "Funny thing is, the drive-thrus are killing more people than the drive-bys . . . I want us all to become *ecolutionary* renegades, gangstas, gangsta gardeners."

Local Municipal Efforts + Direct Reparations

In July 2020, the city council in Asheville, North Carolina, passed a resolution that formed a community reparations commission to recommend short- and long-term interventions "that will make significant progress toward repairing the damage caused by public and private systemic racism." The first step was naming the harms this commission was seeking to address:

> Denied housing through racist practices in the private realty market, including redlining, steering, blockbusting, denial of mortgages, and gentrification;

Displaced or inadequately housed by government housing policies that include discriminatory VA/FHA practices, urban renewal, and a variety of local and federal "affordable" housing
programs . . .

Systematically excluded from historic and present private economic development and community investments, and, therefore, Black-owned businesses have not received the benefits of
these investments . . .

Forced to reside in, adjacent to, or near Brown Zones and other
toxic sites that negatively impact their health and property . . .

Disproportionately suffered from the isolation of food deserts
and . . . whereas, systemic racism was created over centuries
and will take time to dismantle.

The city acknowledged the harm with specificity, apologized publicly,
and committed to intentional action locally and to influencing other state
actors to do the same on a larger scale.

In other instances, the path to reparations is forged in the pain and loss
felt by our elders and ancestors. Several living survivors of the Tulsa Race
Massacre, each over the age of one hundred, filed a lawsuit just months
after the Asheville reparations resolution was passed and adopted. Twenty
years after the violence in Wilmington ended, a period of Black wealth and
multiracial political organizing, white people in Oklahoma unleashed a
similar onslaught, killing hundreds and turning many Black Tulsans into
refugees. After the white mob finished their rampage, property destruction
was widespread, yet neither the city nor private insurance companies ever
gave the victims a cent for their losses.

The suit called on the City of Tulsa, the Tulsa Regional Chamber, the
Tulsa Development Authority, the Tulsa Metropolitan Area Planning
Commission, the Tulsa Board of County Commissioners, the Sheriff of
Tulsa County, and the Oklahoma Military Department "to remedy the on-
going nuisance caused by the 1921 Tulsa Race Massacre in the Greenwood
district of Tulsa." The suit specifically cites the words of Tulsa's mayor,
G. T. Bynum, who said in 2019, "In Tulsa, the racial and economic dis-
parities that still exist today can be traced to the 1921 race massacre."

There were also calls for various declarations admitting harm, and for injunctions to prohibit city and state officials from continuing to profit from the likenesses of the massacre victims through cultural tourism of the desecrated "Black Wall Street." Further, the lawsuit seeks the creation of a Victims Compensation Fund to be used by survivors, descendants, and long-term Greenwood residents who were impacted by subsequent racist intimidation, redlining, and land theft. "In 1923, Defendants again used zoning laws to impede the reconstruction of the Greenwood neighborhood," the lawsuit claims. "This caused overcrowding in the decades that followed. Defendants' unlawful acts and omissions drove up rent prices and mortgage rates to levels most Greenwood residents could barely afford."

Neglect of basic infrastructure and community services left the Greenwood neighborhood in dire need of paved streets, running water, and waste management. The suit went on to expose continued acts of white supremacy and land theft throughout the twentieth century and long after the massacre:

> These unlawful acts and persistent neglect of governmental duties include the continuous dispossession and taking of land owned by Greenwood residents, blighting the Greenwood and North Tulsa neighborhoods and community by causing a steady decline of the Greenwood and North Tulsa neighborhood property values, the fragmentation of the Greenwood and North Tulsa neighborhood and community by placement of a highway that physically divided it, and the destruction of a base of professionals and entrepreneurs who lived and worked in Greenwood and North Tulsa. Defendants, on the other hand, made it possible for property values in predominantly White South Tulsa to appreciate, new housing and commercial developments to sprout, and White professional and entrepreneurial residents to maintain their base in South Tulsa.
>
> Throughout the 1950s, 1960s, and 1970s, Defendants City, County, and Chamber, acting through TDA and the Planning Commission, implemented or promoted policies of "urban renewal" and urban planning initiatives without regard for the health and

safety needs of the Greenwood community and Black Tulsans ...
Defendants used their urban renewal powers to take property from
Greenwood residents for projects that provided no direct benefit to
them ... This taking perpetuated the Defendants' acts that dimin-
ished the enjoyment by Greenwood residents of their property and
further eroded Greenwood's tax base negatively [a]ffecting residents, businesses, and schools in the Greenwood and North Tulsa
Community.

After such evidence, the Black Greenwood community who offered
testimonies included both 107-year-old Lessie Randle and 108-year-old
Viola Fletcher, and a few years after the original suit was filed, a judge
granted a motion to limit the named plaintiffs on the suit to only living
survivors; however, descendants of those killed in Wilmington, Tulsa, and
any other cities leveled by white mobs (such as during the 1919 Red Summer) should all be compensated for what was taken from them, and how it
ignited intergenerational precarity.

The easiest place to start with reparations is with direct compensation
to families who can trace the theft of their land and the violence done to
their ancestors. There is a dangerous myth that reparations cannot be
achieved because it is too difficult to know who was harmed and who
wasn't. In this book alone, I have named a dozen or so such people and
families—the descendants of families who owned property in Central
Park, the descendants of Wilmington Massacre victims, the Jones siblings,
Beverly Moore, the Freeman family, the Black owners of Seabreeze Resort,
farmers discriminated against by the USDA, and my own maternal and
paternal families. The reality is that *all* Black American families were impacted in some way by white supremacy, and many Black Americans can
pinpoint exact moments of theft and exploitation in their genealogical history.

Take the descendants of Charles and Willa Bruce, for example. The
Bruce family operated a lodge for Black vacationers who had few other
options. Bruce's Beach, as they called it, was wildly successful for the
twelve uninterrupted years that they ran the establishment before Manhattan Beach officials condemned the land for a public park in 1924. Yet de-

cades later, the Bruces' land lay undeveloped and vacant before being turned into a park and lifeguard training center by Los Angeles County. The less than $20,000 that the Bruces were given in compensation for their land loss is pennies when considering how beachfront real estate has been a figurative gold mine for white developers.

In 2007, the Manhattan Beach City Council renamed the public park located behind the Bruces' land as "Bruce's Beach" and acknowledged the history of racial discrimination with a small placard. Their recognition and atonement initially stopped there. Years later, local poet and activist Kavon Ward launched a campaign to educate the community about the land theft. At her first rally, Ward called for the return of all land to the Bruce descendants. After applying pressure through media and connecting the family to legal representation, the Bruce family descendants formally teamed up with Ward on the Justice for Bruce's Beach campaign. This advocacy and support led to an unprecedented decision to return the waterfront property to the Bruce family. Many Black Americans praised the move and saw it as a glimmer of hope on the path to communal reparations. What many missed was that returning the property didn't erase the almost century of damage to the land that could never be undone.

In the time since the Bruces had their land unjustly taken from them by local government officials, the Bruce's Beach property was regulated for public use only. This meant that the Bruce heirs were limited in what they could do with the land. While it was legally theirs, legislation ensured they had very few options for profiting from said land. Further, owning the land, even without a mortgage, was a significant expense for the Bruce heirs. All real estate in this country comes with property taxes proportional to the value of the land. The more valuable the land, the more expensive the taxes. The return of the land to the Bruces became more burden than blessing. "They had no choice but to sell it and take whatever they could get out of it, and use it to invest in some other way to develop their family wealth that they've lost," said relative and clan chief Duane Yellow Feather Shepard of the Pocasset Wampanoag Tribe of the Pokanoket Nation. In the end, the family sold the land back to Los Angeles County for approximately $20 million.

In a statement, Ward noted that "while I am disappointed the Bruces have chosen to sell the land, I understand their decision, as the city of Manhattan Beach is anti-Black. Justice, in this case, should afford the family some peace; unfortunately, I don't believe the Bruce family descendants will find peace taking up space in a racist Manhattan Beach." The Bruce family lawyer, George Fatheree III, expressed similar sentiments: "My clients were essentially robbed of their birthright; they should've grown up as part of a hospitality dynasty like the Hiltons," he shared with local radio station KBLA. "The ability to sell the property and invest the funds presents an opportunity for my clients to get a glimpse of that legacy that was theirs."

This case study, seen as both a win and a cautionary tale, signals larger questions that need to be reconciled: *If Black people receive land reparations, how do we ensure families are able to benefit from the returned land? When thinking of the many families who deserve land returned, how do we prevent legal loopholes from taking what should be theirs?* Marginalized people need more than their land back. We need our interest too, as well as exemption from adherence to paternalistic and exploitative strategies. Policy and legislative protections are needed to ensure that Black families don't bear their oppressor's cross.

Policy Recommendations

There are various proposals and recommendations in regard to land grants and allotments to Black Americans. The National African American Reparations Commission has a preliminary ten-point reparations program that includes a call for land, among other things. "We demand substantial tracts of government/public land in the South and other regions of the country . . . [and f]unds to support the restoration and enhancement of agricultural development." The Brookings Institution also outlined several potential avenues for reparations, including down payment grants to Black Americans for building equity in homes and/or refurbishing existing homes.

In 2019, the NAACP called for a national reckoning through a resolution that pushes for a robust series of financial investments, including the following:

Each family of 3 or more individuals (parents & children) shall be granted 40 acres of tillable land. No taxes to be paid on the property for 5 years from the date the land is first bequeathed by the government. If taxes are not paid on the land or land is taken for any other reason (criminal seizure), those of African descent are to be given the first right of refusal and opportunity to purchase the land. Publication of land availability must be in place for one year from the date the tax lien is issued on the property.

California's Reparations Task Force, formed in 2020 by Governor Gavin Newsom, made various preliminary recommendations to address anti-Blackness in state history. There were several land and housing–related proposals:

Estimate the value of Black-owned businesses and property in California stolen or destroyed through acts of racial terror, distribute this amount back to Black Californians, and make housing grants, zero-interest business and housing loans and grants available to Black Californians . . .

Compensate individuals forcibly removed from their homes due to state action, including but not limited to park construction, highway construction, and urban renewal . . .

Establish a state-subsidized mortgage system that guarantees low interest rates for qualified California Black mortgage applicants . . .

Compensate families who were denied familial inheritances by way of racist anti-miscegenation statutes, laws, or precedents, that denied Black heirs resources they would have received had they been white . . .

Establish a cabinet-level secretary position over an African American/Freedmen Affairs Agency tasked with implementing the recommendations of this task force.

The boldest reparations plan being proposed is still a conservative take on repairing harm that has only snowballed over centuries.

We can never adequately quantify the harm, loss, and long-term impacts of enslavement and disenfranchisement. In the last essay he ever published, Dr. King wrote, "When millions of people have been cheated for centuries, restitution is a costly process. This fact has not been fully grasped, because most of the gains of the past decade were obtained at bargain rates." The federal government's penny-pinching approach to addressing and repairing anti-Blackness is why the problem has persisted and compounded. Freedom that can be negotiated isn't freedom at all.

While Black America has the right to reclaim land even if white Americans have settled onto said land unlawfully, except in the cases of direct reparations, that doesn't need to be where we begin. The U.S. federal government owns 640 million acres of land across the country that is managed by the Bureau of Land Management, Fish and Wildlife Service, Forest Service, and National Park Service. Additionally, the U.S. military owns tens of millions of acres, with almost 4.5 million acres across the South. These avenues are also being eyed by various Indigenous nations in their quest for retribution, but there's plenty of land to explore there.

Bill Gates, the largest noncorporate owner of American farmland, regularly expresses interest in racial and environmental justice, despite privately owning more than 242,000 acres. John Malone is a billionaire who is one of the largest private landowners in the country, with acreage mostly in Maine, New Mexico, Colorado, and Wyoming. Malone isn't the only wealthy white American with millions of acreage in his portfolio. Wealthy white families—like the Reed and Emmerson families, who got rich working in lumber and logging—as well as businessmen like CNN founder Ted Turner and Los Angeles Rams owner Stan Kroenke—each own large swaths of land across Kansas, Montana, Nebraska, New Mexico, South Dakota, California, Oregon, and Washington.

Taxing the rich through land seizures is more than feasible, especially when you remember that our government has no issue taking land from working-class Black people who need it. Unless there's a non-racist reason why taking land from poor Black people is a public service, but taking excess land from rich white people is not.

A lack of urgency mixed with right-wing fearmongering is sure to stall the implementation of land reparations, but that doesn't mean pursuing it is futile; rather, in the meantime, other more immediate policy interventions are needed.

Bree Jones is an activist and equitable housing developer who has been working on regenerative migration and Black home ownership for years. For several years, she envisioned and developed a nonprofit real estate firm that would acquire vacant buildings, flip them, and sell them at accessible rates to locals. Parity's program is a mix of direct services and political education, allowing participants a path to true equity while educating them about home ownership and maintenance, as well as the history of redlining and other racist practices. Community members are also connected to legal support to protect their assets in the long term.

Development without displacement—that's Jones's lifelong work. As she worked intimately with Baltimore residents on resisting gentrification, Jones was simultaneously having conversations with elected officials like Maryland state senator Antonio Hayes. While many found her work to be inspirational, Jones knew that larger issues were keeping Black people from accessing generational wealth, namely appraisal disparities that undervalued Black homes and land. In 2021, the Maryland State Legislature officially launched the Appraisal Gap from Historic Redlining Financial Assistance Program, offering financial support to bridge the gap between renovation costs and appraisal values in historically undervalued and underinvested areas.

This work is critical and touched on by other leading academics and researchers. In "The Devaluation of Assets in Black Neighborhoods," Andre Perry, Jonathan Rothwell, and David Harshbarger wrote the following:

> If we can detect how much racism depletes wealth from Black homeowners, we can begin to address bigotry principally by giving Black homeowners and policymakers a target price for redress. Laws have changed, but the value of assets—buildings, schools, leadership, and land itself—are inextricably linked to the perceptions of black people. And those negative perceptions persist.

Jones's reshaping of public policy brings attention to a larger issue of perception. Black property is undervalued because Black people and labor are undervalued. While it's easy to claim we have no control over hearts and minds, it's important to remember that we do have a responsibility to the narratives we allow to persist and the powerful people who greenlight those narratives. Through the loophole of free speech, rogue journalists and legacy media makers alike have been given free reign over Black futures. Media tells the public what to think, legitimizes what it wants to be taken as fact, and discredits Black and Indigenous points of view. All without accountability.

In recent years, several large-scale publications have looked inward and reflected on their role in swaying public opinion in favor of white supremacy. "For at least its first 80 years, the Los Angeles Times was an institution deeply rooted in white supremacy and committed to promoting the interests of the city's industrialists and landowners," the *Los Angeles Times* editorial board wrote in September 2020. *The Baltimore Sun* followed two years later with their own reflections: "We bore witness to many injustices across generations, and while we worked to reverse many of them, some we made worse . . . this newspaper, which grew prosperous and powerful in the years leading up to the Civil War and beyond, reinforced policies and practices that treated African Americans as lesser than their white counterparts—restricting their prospects, silencing their voices, ignoring their stories and erasing their humanity." More local newspapers joined in as well, like *The Oregonian,* which admitted that "the newspaper demonized Black Oregonians and treated them as inferior, celebrating efforts to prevent them from voting, owning homes or having equal rights."

These public acknowledgments are welcome yet insufficient. Maligned Black families and institutions cannot revive lost economic opportunities or tainted legacies with apologies alone. Accountability calls for both awareness and repair; full investigations led by independent Black-led firms should be conducted of all major newspapers, magazines, studios, and stations to unearth the extent of harm caused to the Black community on micro and macro levels. The findings of these investigations should be published for all to see, with recommendations quickly implemented to ensure as much restoration as possible for the survivors and descendants of the media's violence of portrayal. Further, anti-racist trainings facilitated by Black, Indigenous, and other racially marginalized people should be mandated to ensure ethical reporting for the future.

These proposals mark the beginning of a full reimagining of how Black people come to own assets such as property and land. Eliminating property taxes altogether is another way to do away with the hurdles to ownership, but let's not stop there. We have been forced, for centuries, to dream within the limitations of racial capitalism. What is possible if we got rid of all bureaucratic red tape standing in the way of Black people and opportunities to access refuge, wealth, and joy? What if Black and Indigenous people had free hunting and fishing licenses, immunity from eminent domain, and the ability to grow food in their communities without zoning limitations? What if Black and Indigenous farmers and agricultural innovators were seen as climate investments rather than charitable write-offs? What if we dared to dream bigger dreams about our relationship to land?

Emphasizing Stewardship

To be clear, I am not here to praise Black capitalism. (Capitalism of any kind needs no advocates.) It was Audre Lorde who warned that "the master's tools will never dismantle the master's house. They may allow us temporarily to beat him at his own game, but they will never enable us to bring about genuine change." Fred Hampton put it even more plainly: "We're not gonna fight capitalism with Black capitalism." When presented with the horrors of what happened when white people stole land, the answer is not for Black people to follow the same playbook. We must, instead, disrupt the current model of ownership, first by putting land back in the hands of Black and Indigenous people and then by transforming what it means to be stewards of land.

Reparations shouldn't come under the pretense of more Black labor and service to greater society, but that doesn't give us a free pass to be selfish. We still owe a great deal to the Land and should feel responsible for how we treat Her. That level of awareness has to come with a respect for Indigenous people and their land sovereignty as well. Some of the greatest Black revolutionaries to walk the Earth knew that. Kwame Ture declared, "The land upon which we live, on which we inhabit, which we exploit—

that land belongs to the red man. He must come first in any dealings with the land." More recently, Angela Davis called on Black people to honor our collective responsibility to fight for the rights of Indigenous people. Audience members and social media users alike were torn, but I couldn't agree more. Black and Indigenous people are responsible to each other because otherwise any "justice" we receive would be half-baked.

Further, as a people with our own ancestral roots connected to respect for nature, we should never see reparations through a purely economic lens. I talked with a friend and former classmate from college, Rose Bear Don't Walk, about her perspectives on land ownership more generally. Rose is a Bitterroot Salish and Crow ethnobotanist working as a tribal foods consultant; she studies traditional knowledge of native plants as well as their many uses, focusing on the importance of Salish ethnobotanical knowledge to community well-being.

"I know that Native people could technically be like, 'No one owns the land because it's all just for everybody' but right now that's not applicable in a modern context," Rose said, leveling with me, "because we live in a Western world and we have these borders and zones and things like that. So we have to think about ownership in those senses." There could be a future where more communal styles of ownership are the norm, but right now we need immediate interventions for displaced, landless people. That includes both Black and Indigenous Americans. "But still," Rose continued, "I would hope that [landowners] would respect the land just how we have as Indigenous people, even though the way that land is owned and looked at right now is very, very different."

Derecka Purnell wrote something similar in her book *Becoming Abolitionists:* "The end goal is collective ownership and responsibility for the land but in the meantime, redistributing land among Black and Indigenous communities is a must to reverse [white] man-made environmental destruction and to achieve more economic equity." To see reparations as such will require many Black people to unlearn and heal from the agricultural trauma blocking us from connecting with the land.

While writing this book, I happened upon an Instagram story posted by a friend, Carlos, who had posted imagery of cotton bolls. Carlos's post sparked a lot of questions and jokes, with some social media users calling cotton a "slave plant" that shouldn't be in his home as decor. Carlos used the moment to call out what he saw as "plant trauma." With cotton so prevalent in our everyday life, from clothes to menstrual products and beyond, why did seeing cotton in its natural form spark such a visceral response?

Many Americans, including Black people, are happy to have an apartment sandwiched between other dwellings, the nearest green space being road verges or local parks. Some of us have learned to hate anything related to agriculture because of how white people forced it upon our ancestors. Either that, or we associate being outdoors with "white people stuff." That's not to shame those who opt for city living, but rather to acknowledge that we are often given the illusion of choice. We think of agriculture as either a necessary burden or an occasional excursion. Some people *have* to grow what we all eat, and other people get to experience nature as ecotourism. Many of us have become so desensitized, we wouldn't know where to begin even if we had full access to the land again.

A dear friend, Brian McAdoo, PhD, invited me to speak to his Duke students about my research on land theft alongside other researchers and advocates. Through that guest lecture panel, I met an incredible farmer named Delphine Sellars. Sellars is the co-owner of Urban Community AgriNomics (UCAN) alongside her sister Lucille Patterson. During the Duke panel, Delphine spoke about the systemic racism she's seen up close and how she set out to create both a haven and a source of nourishment for the North Durham community via the Catawba Trail. With the help of volunteers, UCAN has donated over thirty thousand pounds of fresh vegetables and fruits, through local harvesting and gleaning events. Delphine and Lucille prioritize collaborating with Black young people to get them out on the land and working with their hands.

During a research trip, I stopped by the Catawba Trail for a Saturday volunteer session. I scanned a crowded space full of volunteers bent over raised gardening beds. Everyone seemed to be busy at work, and, after greeting Delphine, I jumped in as well. After a few hours in the sun, I prepared to get back on the road. Delphine sent me off with a bag of cucumbers and I was left feeling so hopeful about the future. Sitting in my hotel room later that evening, I scanned UCAN's website and saw an infographic

developed by Dr. Brian McAdoo and his students about the history of
Black land tenure in the area and UCAN's work to address food injustice.
The image offers a breakdown of soil quality statewide alongside a time-
line of land tenureship, with the hope of making connections around food
insecurity and ownership.

I was struck by the mention of a partnership with the Triangle Land
Conservancy (TLC), which Delphine had also brought up in conversation
with me. "Since 1983," their website reads, "Triangle Land Conservancy
has worked to save the places you love and the land we need to safeguard
clean water, protect natural habitats, support local farms and food, and
connect people with nature." TLC often does this through land-acquisition
projects to protect said land from development. Most of the land purchased by TLC is turned into nature preserves, but in recent years they've
also begun leveraging creative partnerships to enlist Black farmers and
Indigenous tribes to be stewards of the land. Delphine and UCAN, for
example, were given the right to develop TLC's Snow Hill IV property
into the Catawba Trail Farm for the benefit of the community.

I reached out to the Triangle Land Conservancy team, curious about
what first brought them to land redistribution and conservation. Sandy
Sweitzer is TLC's executive director and has been with the organization
since 2013 after working in conservation for quite some time. Margaret
Sands joined TLC two years after Sandy and has worked intimately on
developing new community partnerships and acquiring more land.

Kierra Hyman, a recent college graduate working closely on creating
opportunities for BIPOC land stewards, said, "We want to be able to support people of color in having access and having the ability to promote
their ancestral knowledge." She continued, "The reality is that we live in a
world where you need to have capital to afford land. And you need to have
all these different connections." Kierra hails from Greensboro, where she
helped her maternal grandparents work their plot of land. "I would go out
there and help [my grandfather] grow things and we had some chickens
back then too, we gave each of them little birth certificates," she said between chuckles.

The TLC team makes clear that their work is not a replacement for
reparations, and yet I see great value in climate funders and investors pur-

suing similar models of returning land to Black and Indigenous people with little to no strings attached. In general, we need more stewards and a drastically different consumer relationship to the land. The USDA estimates that a third of all farmland in America is leased out, which means the land is owned by people and companies who cannot or don't wish to be involved in its cultivation. This may not seem like an inherently bad thing to some, but short-term farmers leasing the land are less incentivized to invest in practices that conserve and add to the land. Landowners with no real tie to their land are likewise less likely to be vigilant for signs that the land is stripped and in need of repair, because they are more focused on keeping the land occupied and turning a profit.

We need what Ayana Albertini-Fleurant and Destiny Hodges, cofounders of Generation Green, called *environmental liberation,* the intersection of environmental justice and Black liberation. This foundational ideology pushes us toward a "decolonized, regenerative, and autonomous future" where Black people are able to return to our ancestral relationship with Earth. Put plainly, environmental liberation is the belief that climate justice and Black liberation can only be achieved together, and that the result will be liberating for everyone. As Leah Penniman often says, "To free ourselves, we must feed ourselves." To free ourselves, we must reclaim who we were pre-colonization: land stewards.

Long before the contemporary examples and innovation came to be, Black and Indigenous seed librarians were the OG gardeners. Filing away seeds ranging from readily available to more rare, heirloom seeds, seed librarians ensure regenerative growing that emphasizes ancestral produce. Collectively preserving rich cultural traditions and the foods central to them, seed libraries around the nation are time capsules of a sort. As American agriculture incentivizes the same few crops, these community activists have protected various fruits, vegetables, and grains from extinction through an open data model reinforcing everyone's right to the seeds.

Accessibility is core to the collectivist styles of work and leadership known to characterize cooperatives and other worker-owned land projects. Soul Fire Farm similarly engages in resource sharing, so that the ancestral knowledge they've curated can be used by all. On their website, SFF lists various farming practices that guide their work. "The work of a generative farmer is to call the life and carbon back in," Penniman shared with me during an interview. The technologies and planting strategies used by SFF are a reflection of that belief. Ultimately, though, "the land has veto power over all practices," Penniman reiterated. The work of a farmer can never be cookie-cutter and must respond to what the Land is expressing, like a conversation.

Reverend Eddie McNair of New Life Agribusiness Center knows the conversation; he considers farming a ministry. In an interview with RAFI-USA, an organization tackling unjust food systems, Reverend McNair shared his journey of moving back to North Carolina and growing produce with his congregation. McNair told his team, "Let's take that land and use it to build the capacity of our neighbors." Instead of investing in a physical edifice for their church, McNair's congregation worships through soil. "I call myself a renegade preacher. I believe if I can build the capacity of people first, and get them to a place with a good quality of life, they will get to a point of being able to build a ministry and a church."

McNair speaks of liberation theology, the application of Christian texts and interpretation toward justice for oppressed people. In this case, it's not abstract at all; a fed congregation can find God better than a hungry one. William Barber III acknowledged this dynamic in a conversation with me where he recognized unmet material needs as the biggest barrier to Black political participation. "Land ownership and the production of food are foundational to any conversation around political autonomy," Barber told me. He is the founder and CEO of Rural Beacon Initiative, a Black-led climate consulting firm, as well as the co-chair of the Ecological Devastation Committee for the North Carolina Poor People's Campaign, a state chapter of the economic justice movement that his father is chairing. Long before his degrees and board appointments, Barber's love for land and planet was instilled in him as a child. As a son of the South, he describes climate justice as his first love. "I come from areas that are considered on the front lines of the climate crisis," Barber said. "But our stories are more than just displacement. We are incredible sources of entrepreneurship, leadership, and genius."

Barber's mission has been BIPOC-led social enterprise, an idea popularized by Dr. Muhammad Yunus. In order to do this work, one must have capital without making it the primary goal of any given venture. For Barber, social impact is always the central objective, with profit coming secondarily or even tertiarily. Through Rural Beacon Initiative, Barber and the team seek to bridge climate investment and social equity through scalable and replicable models like the Free Union Farm. Sitting on just over fifty acres of land, the farm is a hub for renewable energy and cutting-edge sustainability practices. The location, northeastern North Carolina, is an economically distressed region where Black landowners were decimated by exclusionary practices. This initiative rights that wrong by putting Black farmers at the helm of regenerative agriculture. Just because the industry was once a site of extraction doesn't mean it always has to be. "Systems are responsive to input by humans, so we aren't bound in perpetuity to certain bad systems," Barber says of those stuck in the cycle of tradition. "Do we have the courage to question those systems and add new inputs?"

Through the Free Union Farm, Barber knows intimately how much money is required to transport projects like this and get land back into the hands of Black Americans. "Our communities weren't destined to be in these situations," he reiterated. "One-time payments would be a very slow drip when we're facing a flood." People will need to get uncomfortable if we are serious about repairing the intergenerational harm of slavery. But that process can be redemptive all-around. "Reparations won't be a zero-sum game," Barber said. "It's not taking some of the pie from one group and giving it to another. We actually grow the pie by uplifting these marginalized groups."

IT IS OUR DUTY TO FIGHT
FOR OUR FREEDOM

===

**Within white supremacist capitalist culture in the
United States there has been a concentrated effort to
bury the history of the black farmer.**

—BELL HOOKS, *BELONGING: A CULTURE OF PLACE*

Reparations is no pie-in-the-sky idea; the call for reparations is a racial,
economic, and environmental imperative. When people operate off of half-
stories and whitewashed histories, they block the more equitable, "post-
racial" future they claim to already be living in. We also doom ourselves to
repeating history. This book centers the Black American experience because that is the one I know, and because I believe any just future, particularly in the United States, is predicated on repairing the centuries of harm
we've been subjected to. But we are not the only victims of land theft and
labor under duress. The practices first perfected on stolen Indigenous
land and against Black laborers are now being weaponized against Latine,
Asian, and Pacific Islander people.

Everywhere you turn, verdurous ancestral land is being turned into
playgrounds for the rich at the expense of communities of color. There is
ongoing land theft across Puerto Rico, the occupied kingdom of Hawai'i,
West Papua, Palestine, Guam, Samoa, and various other island-nations-
turned-American-colonies. Land is taken to establish and expand industries that profit white American and other foreign businessmen first and
foremost. This almost always results in Indigenous people and communities of color being left out of ownership and forced into low-wage labor.

From the Marshallese poultry workers in Arkansas to the Chicano farm-workers in California, we continue to see the insatiable thirst for wide-spread landholdings and cheap labor. One of America's oldest pastimes continues on . . . unless we decide it won't.

Black America was the forced architect of this society, building capital against our will, only to turn around and watch the crumbs we held on to be snatched from us. No Black person should be unhoused in a country where our ancestors were forced, under great duress and racial violence, to work the land and make the American economy what it is today. No Indigenous person should live in poverty while wealthy institutions oversee billion-dollar endowments and centuries-old (stolen) land grants. We need a re-redistribution to correct for the centuries-long theft that both groups have been subjected to. We must demand a re-redistribution of land back to those who cultivate with care and in service of community as opposed to greed.

The most bittersweet aspect of my research has been conversations with Black elders who have long loved and worked the land. When I ask these elders what the biggest threats to the tradition of land ownership are, most named the void of young Black people interested in it. Many older Black people have died with no one to pass their land on to, or with said land falling into the hands of people who couldn't appreciate it enough to hold on to it. *Who is there to pass the baton to?*, they ask themselves.

Young Black people across this country are reclaiming our connections to land and our role in the agrarian economy. From testing our green thumbs with potted plants and home gardens, to becoming family histori-ans and retracing our pre–Great Migration roots, there is a hunger for these ancestral connections. Black celebrities like the singer Kelis, mogul Rick Ross, rapper Waka Flocka, and many others have purchased expan-sive fields that they grow food and raise livestock on. Farmer-influencers and public educators—like Abril Donea (the Girly Black Farmer) and Nel-son ZêPequéno of Black Men With Gardens—are demystifying what it means to be a young Black farmer and landowner. Organizations like GirlTREK, Vibe Tribe Adventures, Hike Clerb, Outdoor Afro, Outdoorsy Black Women, and many others are bridging the divides and exposing Black youth to experiences in nature that have otherwise been dubbed "white people shit." Collectives centered around regenerative agriculture and land justice, like Jubilee Justice and Soul Fire Farm, are championing collective ownership and bringing resources to Black agricultural workers. We are here and we are ready.

Lauren Rosa Miller is the quintessence of picking up the mantle and running with it. A self-proclaimed legacy keeper and second-generation business owner, Miller and her brother have expanded the work their father, Dave James Miller Sr., began decades before. Dave Sr. founded D. J. Miller & Associates, Inc., in 1986 after years working for the City of Atlanta in high-level contracting and procurement positions under the Maynard Jackson administration. When he was less than a decade into leading his firm, D. J. Miller & Associates was commissioned by the USDA to study racial disparities in agriculture. The comprehensive report—analyzing fourteen million records, anecdotal interviews across twenty-five states, and feedback from seven town halls—wasn't released at the time, at the direction of the USDA. A decade later, this research served as the basis for Supreme Court cases demanding equal access and opportunity for Black farmers and landowners.

Miller's deeply rooted commitment to Black farmers was personal, an extension of his love for his own family's century-old landholdings, which were once the largest Black-owned farm in the Southeast. He raised his children, including Lauren, to appreciate the legacy on which they stand and to be good stewards. "My dad walked like he knew who he was," Lauren told me. "Owning land is so grounding when it comes to generational legacy because it's a tangible connection to the past. When I'm on land, I can say that my dad walked here and my grandfather walked here, and my great-grandmother."

Knowing the one-hundred-and-fifty-year history of her family's land has put Miller face-to-face with both the good and the bad of being a Black landowner in this country. She recognizes that her elders have survived versions of this world that she didn't, and thus operate from a level of over-caution. "They hold the baton tight because they've had to be protective." Because Miller understands the history of disenfranchisement and violence they've endured, she is patient and attentive in intergenerational estate planning. "I see it as an opportunity to dream across generations," she says.

The younger Miller is invested in land ownership not only as an economic tool taught to her by her father, but also for her mental health. A believer in ecotherapy, or nature therapy, Lauren Miller recognizes that being in nature of any kind is incredibly healing. But for Black people, the positive impact of being on land you and your family own is exponentially greater. "There's a huge sense of pride for people who are constantly being told not to be proud of who we are," she explained. "That ancestral land is positive reinforcement."

For the extended Miller family—even those who didn't grow up *on* the land—the fellowship and recognition that a slice of this world is yours have extended a deep sense of pride in self and community. Priceless. "Owning land is a spiritual thing, not a get-rich industry," Lauren noted before quickly adding, "That doesn't mean you can't make money, but the narrative around land ownership has to become more intrinsic than purely financial benefit." That's what keeps land in the family across generations.

Death can be a scary time in Black families. Amid grief, asset loss and predatory outsiders can make families vulnerable. That's why talking openly about transitions is critical for Miller. "There's nothing wrong with people wanting to cash out at some point, because a lot of us are asset rich but cash poor or have other things they want to do. But how do we create liquidity opportunities that don't hurt the family?" Her family's primary approach has been to sell and transfer land inwardly while encouraging people to remain stakeholders even if they don't wish to live on the land.

We need to remove the negative connotations around being in the field and farming. Black people have always been farmers and are one with the land. Long before we did so under duress, we spoke the language of the world around us and stewarded life. We've foraged for mushrooms and herbs, made medicine out of our food, and fed ourselves from the land. We've owned and worked collectively and were all the better for it. What white men saw as a gullible value system to be preyed upon is actually the relationship and mindset we all desperately need to find our way back to. For the sake of a planetary future.

Lex Barlowe is a dear friend, a seed librarian, and an archivist working to retain our connections to land. Barlowe's ancestral roots span from Virginia to South Carolina and the Caribbean, which informs her work preserving wisdom and histories that young people can learn from. I myself have learned so much from Barlowe, particularly around the need for intergenerational community building and cooperative economics. As a facilitator and community liaison, Barlowe sees firsthand the challenges in not only owning land but holding on to it. "Black farmers who are doing this *love* the land," she once told me. "The work is so hard, so you don't do it if you don't love it." Her words reminded me of the late bell hooks, a native Kentuckian and prolific writer, who said, "When we love the Earth, we are able to love ourselves more fully. I believe this. The ancestors taught me it was so."

———

From 2016 to 2018, my grandparents began building their dream home on Bakers' Acres, a plot of land they purchased years prior as a larger family plot to the acreage we are heirs' property owners to.

My grandmother Jenail Baker, standing on some of the cleared land before her and Albert's home was built.

In early 2018, following the devastating loss of my cousin Linnaye, our family was preparing to send another loved one home to the Lord: Alfred Baker. Unbeknownst to me leading up to that time, Grandpa was silently losing his own battle with cancer, one he seemed to have tried to will away rather than addressing head-on. With everything happening so suddenly, I never did get to say goodbye.

My Auntie Deanna, joined by my grandmother and uncles, was there by his side holding his hand as he slipped away from this life and into the next. "I remember him on the hospital bed barely able to talk or walk but still asking someone to go pay the land's taxes," she said while laughing and wiping away tears. I smiled with her, though the pain was palpable, because this is who Grandpa had always been. "When he was dying," she added, "he said, 'Take care of the house' and I took that to mean take care of Grandma. He said, 'I'm not worried about Grandma because I know that she'll be okay. I'm talking about the house and the land. Don't sell it.'" The last words he shared with his daughter were to never forget the land. "Until my last breath," she replied, before watching her father take his.

"I will retire and die on this land, God willing," Grandpa often said. And he did. My grandfather's vision was that no one in our family would ever lack for a home base to turn to when in need or want. Though Grandpa didn't live long enough to fully enjoy the home he spent his entire life working toward, he did succeed in passing on that love and fervor to his children and grandchildren. "It's only brick and mortar to one person," my father always told me, "but, to me, his soul lives on this land, so it's out of the question to sell it." On the day of my grandfather's funeral, a trail of cars drove from Bakers' Acres to the land he paid for and the church he built with his brothers. On that day, we returned him to the earth he loved so much while he was alive.

Since his passing, Bakers' Acres has been home to two weddings (including my own!) and countless family gatherings. We still cook fried chitterlings around holidays and celebratory moments, just like Grandma Martha learned from her father, Plummer Spruill. My Auntie Karen's greenhouses and gardening beds on the land have brought new life to visits, and we all line up for batches of hot sauce made with peppers her hands and this land brought forth. "I feel him in the garden," she once told me with a lump in her throat. We sit around the patio and dream of where we'll all put our own homes. I talk of inviting my father-in-law to do some hunting while my aunts and uncles dream of fixing the dam and building a dock. Grandma laughs as baby Zen coos up at her; all on the land she and her husband made possible for us. Life isn't perfect, but we have so much.

What my grandfather wanted and created for my family is what I want for every Black American. To know where you come from and to never worry about where you're going. To live an untethered life full of choice. To eat good food, breathe good air, and drink good water. To know the feeling of grass between one's toes and to call a plot of land your own. As Dr. Sarah Elizabeth Lewis once wrote: "Here's to doing what the ancestors asked for, what the present demands, and what the future requires."

EPILOGUE

====

**My mission in life is not merely to survive,
but to thrive; and to do so with some passion,
some compassion, some humor, and some style.**

—MAYA ANGELOU

My cousin-in-law Maria's union was the third wedding I was lucky enough to witness on Black-owned land. I've always associated weddings with churches—long aisles lined with wooden pews, an altar ordained by God. But churches are edifices, static buildings that keep out the outdoors, constructed by man. Love is verdant. Lush. Constantly evolving, growing, and adapting.

What made Maria's wedding even more special was that it was taking place on Juneteenth weekend, the same year that it became a federal holiday. Though wide recognition of this holiday came only after a Black youth–led uprising in response to extrajudicial killings, I and many other Black Americans had been observing the holiday for much longer. While Juneteenth certainly calls attention to justice delayed, the day has also served as a north star guiding Black Americans toward truer versions of liberation. Celebrations—especially those in Texas, where the holiday originated—routinely involved purchasing large swaths of land, coming together for community-wide feasts, and recommitting to doing what the U.S. government never could: securing a vibrant Black future.

With the backdrop of this history, we'd be celebrating love, family, and Blackness on land made possible through the foresight of elders.

This was also my first time in the state of West Virginia, a place I'd previously only associated with blatant racism, guns, and coal mines. I desperately wanted the "story" of the land, and because these were my in-laws, there were a lot of blanks to fill in.

I didn't know what to expect as my father-in-law's Toyota rolled into Shepherdstown, but I'd heard it called the most haunted town in America. I had read that the town was established before the American Revolution and named after the European settler who was "granted" 222 acres of sto-len land by the colonial government. The land, nourished by a meander-ing brook, became home to Europeans and the United States Armory before it was destroyed during the Civil War. It served as a setting for sev-eral of the bloodiest battles in American history, many of which furthered colonialist visions. Decimated battlefields and fallen soldiers loomed in their backyard—no wonder it was a ghost town.

Though most of the battles in the northern part of the state were fought by and for white men, a handful of others contributed greatly to the story of Black liberation. None more so than white abolitionist John Brown's raid and attempt at sparking a mass revolt against the institution of slavery. John Brown, believing himself to be sent by God to end American slavery, tried everything to convince his fellow Americans that they were engaging in a deeply immoral practice. After years of making his case through non-violent measures, Brown was convinced that violence was the only lan-guage slavers spoke.

Having fought in the Bleeding Kansas conflict and assassinated several slavers, John Brown decided it was time to take things up a notch. For years, he had dreamt of liberating the South's plantations and establishing a new, just government. He didn't share his full plans with anyone—not even his wife and sons, who were regular collaborators of his. But from what is known, Brown planned to first take over Harpers Ferry and use the artillery to arm nearby enslaved people. The next phase involved traveling deeper and deeper into the South, attacking more plantations and arming more Black soldiers until all were free. Unfortunately, Brown's plans were stopped before he and his men could even leave the armory. John Brown was charged with murder and treason and convicted in less than forty-five minutes of deliberation. His last words before being hanged were "I, John

Brown, am now quite certain that the crimes of this guilty land will never be purged away but with blood."

My sister-in-law, Casey, and I visited the John Brown Museum, which sits at Harpers Ferry and honors Brown's legacy. There was a whiteboard available for the general public to reflect on what Juneteenth means to us. I scribbled something earnest about justice delayed, but over the next few days, what I'd come to feel was a newfound appreciation for the pure joy and love that Black Americans deserve to relish in, when commemorating the day.

Maria's ceremony was scheduled to take place at a quarry, followed by a reception at another location. Quarries are massive pits of excavated land—often the result of mining for stone or other underground materials. As we drove up to the site, the main road turned to wooded paths and opened up to a crater filled with blue-green water that glimmered. Sloping earth created a pathway for vehicles, people, and animals alike to get from the waterfront area in the valley to the street-level peaks.

Photos taken by author,
Juneteenth weekend, 2021.

The day after the ceremony, Juneteenth, we returned to the same place for the family reunion, spending most of the day and a good portion of the evening at the quarry. I had set out on interviewing family to understand their land history.

Pat Pat Walker, the patriarch of his family, learned of an opportunity to buy a high-quality quarry sitting on approximately one hundred acres. He called on his sons to join him, and the Walker men not only agreed on the collective purchase, but also on making the land work for them. They started by leasing land for cell towers and soon expanded into extracting rocks from the ground. The rocks pulled from the Walkers' land became what is now WV Route 9, a state highway connecting the northern panhandle. Their early ingenuity allowed them to pay off the land far more quickly than they'd anticipated. Now—except for renting out passes to campers, hunters, and anglers—the Walkers and all of their married-in loved ones get to revel in the land.

It's impossible for this book to tell every story, say every name, and document every act of thievery and every act of resilience. But in scratching the surface, my hope is to remind everyone that, on a mainstream level, we are not only underestimating white supremacy and how pervasive it is; we are denying ourselves the land, and vice versa.

My hope is that these glimpses will encourage you each to dig deep into understanding your connection to this sordid past. The more we know and uncover, the more we can rectify and redress. When, for so long, those in power have obfuscated people by rewriting history, we haven't even begun to make a true turn toward justice. In life, when the path forward is fuzzy, seers are placed in our path to grow our imagination for what freedom smells, tastes, sounds, looks, and feels like.

Though mining made roadways and financial autonomy possible for the Walkers, the family were environmentalists and adventurers first. Most of the land has remained untouched by the excavation processes, allowing for a vibrant ecosystem of animals, fish, and birds. Our cousin, Logan, recalls walking the trails, fishing with minnows, and watching the wildlife on the quarry. Deer, foxes, groundhogs, bobcats, wild turkeys, cardinals, and owls all call the land home. Logan recalled a memory with her sister, Maria. The two of them had been hiking with their dad when they came upon a small cave. They never saw an animal entering or exiting the mouth of the cave, but they convinced themselves that a mountain lion lived there, she told me with a laugh.

The evening of Juneteenth, as the sun set and darkness took over, I found an open grassy area at the base of the quarry and lay down on my back to look up at the stars. The family was setting off fireworks not too far away, and a cacophony of booms and whistle sounds filled the air. Bright shades of red, orange, and purple lit up the sky, disrupting the constellations. There, surrounded by family, I marveled at the life those Walker men made possible. The slice of heaven they carved out for generations to come. May we all get to experience such peace.

ACKNOWLEDGMENTS

===

**Everything worthwhile is done
with other people.**

—MARIAME KABA

I grew up in the church, so I must first give honor to God, who is the head of my life and the architect of my greatest accomplishments. Thank you for using me as a vessel.

Secondly, to the Land, which has made *all* life possible. Your wonders never cease to amaze me and you serve as my greatest reminder of a Creator.

Thank you to the Black women writers before me who encouraged my own audacity. When the path felt murky, it was the words of Octavia Butler that whispered, "So be it, see to it." When I questioned my place in the publishing world, it was Toni Morrison ringing in my ear, reminding me that "if there's a book that you want to read, but it hasn't been written yet, then you must write it." When self-doubt pressed upon my heart, I leaned on Maya Angelou's understanding that "there is no greater agony than bearing an untold story inside you." I stand on the shoulders of giants, and that will never be lost on me.

At the heart of it, this book is about family, and it wouldn't be possible without my wife, siblings, parents, aunts, uncles, and cousins, who lent their memories toward making this possible. Specifically:

Mariah: You have loved me in ways I didn't even have the foresight to pray for. Throughout this book journey, you've joined me on research trips, edited my messy first drafts, analyzed maps, and been the best sounding board in shaping this work. Best of all, you inspired me through your own love for land—often reminding me to get my hands dirty. You have shared me with this writing process so selflessly, and I don't take that for granted.

Auntie Karen and Grandma: You both have been bridges to Grandpa's memory and helped fill in the gaps that written records couldn't. Exploring North Carolina through your eyes made me fall in love all over again with Bakers' Acres. This book is as much yours as it is mine.

Mommy: Way way *way* back, I told you I had the dream to be an author. My first story about a magical boy and the seven seas was written in elementary school and you had it, along with my stick-figure drawings, bound. Several years later, I dreamt up a young adult romance novel and you scrounged the money to get a professional cover made. You've always taken me and my dreams seriously and though those books never came to fruition, your unfettered belief made all of this possible.

Daddy: Thank you for sharing your love for North Carolina with us and ensuring we made it down south as kids. Who knew it would become all of this?!

Auntie Tammy: Thank you for introducing me to Black literary icons. You first introduced me to *The Bluest Eye* and let me borrow your tattered Carter G. Woodson books. You encouraged me to challenge myself, and I can't imagine being who I am now without having had that foundation at such a young age.

This story would not have made it to the finish line without each person who agreed to be interviewed and, in doing so, opened up their hearts and minds to tell me the most beautiful, tragic, harrowing, and inspiring stories I've ever heard:

My daddy, Steven Baker. Ed Baker. Sue Baker. Jenail Baker. William Baker. Ernest Baker. David Baker. Karen Baker. Deanna DeVore.

Ashley Baker. My poppy, Apostle Ronald H. Carter. Miriam "Aunt Tina" Flowers. (Uncle) Bruce Carter. Kavon Ward. Leah Penniman. Lauren Miller. Tony Harris. Paula Harris. Mariah Harris. Casey Harris. Lee Hicks. Rico Hicks Sr. Logan Ann Hicks. Ashtan Towles. Barry Glenn Towles. Rose Bear Don't Walk.

When embarking on this journey, there were so many times when I second-guessed myself:

To my literary agent, Johanna Castillo: You believed in my ability to produce a book like this before I believed in it for myself. Thank you for answering every silly question, offering priceless feedback, and championing this project. You not only trusted this vision, but helped me make it a reality. I pray that every writer finds their Johanna.

To Nicole Counts and Oma Beharry, my brilliant editors: To work on this book with a Black woman has been a dream. You never diluted my voice, and your confidence allowed me to walk boldly toward the stories that most needed to be told. More than that, you never stopped seeing me as a person, and reminded me that writing great things doesn't need to come at the expense of my wellness.

The integrity of this project was sustained thanks in large part to my research assistant, Hannah Greene. You are a sister-friend in every sense of the word and I'm so grateful to be on this walk with you!

Tony, you are the best father-in-law that a young woman could ask for. Not only have you bounced ideas with me and shared your own love for land with me, but you also were the most diligent and meticulous copywriter ever! (Those *degreesssss* continue to come in handy.) Thank you for loving me and this project so deeply, and lending your time to ensure that no Oxford comma was left behind.

To my informal book advisory committee: Taylor K. Shaw. Nic Ashe. Denisha Gingles. Terisa Siagatonu. Philip McHarris. Jorel Holmes. Lucy Carmelo. Lex Barlowe. Thank you for graciously and diligently reading and reviewing chapters. You sharpened my raw thoughts and helped ensure that my intentions translated. Individually and collectively, you have made me better.

To Mr. Spanier, my eleventh-grade AP English teacher: Your class has served as my unofficial MFA and I lean on many of your lessons to this day. Thank you for pushing me all those years ago and honing my writing voice.

My first job out of college was serving as a Dean's Fellow at a now-defunct university called Yale-NUS College in Singapore. One of the most unexpected blessings was connecting with and befriending Professor Brian McAdoo who, at the time of writing, is an associate professor of earth and climate sciences at Duke University. Writing a research-heavy book without being affiliated with a university would have been considerably more difficult had you not graciously opened up your classroom and institutional access to me. I can't begin to thank you enough but I hope that, together, we can tell a new story about land and how we begin the process of rehabilitating our planet. #FreeTheSoil

I'm surrounded by people who have lifted me up and held me there. Thank you to everyone who sent me articles, book recommendations, connected me to interviewees, or simply sent good energy my way. Your passion electrified me and hammered home just how necessary a book like this is.

And lastly, but certainly not least, there has been no greater influence on me, and thus on this book, than my ancestors. You lift, guide, shield, and love me every single day. Everything I do is in service of the legacy you've left behind. I vow to leave this country safer and more free than I received it.

Asé

NOTES, INFLUENCES,
AND FURTHER READING

====

> [The] politics of citation is also about the politics of
> access and reading. Not only should we share the names
> of and read more voices, we can also take more care
> in how they are described.

—MINDY SEU

This book could not have been written without the scholarly and advocacy work of Kavon Ward of Where Is My Land, Robin D. G. Kelley, Dr. Alaina E. Roberts, Leah Penniman of Soul Fire Farm, Leah Thomas of the Intersectional Environmentalist, Isabel Wilkerson, the Slow Factory, Decolonial Atlas, Ta-Nehisi Coates, Lex Barlowe, and many other people and organizations. Their contributions, individually and collectively, have helped to frame my understanding of white supremacy, land theft, wealth gains, and environmental injustice in ways I can't fully articulate, though I've tried my best throughout these pages. Readers seeking to dive deeper, and those wanting to take action and fund meaningful work, should begin with them.

Each of the below resources contributed to my knowledge and understanding of when and how land was systematically stolen from Black and Indigenous people. Every speech, social media account (or post), journal entry, book, documentary, oral anecdote, personal photograph, letter, article, public record, interview, academic study, and other form of documentation helped make this book possible.

CHAPTER ONE

Amos, Jonathan. "America Colonisation 'Cooled Earth's Climate,'" BBC News, January 31, 2019, https://www.bbc.com/news/science-environment-47063973.

Barlowe, Arthur. *The First Voyage to Roanoke* (pamphlet, 1584), Old South Leaflets no. 92, Documenting the American South, University of North Carolina at Chapel Hill, https://docsouth.unc.edu/nc/barlowe/barlowe.html.

Cox, Anna-Lisa. *The Bone and Sinew of the Land: America's Forgotten Black Pioneers and the Struggle for Equality* (PublicAffairs, 2018), pp. 45–52, 87–89, 199–201, 210.

Dunbar, Gary S. "The Hatteras Indians of North Carolina," *Ethnohistory*, vol. 7, no. 4, 1960, pp. 410–18, https://doi.org/10.2307/480877.

Gilbert, Jess, Spencer D. Wood, and Gwen Sharp. "Who Owns the Land? Agricultural Land Ownership by Race/Ethnicity," *Rural America*, vol. 4, no. 17, Winter 2002, pp. 55–62.

Hall, Gwendolyn Midlo. *Africans in Colonial Louisiana: The Development of Afro-Creole Culture in the Eighteenth Century* (Louisiana State University Press, 1995).

Hannah-Jones, Nikole. *The 1619 Project: A New Origin Story* (One World, 2021), p. 124.

Harris, Katherine J. "Colonization and Abolition in Connecticut," in Elizabeth J. Normen et al. (eds.), *African American Connecticut Explored* (Wesleyan University Press, 2014), p. 64.

"History Through the Ages." *Outer Banks Guide,* September 19, 2017, https://obxguides.com/articles/what-are-outer-banks.

hooks, bell. "Touching the Earth," *Orion,* vol. 15, no. 4, Autumn 1996, pp. 21–23.

Katz, William Loren. *Black Indians: A Hidden Heritage,* rev. ed. (Atheneum Books for Young Readers, 2012), pp. 152–54, 160–64, 207–9.

King, Martin L., Jr. "We Are Coming to Get Our Check" (speech in Mississippi, 1968).

Koch, Brierley, and Lewis Maslin. "Earth System Impacts of the European Arrival and Great Dying in the Americas After 1492," *Quaternary Science Reviews*, vol. 207, 2019, pp. 13–36, https://doi.org/10.1016/j.quascirev.2018.12.004.

Nichols, Patrick. "Freedom as Marronage as Anti-Capitalism," African American Intellectual History Society, January 21, 2017, https://www.aaihs.org/freedom-as-marronage-as-anti-capitalism/.

Nugent, Ciara, and Thaís Regina. "How Black Brazilians Are Looking to a Slavery-Era Form of Resistance to Fight Racial Injustice Today," *Time,* December 16, 2020, https://time.com/5915902/brazil-racism-quilombos/.

Opala, Joseph. *The Gullah: Rice, Slavery, and the Sierra Leone-American Connection* (United States Information Service, 1987).

Purnell, Derecka. *Becoming Abolitionists* (Verso Books, 2021), pp. 53, 57, 107–8.

Roberts, Alaina E. *I've Been Here All the While: Black Freedom on Native Land* (University of Pennsylvania Press, 2021), pp. 6–7, 16, 29, 50, 67, 85.

Roberts, Neil. *Freedom as Marronage* (University of Chicago Press, 2015).

Rodrigue, John C. *In Reconstruction in the Cane Fields: From Slavery to Free Labor in Louisiana's Sugar Parishes, 1862–1880* (Louisiana State University Press, 2001), p. 320.

Saunders, Corinne. "Roanoke-Hatteras Algonquian: The Tribe That Never Left," *Island Free Press,* October 18, 2021, https://islandfreepress.org/hatteras-island-features/roanoke-hatteras-algonquian-the-tribe-that-never-left/.

Smith, Clint. *How the Word Is Passed: A Reckoning with the History of Slavery Across America* (Little, Brown, 2022), pp. 210–11, 231–34.

Smith, Ryan P. "How Native American Slaveholders Complicate the Trail of Tears Narrative," *Smithsonian Magazine,* March 6, 2018, https://www.smithsonianmag.com /smithsonian-institution/how-native-american-slaveholders-complicate-trail-tears -narrative-180968339/.

Weiner, Dana Elizabeth. "A Second Look: The Bone and Sinew of the Land: America's Forgotten Black Pioneers and the Struggle for Equality," *Civil War Book Review,* vol. 20, no. 4, 2018, doi:10.31390/cwbr.20.4.18.

Zora's Daughters Podcast. Instagram account.

CHAPTER TWO

Calhoun, John C. *Speeches of John C. Calhoun* (Harper & Brothers, 1843), p. 225, https:// archive.org/details/speechesofjohncc00incalh/page/224/mode/2up?view=theater.

Freedom's Journal, vol. 1, no. 34, November 2, 1827, https://www.wisconsinhistory.org /Records/Article/CS4415.

hooks, bell. "Touching the Earth," *Orion,* vol. 15, no. 4, Autumn 1996, pp. 21–23.

"National Register Properties in South Carolina: Patrick Calhoun Family Cemetery, Abbeville County (S.C. Hwy. 823, Abbeville Vicinity)." South Carolina Department of Archives and History, http://www.nationalregister.sc.gov/abbeville/S10817701006 /index.htm, accessed November 13, 2023.

Penniman, Leah. *Farming While Black: Soul Fire Farm's Practical Guide to Liberation on the Land* (Chelsea Green Publishing, 2018).

Remnick, Noah. "Yale Will Drop John Calhoun Name from Building," *New York Times,* February 11, 2017, https://www.nytimes.com/2017/02/11/us/yale-protests-john-calhoun -grace-murray-hopper.html.

U.S. Census. "Population of the United States in 1890: North Carolina," https://www .census.gov/library/publications/1864/dec/1860a.html, accessed November 13, 2023.

CHAPTER THREE

Aptheker, Herbert. "Negro Casualties in the Civil War," *Journal of Negro History,* vol. 32, no. 1, January 1947, pp. 3–6.

Baker, Ella. "Oral History Interview with Ella Baker," interview conducted by Sue Thrasher and Casey Hayden, April 19, 1977, Southern Oral History Project, University of North Carolina at Chapel Hill, https://docsouth.unc.edu/sohp/html_use/G-0008.html.

Baker, Jenail. Interview conducted by Brea Baker, October 2, 2021.

Balfour, Alan. *The Walls of Jerusalem: Preserving the Past, Controlling the Future* (Wiley-Blackwell, 2019), pp. 137–226.

Barnett, Jim, and H. Clark Burkett. "The Forks of the Road Slave Market at Natchez," *Journal of Mississippi History,* vol. 63, no. 3, Fall 2001, pp. 169–87.

Browne, Frederick W. *My Service in the U.S. Colored Cavalry: A Paper Read Before the Ohio Commandery of the Loyal Legion, March 4, 1908* (Project Gutenberg, 2010), p. 3.

"Buffalo Soldiers." National Museum of the United States Army. https://www.thenmusa .org/articles/buffalo-soldiers/, accessed November 13, 2023.

Cantrell, Gregg, Elizabeth Turner, and W. F. Brundage. "Juneteenth," in Gregg Cantrell and Elizabeth Turner (eds.), *Lone Star Pasts* (Texas A&M University Press, 2007), pp. 147–48.

Cox, Anna-Lisa. *The Bone and Sinew of the Land: America's Forgotten Black Pioneers and the Struggle for Equality* (PublicAffairs, 2018).

Davis, Ronald L. *The Black Experience in Natchez, 1720–1880: A Special History Study* (Eastern National, 1999).

Dobak, William A. *Freedom by the Sword: The U.S. Colored Troops, 1862–1867* (Skyhorse Publishing, 2013).

Du Bois, W. E. B. *Black Reconstruction in America: An Essay Toward a History of the Part Which Black Folk Played in the Attempt to Reconstruct Democracy in America, 1860–1880* (Oxford University Press, 2007).

Federal Writers' Project. *A Folk History of Slavery in the United States from Interviews with Former Slaves, Assembled by the Library of Congress,* vol. 2, *Arkansas Narratives,* part 1 (Library of Congress, 1941), p. 2.

Federal Writers' Project. *Slave Narratives: A Folk History of Slavery in the United States from Interviews with Former Slaves,* vol. 11, *North Carolina Narratives,* part 1 (Library of Congress, 1941), https://tile.loc.gov/storage-services/service/mss/mesn/mesn-111/mesn-111.pdf.

Ferguson, Paul-Thomas. "A History of African American Regiments in the U.S. Army," U.S. Army, February 11, 2021, https://www.army.mil/article/243284/.

Gates, Henry Louis, Jr. "The Truth Behind '40 Acres and a Mule,'" PBS, https://www.pbs.org/wnet/african-americans-many-rivers-to-cross/history/the-truth-behind-40-acres-and-a-mule/, accessed November 13, 2023.

Hannah-Jones, Nikole. *The 1619 Project: A New Origin Story* (One World, 2021), pp. 25–26.

Horhn, John. "They Had No King: Ella Baker and the Politics of Decentralized Organization Among African-Descended Populations," thesis, Georgia State University, 2016, https://scholarworks.gsu.edu/aas_theses/36.

Ingraham, Joseph Holt. *The South-West: By a Yankee,* 2 vols. (New York: Harper & Brothers, 1835; reprint, Readex, 1966).

International Committee of the Red Cross. "2021 Olive Harvest Season in the West Bank Amidst a Triple Challenge," news release, October 12, 2021, https://www.icrc.org/en/document/2021-olive-harvest-season-west-bank-amidst-triple-challenge.

Katz, William Loren. *Black Indians: A Hidden Heritage,* rev. ed. (Atheneum Books for Young Readers, 2012), pp. 160–64.

Kaur, Harmeet. "Kanye West Just Said 400 Years of Slavery Was a Choice," CNN, May 4, 2018, https://www.cnn.com/2018/05/01/entertainment/kanye-west-slavery-choice-trnd/index.html.

Lincoln, Abraham. "Transcript of the Proclamation," January 1, 1863, National Archives, https://www.archives.gov/exhibits/featured-documents/emancipation-proclamation/transcript.html.

Manuscript Division, Library of Congress. *Born in Slavery: Slave Narratives from the Federal Writers' Project, 1936–1938,* vol. 2, *Arkansas,* pt. 1, pp. 1–2; vol. 11, *North Carolina,* pt. 1, pp. 59–62 (Library of Congress, 2001).

Myers, Barton. "Sherman's Field Order No. 15." *New Georgia Encyclopedia,* last modified September 30, 2020, https://www.georgiaencyclopedia.org/articles/history-archaeology/shermans-field-order-no-15/.

Nathans, Sydney. *A Mind to Stay: White Plantation, Black Homeland* (Harvard University Press, 2017).

Purnell, Derecka. *Becoming Abolitionists* (Verso Books, 2021), pp. 53, 101.

Queen Quet. "Gullah/Geechee Sea Island Stand for Land: 150 Years Since Sherman's Meeting in Savannah, GA," Gullah/Geechee Nation, January 13, 2015, https://gullahgeecheenation.com/2015/01/13/gullahgeechee-sea-island-stand-for-land-150-years-since-shermans-meeting-in-savannah-ga/.

Ransby, Barbara. *Ella Baker and the Black Freedom Movement* (University of North Carolina Press, 2003), p. 31.

Roberts, Alaina E. *I've Been Here All the While: Black Freedom on Native Land* (University of Pennsylvania Press, 2021), pp. 4–5, 45, 74–76.

Simon, Dan. "How Octavia Butler's Sci-Fi Dystopia Became a Constant in a Man's Evolution," NPR, February 18, 2021, https://www.npr.org/transcripts/968498810?t=1657550250768.

Smith, Clint. *How the Word Is Passed: A Reckoning with the History of Slavery Across America* (Little, Brown, 2022), pp. 191–93, 199–203.

Smith, John David. *Black Soldiers in Blue: African American Troops in the Civil War Era* (University of North Carolina Press, 2001).

Stephenson, Wendell, and Isaac Franklin Holmes. *Slave Trader and Planter of the Old South* (Peter Smith Publishing, 1968).

"To Colored Men! Freedom, Protection, Pay, and a Call to Military Duty!" (flyer), National Archives, Record Group 94, Records of the Adjutant General's Office, Letters Received 1863–1888, Consolidated File for Major Martin Delaney, 104th USCT Infantry Regiment, https://catalog.archives.gov/id/1497351, accessed November 13, 2023.

Tour of Historic Stagville Plantation, Durham, NC.

Tyler, Ron C., and Lawrence R. Murphy (eds.). *The Slave Narratives of Texas* (Encinitas Press, 1974), pp. 114, 121.

CHAPTER FOUR

Aguilar, Ben. Interview conducted by Brea Baker, Berry Center Bookstore, New Castle, KY, December 11, 2021.

Akerman, Amos T. Letter, Amos T. Akerman to Todd R. Caldwell, December 26, 1871, Walt Whitman Archive, Matt Cohen, Ed Folsom, and Kenneth M. Price (eds.), http://www.whitmanarchive.org.

"Amos T. Akerman (1870–1871)." Miller Center, University of Virginia, https://millercenter.org/president/grant/essays/akerman-1870-attorney-general#:~:text=Though%20he%20opposed%20secession%2C%20Akerman,attorney%20for%20Georgia%20in%201869, accessed November 13, 2023.

Ayah A. "Inside the Wormley Hotel: America's First Known Upscale Black-Owned Hotel," *Travel Noire*, February 15, 2021, https://travelnoire.com/wormley-hotel-first-black-owned-upscale-hotel.

Baker, Nancy V. *Conflicting Loyalties: Law and Politics in the Attorney General's Office, 1789–1990* (University Press of Kansas, 1992).

Baldwin, James. "Nothing Personal," *Contributions in Black Studies*, vol. 6, art. 5, 2008.

Carter, Bruce. Interview conducted by Brea Baker, May 13, 2021.

Carter, Ronald. Interview conducted by Brea Baker, May 6, 2021.

"Desperate Work: Murder of an Old Man by a Masked Mob at Midnight." *Pittsburgh Commercial Gazette,* October 10, 1878.

Farris, Scott. *Freedom on Trial* (Lyons Press, 2020), p. 79.

Foner, Eric. *Reconstruction: America's Unfinished Revolution, 1863–1877* (HarperCollins, 1988), p. 458.

Gelderman, Carol. *A Free Man of Color and His Hotel* (Potomac Books, 2012), p. 28.

Grant, Ulysses S. *Papers of Ulysses S. Grant,* vol. 22, edited by John Y. Simon (Southern Illinois University Press, 1998).

Kaczorowski, Robert J. "Federal Enforcement of Civil Rights During the First Reconstruction," *Fordham Urban Law Journal,* vol. 23, no. 1, 1995.

Lincoln, Abraham. "Transcript of the Proclamation," January 1, 1863, National Archives, https://www.archives.gov/exhibits/featured-documents/emancipation-proclamation/transcript.html.

Martinez, Michael J. *Carpetbaggers, Cavalry and the Ku Klux Klan* (Rowman & Littlefield, 2007).

"Protecting Life and Property: Passing the Ku Klux Klan Act." Ulysses S. Grant National Historic Site, National Park Service, https://www.nps.gov/articles/000/protecting-life-and-property-passing-the-ku-klux-klan-act.htm.

Ryan, Allan A. "Reconstruction Radical," *Dartmouth Alumni Magazine,* March–April 2021, https://dartmouthalumnimagazine.com/articles/amos-akerman-reconstruction-radical.

U.S. Congress. *Report of the Joint Select Committee to Inquire into the Condition of Affairs in the Late Insurrectionary States* (Government Printing Office, 1872), pp. 1599–1601.

Zuczek, Richard. "The Federal Government's Attack on the Ku Klux Klan: A Reassessment," *South Carolina Historical Magazine,* vol. 97, no. 1, 1996, pp. 47–64, http://www.jstor.org/stable/27570136.

CHAPTER FIVE

"Abandoned Plantations—A Virginia Case." *Chicago Tribune,* October 13, 1865.

Ager, Philipp, Leah Boustan, and Katherine Eriksson. "The Intergenerational Effects of a Large Wealth Shock: White Southerners After the Civil War," *American Economic Review,* vol. 111, no. 11, 2021, pp. 3767–94.

Ahtone, Tristan, and Robert Lee. "Land-Grab Universities," *High Country News,* March 30, 2020, https://www.hcn.org/issues/52.4/indigenous-affairs-education-land-grab-universities.

Allen, Walter Recharde, and Joseph O. Jewell. "A Backward Glance Forward: Past, Present and Future Perspectives on Historically Black Colleges and Universities," *Review of Higher Education,* vol. 25, no. 3, 2002, pp. 241–61, doi:10.1353/rhe.2002.0007.

"Before Central Park: The Story of Seneca Village." Central Park Conservancy, January 18, 2018, https://www.centralparknyc.org/articles/seneca-village.

Bell, Karen Cook. *Claiming Freedom: Race, Kinship, and Land in Nineteenth-Century Georgia* (University of South Carolina Press, 2018), pp. 63–68.

Berlin, Ira, Joseph P. Reidy, and Steven F. Miller. *The Wartime Genesis of Free Labor: The Upper South,* vol. 2 (Cambridge University Press, 1993), excerpts at https://goo.gl/hX90D7.

Connolly, Colleen. "The True Native New Yorkers Can Never Truly Reclaim Their Homeland," *Smithsonian Magazine,* October 5, 2018, https://www.smithsonianmag.com /history/true-native-new-yorkers-can-never-truly-reclaim-their-homeland-180970472/.

DeSantis, John. *The Thibodaux Massacre: Racial Violence and the 1887 Sugar Cane Labor Strike* (History Press, 2016).

Du Bois, W. E. B. *Economic Co-Operation Among Negro Americans: Report of a Social Study Made by Atlanta University, Under the Patronage of the Carnegie Institution of Washington, D.C.* (Atlanta University Press, 1907).

Engs, Robert Francis. *Educating the Disfranchised and Disinherited: Samuel Chapman Armstrong and Hampton Institute, 1839–1893* (University of Tennessee Press, 1999).

Engs, Robert Francis. *Freedom's First Generation: Black Hampton, Virginia, 1861–1890* (Fordham University Press, 2004).

Evans, Booker. "Differing Approaches: Native American Education at Carlisle and Hampton," Educ 300: Education Reform, Past and Present, Trinity College, May 3, 2012, https://commons.trincoll.edu/edreform/2012/05/2562/.

Fleisher, Chris. "The Recovery of Southern Wealth After the Civil War," American Economic Association, November 10, 2021, https://www.aeaweb.org/research/southern -wealth-persistence-civil-war-leah-boustan.

Foreman, P. Gabrielle, et al. *The Colored Conventions Movement: Black Organizing in the Nineteenth Century* (University of North Carolina Press, 2021), pp. 284–88.

Frances, M. F. *Hampton Institute, 1868 to 1885: Its Work for Two Races* (Normal School Press Print, 1885), 9–17, 31–32, excerpt at https://www.americanantiquarian.org /Manuscripts/hampton2races.html.

Franklin, John Hope, and Alfred A. Moss. *From Slavery to Freedom: A History of Negro Americans* (Knopf, 1988).

Gates, Henry Louis, Jr. "The Black Church," PBS, February 16, 2021, https://www.pbs.org /show/black-church/.

Horhn, John. "They Had No King: Ella Baker and the Politics of Decentralized Organization Among African-Descended Populations," thesis, Georgia State University, 2016, pp. 104–112, https://scholarworks.gsu.edu/aas_theses/36.

Horton, Scott. "Douglass—Rising Against Oppression," *Harper's Magazine,* February 19, 2008, https://harpers.org/2008/02/douglass-rising-against-oppression/.

Humphries, Frederick S. "1890 Land-Grant Institutions: Their Struggle for Survival and Equality," *Agricultural History,* vol. 65, no. 2, 1991, p. 3.

Jenkins, Jeffery A., and Justin Peck. *Congress and the First Civil Rights Era, 1861–1918* (University of Chicago Press, 2021).

Johnston (Frances Benjamin) Photograph Collection. Library of Congress, Prints and Photographs Division, https://www.loc.gov/pictures/collection/fbj/, accessed November 13, 2023.

Kahrl, Andrew W. *The Land Was Ours: How Black Beaches Became White Wealth in the Coastal South* (Harvard University Press, 2012), pp. 4–9, 22–29.

Katz, William Loren. *Black Indians: A Hidden Heritage,* rev. ed. (Atheneum Books for Young Readers, 2012), pp. 166–67.

Lee, Robert, and Tristan Ahtone. "How They Did It: Exposing How U.S. Universities Profited from Indigenous Land," Pulitzer Center, May 19, 2020, https://pulitzercenter .org/stories/how-they-did-it-exposing-how-us-universities-profited-indigenous-land.

Lee, Robert, and Tristan Ahtone. "Land Grab Universities," *High Country News,* March 30, 2020, https://www.hcn.org/issues/52.4/indigenous-affairs-education-land -grab-universities.

Lindsey, Donal F. *Indians at Hampton Institute, 1877–1923* (University of Illinois Press, 1995).

Lovett, Bobby L. *America's Historically Black Colleges and Universities: A Narrative History from the Nineteenth Century into the Twenty-First Century* (Mercer University Press, 2015).

Ludlow, Helen W., and Elaine Goodale Eastman. *Hampton Institute, 1868 to 1885: Its Work for Two Races,* edited by M. F. Armstrong (Normal School Press Print, 1885), www.loc .gov/item/07042231/.

Maps of Captured and Abandoned Properties. Department of the Treasury, Division of Captured Property, Claims, and Lands (1885–1887), NAID 960291.

Medlin, Eric. "Rosenwald Schools in North Carolina," *NCpedia,* September 2022, https:// www.ncpedia.org/anchor/rosenwald-schools-north.

Nathans, Sydney. *A Mind to Stay: White Plantation, Black Homeland* (Harvard University Press, 2017).

Nembhard, Jessica Gordon. *Collective Courage: A History of African American Cooperative Economic Thought and Practice* (Penn State University Press, 2014), p. 60.

Perry, Imani. *South to America: A Journey Below the Mason-Dixon to Understand the Soul of a Nation* (Harper Large Print, 2022).

Roberts, Alaina T. *I've Been Here All the While: Black Freedom on Native Land* (University of Pennsylvania Press, 2021), pp. 50, 67, 112–14, 122.

Rosales Castañeda, Oscar. "The IWW in the Fields, 1905–1925," Seattle Civil Rights and Labor History Project, University of Washington, https://depts.washington.edu/civilr /farmwk_ch2.htm, accessed November 13, 2023.

"The Rosenwald Schools: Progressive Era Philanthropy in the Segregated South (Teaching with Historic Places)." National Park Service, last updated September 19, 2023, https://www.nps.gov/articles/the-rosenwald-schools-progressive-era-philanthropy-in -the-segregated-south-teaching-with-historic-places.htm.

Schweninger, Loren. *Black Property Owners in the South, 1790–1915* (University of Illinois Press, 1997), pp. 143–233, 236.

Slocum, Karla. *Black Towns, Black Futures* (University of North Carolina Press, 2019), p. 19.

Smith, Clint. *How the Word Is Passed: A Reckoning with the History of Slavery Across America* (Little, Brown, 2021), pp. 231–33.

Staples, Brent. "In Search of the Black Utopia," *New York Times,* January 8, 2022, https:// nytimes.com/2022/01/08/opinion/seneca-village-central-park-new-york.html.

Stuart, Reginald. "HBCUs' Mission Rooted in Reconstruction," *Diverse Issues in Higher Education,* February 18, 2016, https://www.diverseeducation.com/demographics /african-american/article/15097997/hbcus-mission-rooted-in-reconstruction.

Wall, Diana diZerega, Nan A. Rothschild, and Cynthia Copeland. "Seneca Village and Little Africa: Two African American Communities in Antebellum New York City," *Historical Archaeology,* vol. 42, no. 1, 2008, pp. 97–107, http://www.jstor.org/stable /25617485.

Wills, Shomari. *Black Fortunes: The Story of the First Six African Americans Who Survived Slavery and Became Millionaires* (Amistad/HarperCollins, 2019), pp. 145–46.

Wright, Chester W. "A History of the Black Land-Grant Colleges 1890–1916," American University, 1981.

CHAPTER SIX

Bell, Karen Cook. "Local Politics and Black Freedom After the Civil War," Black Perspectives, July 10, 2019, https://www.aaihs.org/local-politics-and-black-freedom-after-the-civil-war/.
Bell, Karen Cook. "Slavery, Land Ownership, and Black Women's Community Networks," African American Intellectual History Society, October 25, 2018, https://www.aaihs.org/slavery-land-ownership-and-black-womens-community-networks/.
Morrison, Toni. *Beloved* (Bloom's Literary Criticism, 2009).
Shearer, Damon. "Standing in Defiance: The Legacy of Lucy Hicks Anderson," San Diego Black LGBTQ Coalition, June 14, 2019, https://www.sdblackcoalition.org/post/standing-in-defiance-the-legacy-of-lucy-hicks-anderson.

CHAPTER SEVEN

"Alex Manly and His Brother, Frank." Photograph, 1890–1898, Alex L. Manly Papers, 0065-b1-fa-i2, East Carolina University Digital Collections, https://digital.lib.ecu.edu/4181.
Ancestry.com. "North Carolina, U.S., Marriage Records, 1741–2011," database online.
Bell, Karen Cook. *Claiming Freedom: Race, Kinship, and Land in Nineteenth-Century Georgia* (University of South Carolina Press, 2018), pp. 69–87.
Complaint of Harry Nixon, September 19, 1865; complaint of Charles Fryar, September 21, 1865; complaint of John Caldwell, September 30, 1865; complaint of Edmond Newkerk, September 30, 1865; complaint of Charles Haws, October 1, 1865; complaint of Joseph Williams, October 1, 1865. National Archives, Records of the Bureau of Refugees, Freedmen, and Abandoned Lands, Record Group 105, Wilmington, NC, Superintendent of the Southern District, Registers of Complaints, series 2903, vol. 268, pp. 16–17, 21–23.
Cox, Anna-Lisa. *The Bone and Sinew of the Land: America's Forgotten Black Pioneers and the Struggle for Equality* (PublicAffairs, 2018), pp. 88–89.
DeSantis, John. *The Thibodaux Massacre: Racial Violence and the 1887 Sugar Cane Labor Strike* (History Press, 2016).
Einstein, Katherine Levine, and Maxwell Palmer, 2021. "Land of the Freeholder: How Property Rights Make Local Voting Rights." *Journal of Historical Political Economy*, vol. 1, no. 4, 2021, pp. 499–530.
Everett, Christopher (dir.). *Wilmington on Fire,* Speller Street Films, 2017, clip available at Vimeo, https://vimeo.com/151997669.
Franklin, John Hope, and Alfred A. Moss. *From Slavery to Freedom: A History of Negro Americans* (Knopf, 2000), pp. 245–53.
Gara, Antoine. "The Baron of Black Wall Street," *Forbes,* May 31, 2021, https://www.forbes.com/sites/antoinegara/2020/06/18/the-bezos-of-black-wall-street-tulsa-race-riots-1921/.
Hannah-Jones, Nikole. *The 1619 Project: A New Origin Story* (OneWorld, 2021), p. 85.
Kahrl, Andrew W. *The Land Was Ours: How Black Beaches Became White Wealth in the Coastal South* (Harvard University Press, 2012), p. 85.

Katz, William Loren. *Black Indians: A Hidden Heritage,* rev. ed. (Atheneum Books for Young Readers, 2012), pp. 196–97.

"Majority; Oklahoma Territory; Condition." *American Citizen,* June 7, 1889, p. 1.

"News Summary." *American Citizen,* May 31, 1889, p. 1.

O'Neal, Heather, et al. Facsimiles of historic block maps from the New Hanover County (NC) Register of Deeds.

"Ownership of Land as a Prerequisite to the Right to Vote: Equal or Unequal Protection." *University of Pennsylvania Law Review,* vol. 117, no. 4, 1969, https://scholarship.law.upenn.edu/penn_law_review/vol117/iss4/4.

"Poultry-Raising and Market-Gardening by Women in Oklahoma." *Plantation Missionary,* vol. 19, no. 3, May 1908, pp. 47–49.

Reaves, Bill. *"Strength Through Struggle": The Chronological and Historical Record of the African-American Community in Wilmington, North Carolina 1865–1950* (New Hanover County Public Library, 1998).

Registers of Signatures of Depositors in Branches of the Freedman's Savings and Trust Company, 1865–1874. National Archives, Record Group 101, Records of the Office of the Comptroller of the Currency, 1863–2006, ARC Identifier: 566522.

Roberts, Alaina T. *I've Been Here All the While: Black Freedom on Native Land* (University of Pennsylvania Press, 2021), pp. 82–89.

Sarkeesian, Anita, and Ebony Adams. *History vs Women: The Defiant Lives That They Don't Want You to Know* (Feiwel and Friends, 2018), p. 31.

Schermerhorn, Calvin. "The Thibodaux Massacre Left 60 African-Americans Dead and Spelled the End of Unionized Farm Labor in the South for Decades," *Smithsonian Magazine,* November 21, 2017, https://www.smithsonianmag.com/history/thibodaux-massacre-left-60-african-americans-dead-and-spelled-end-unionized-farm-labor-south-decades-180967289/.

"To the Colored Men of the South." *American Citizen,* June 28, 1889, p. 1.

U.S. Census. Year: 1870; Census Place: Wilmington, New Hanover, North Carolina; Roll: M593_1151; page 385B. Year: 1880; Census Place: Wilmington, New Hanover, North Carolina; Roll: 974; page 12D; Enumeration District: 140.

Wills, Shomari. *Black Fortunes: The Story of the First Six African Americans Who Survived Slavery and Became Millionaires* (Amistad/HarperCollins, 2019), pp. 129–32, 191–204, 235–36.

CHAPTER EIGHT

@BlackMassacreProject Instagram account.

Anderson, Ryan K. "Lumbee Kinship, Community, and the Success of the Red Banks Mutual Association," *American Indian Quarterly,* vol. 23, no. 2, 1999, pp. 39–58, https://doi.org/10.2307/1185966.

Cody, Sue Ann. "After the Storm: Racial Violence in Wilmington, North Carolina and Its Consequences for African Americans, 1898–1905," M.A. thesis, University of North Carolina at Wilmington, 2000.

Cox, Anna-Lisa. *The Bone and Sinew of the Land: America's Forgotten Black Pioneers and the Struggle for Equality* (PublicAffairs, 2018).

Davis, Molly. "Owning Up to a Violent Past," *Endeavors,* May 1, 2007, https://endeavors.unc.edu/spr2007/tyson.php.

Du Bois, W. E. B. *The Negro* (West Margin Press, 2021), p. 224.

Everett, Christopher (dir.). *Wilmington on Fire,* Speller Street Films, 2017, clip available at Vimeo, https://vimeo.com/151997669.

Historical Database of Sundown Towns. Site created by Matt Cheney, revised by OddBird, copyrighted by James W. Loewen and heirs (Nick Loewen), maintained by Phil Huckelberry and Stephen Berrey, hosted by Tougaloo College, Tougaloo, Mississippi, and facilitated by Pantheon, https://justice.tougaloo.edu/map/.

"A Horrid Slander." *Wilmington Star,* October 15, 1898, https://exhibits.lib.unc.edu/items /show/2158.

Jaspin, Elliot. *Buried in the Bitter Waters: The Hidden History of Racial Cleansing in America* (Basic Books, 2007).

Kirk, J. Allen. "A Statement of Facts Concerning the Bloody Riot in Wilmington, N.C. of Interest to Every Citizen in the United States," 1898, Documenting the American South, University of North Carolina at Chapel Hill, https://docsouth.unc.edu/nc/kirk /kirk.html.

Krouse, Lauren. "A History of Hatred and Love in Wilmington, North Carolina," *Shenandoah,* vol. 69, no. 2, Spring 2020, https://shenandoahliterary.org/692/a-history-of -hatred-and-love-in-Wilmington-north-carolina/.

LaFrance, Adrianne. "The Lost History of an American Coup d'État," *The Atlantic,* August 12, 2017.

Lee, Trymaine. "How America's Vast Racial Wealth Gap Grew: By Plunder," *New York Times,* August 14, 2019, https://www.nytimes.com/interactive/2019/08/14/magazine /racial-wealth-gap.html.

Lowery, Malinda Maynor. "How the Lumbee Tribe Armed Themselves Against the KKK in 1958—and Won," *Scalawag,* July 20, 2021, https://scalawagmagazine.org/2020/01 /ambush/.

Lowery, Malinda Maynor. *Lumbee Indians in the Jim Crow South: Race, Identity, and the Making of a Nation* (University of North Carolina Press, 2010), pp. 251–65.

McCoy, David B. *The 1898 Wilmington, North Carolina Coup d'État* (Spare Change Press, 2018).

Oyer, Kalyn. "New Documentary on Wealthy SC Black Cotton Farm Owner Who Was Lynched for Success," *Post and Courier,* November 17, 2020, https://www .postandcourier.com/charleston_scene/new-documentary-on-wealthy-sc-black -cotton-farm-owner-who-was-lynched-for-success/article_7ce0fb88-1f94-11eb-ab94 -fba480869e15.html.

Phillip, Abby. "This Duke Dorm Is No Longer Named After a White Supremacist Former Governor," *Washington Post,* July 14, 2014, https://www.washingtonpost.com/news /post-nation/wp/2014/06/17/this-duke-dorm-is-no-longer-named-after-a-white -supremacist-former-governor/.

Prather, H. Leon. *We Have Taken a City: Wilmington Racial Massacre and Coup of 1898* (Fairleigh Dickinson University Press, 1984).

Reaves, Bill. *Post Riot (November 10, 1898) News, from Newspapers Dated January 1899 to June 1899* (B. Reaves, 1999).

Suiter, Geoff. "Outside Newspaper Coverage of the 1898 Coup in Wilmington, North Carolina," paper written for History 605, "Gilded Age," Prof. Hyser, Graduate School, James Madison University, Harrisonburg, VA, Spring 1999.

Traxel, David. *1898: The Birth of the American Century* (Knopf Doubleday, 1999), p. 280.

Tyson, Timothy B. "The Ghosts of 1898: Wilmington's Race Riot and the Rise of White Supremacy," *News and Observer,* November 17, 2006, https://media2.newsobserver .com/content/media/2010/5/3/ghostsof1898.pdf.

Umfleet, LeRae Sikes. *A Day of Blood: The 1898 Wilmington Race Riot* (University of North Carolina Press, 2020).

U.S. Census Bureau. Population statistics for 1880–1920.

Wilkerson, Isabel. *The Warmth of Other Suns: The Epic Story of America's Great Migration* (Knopf Doubleday, 2011), p. 181.

Zucchino, David. *Wilmington's Lie: The Murderous Coup of 1898 and the Rise of White Supremacy* (Grove Press, 2021).

CHAPTER NINE

Asante-Muhammad, Dedrick, and Briana Shelton. "Why the Great Migration Did Little to Bridge the Great Racial Divide," Inequality.org, August 1, 2022, https://inequality.org /research/great-migration-racial-wealth-divide/.

Derenoncourt, Ellora. "Can You Move to Opportunity? Evidence from the Great Migration," *American Economic Review,* vol. 112, no. 2, 2022, https://pubs.aeaweb.org/doi /pdfplus/10.1257/aer.20200002.

Evans, William McKee. *To Die Game: The Story of the Lowry Band, Indian Guerillas of Reconstruction* (Syracuse University Press, 1995).

"The Great Migration, 1900–1929" (map). Schomburg Center for Research in Black Culture, Jean Blackwell Hutson Research and Reference Division, New York Public Library, 2005, https://digitalcollections.nypl.org/items/85f0908d-8265-f747-e040-e00a18062131.

La Vere, David. *The Tuscarora War: Indians, Settlers, and the Fight for the Carolina Colonies* (University of North Carolina Press, 2013).

Lowery, Malinda Maynor. *Lumbee Indians: An American Struggle* (University of North Carolina Press, 2018).

Rountree, Helen C., with Wesley D. Taukchiray. *Manteo's World: Native American Life in Carolina's Sound Country Before and After the Lost Colony* (University of North Carolina Press, 2021).

Sabelhaus, John, and Alice Henriquez Volz. "Are Disappearing Employer Pensions Contributing to Rising Wealth Inequality?," Board of Governors of the Federal Reserve System, February 1, 2019, https://www.federalreserve.gov/econres/notes/feds-notes /are-disappearing-employer-pensions-contributing-to-rising-wealth-inequality -20190201.html.

Wilkerson, Isabel. *The Warmth of Other Suns: The Epic Story of America's Great Migration* (Vintage Books, 2014), pp. 274–75.

Wills, Shomari. *Black Fortunes: The Story of the First Six African Americans Who Survived Slavery and Became Millionaires* (Amistad/HarperCollins, 2019), pp. 137–38, 253, 261.

CHAPTER TEN

Artonline, Ramsess. "Black Farmers' Appeal: Cancel Pigford Debt Campaign," Acres of Ancestry Initiative/Black Agrarian Fund, https://acresofancestry.org/black-farmers -appeal-cancel-pigford-debt-campaign/, accessed November 13, 2023.

Board of Governors, Federal Reserve System. "Survey of Consumer Finances (SCF)," https://www.federalreserve.gov/econres/scfindex.htm, accessed November 2020.

Browning, Pamela, et al. *The Decline of Black Farming in America,* U.S. Commission on Civil Rights (Government Printing Office, 1982), pp. 8, 9, 94, 107, 182, https://files.eric .ed.gov/fulltext/ED222604.pdf.

Daniel, Pete. *Dispossession: Discrimination Against African American Farmers in the Age of Civil Rights* (University of North Carolina Press, 2013), p. 6.

Farm Service Agency. "History of USDA's Farm Service Agency," September 23, 2020, https://fsa.usda.gov/about-fsa/history-and-mission/agency-history/index.

Ficara, John Francis. *Black Farmers in America* (University Press of Kentucky, 2006).

Frey, William H. Analysis of US Census Bureau's Decennial Censuses, 1920–2000, and 2008–2012 American Community Survey, Drawn from IPUMS-USA, University of Minnesota, www.ipums.org, and American Community Survey Public Use Microfiles, Brookings Institution.

Holloway, Kali. "How Thousands of Black Farmers Were Forced Off Their Land," *The Nation,* November 1, 2021, https://www.thenation.com/article/society/black-farmers -pigford-debt/.

Penniman, Leah. Zoom interview conducted by Brea Baker, December 2022.

Staats, Elmer B. "Farmers Home Administration's (FmHA) Operation of the Rural Construction and Improvement Loan Programs," Office of the Comptroller General, B-115398, September 28, 1976, https://www.gao.gov/products/b-115398-50.

USDA. "About the U.S. Department of Agriculture," https://www.usda.gov/our-agency /about-usda, accessed December 12, 2022.

USDA. "Non-Discrimination Statement," U.S. Department of Agriculture, https://www .usda.gov/non-discrimination-statement, accessed December 12, 2022.

USDA. "Priorities," U.S. Department of Agriculture, https://www.usda.gov/priorities, accessed December 12, 2022.

USDA National Commission on Small Farms. *A Time to Act: A Report of the USDA National Commission on Small Farms* (USDA, 1998), p. 40, https://static.ewg.org/reports /2021/BlackFarmerDiscriminationTimeline/1998-NCSF-Report.pdf?_ga=2.72965467 .959248329.1648422523-2123137255.1639662520.

Vilsack, Tom. "Secretary's Column: 'The Peoples' Department: 150 Years of USDA,'" May 11, 2012, https://www.usda.gov/media/blog/2012/05/11/secretarys-column-peoples -department-150-years-usda.

Wilkerson, Isabel. *The Warmth of Other Suns: The Epic Story of America's Great Migration* (Random House, 2010), pp. 274–75, 372–75.

CHAPTER ELEVEN

@AcresOfAncestry Instagram account.

"About Heirs Property." Georgia Heirs Property Law Center, https://www.gaheirsproperty .org/heirs-property, accessed November 13, 2023.

Evans, William McKee. *To Die Game: The Story of the Lowry Band, Indian Guerillas of Reconstruction* (Syracuse University Press, 1995).

Fullilove, Mindy Thompson. "Eminent Domain and African Americans: What Is the Price of the Commons?," Perspectives on Eminent Domain Abuse, Institute for Justice, March 2015, https://ij-org-re.s3.amazonaws.com/ijdevsitestage/wp-content/uploads /2015/03/Perspectives-Fullilove.pdf.

Germain, Jacqui. "What Is Disaster Capitalism? A Cycle of Crisis, Exploitation, and Priva-

tization," *Teen Vogue,* September 2, 2021, https://www.teenvogue.com/story/what-is
-disaster-capitalism.

Hennessy-Fiske, Molly. "The Many Chapters Marked by Racism in George Floyd's Family
History," *Los Angeles Times,* June 3, 2020, https://www.latimes.com/world-nation
/story/2020-06-03/the-many-chapters-marked-by-racism-in-george-floyds-family
-history.

"History of Seabreeze Inspires a Call for Stories," *Wilmington Star-News,* November 9, 2014,
https://www.starnewsonline.com/story/news/2014/11/10/history-of-seabreeze-inspires-a
-call-for-stories/30974320007/.

Holloway, Kali. "How Thousands of Black Farmers Were Forced Off Their Land," *The
Nation,* November 8, 2021, https://www.thenation.com/article/society/black-farmers
-pigford-debt/.

Jones Family. Interview conducted by Where Is My Land, December 14, 2022.

"Jordan Lake State Recreation Area." North Carolina Division of Parks and Recreation,
https://www.ncparks.gov/state-parks/jordan-lake-state-recreation-area, accessed November 13, 2023.

Kahrl, Andrew W. *The Land Was Ours: How Black Beaches Became White Wealth in the
Coastal South* (University of North Carolina Press, 2016), pp. 162–65.

La Vere, David. *The Tuscarora War: Indians, Settlers, and the Fight for the Carolina Colonies* (University of North Carolina Press, 2013).

Lowery, Malinda Maynor. *Lumbee Indians: An American Struggle* (University of North
Carolina Press, 2018).

Moore, Beverly. Interview conducted by Where Is My Land, December 16, 2022.

Purnell, Derecka. *Becoming Abolitionists: Police, Protests, and the Pursuit of Freedom*
(Verso, 2021), pp. 120–25.

Rountree, Helen C., with Wesley D. Taukchiray. *Manteo's World: Native American Life in
Carolina's Sound Country Before and After the Lost Colony* (University of North Carolina Press, 2021).

Snowden, Archie. "Black Family Claims Their Land, Well Was Stolen by Madison County
Officials Decades Ago," WHNT, Huntsville, AL, February 1, 2023, https://whnt.com
/news/huntsville/black-family-claims-their-land-well-was-stolen-by-madison-county
-officials-decades-ago/.

WWAY News. "Black History: The History of Freeman Beach," WWAY, February 22,
2019, https://www.wwaytv3.com/black-history-the-history-of-freeman-beach/.

CHAPTER TWELVE

"(1901) Congressman George H. White's Farewell Address to Congress," BlackPast, January 28, 2007, https://www.blackpast.org/african-american-history/1901-george-h-whites
-farewell-address-congress/.

Aminetzah, Daniel, Jane Brennan, Wesley Davis, Bekinwari Idoniboye, Nick Noel, Jake
Pawlowski, and Shelley Stewart. "Black Farmers in the US: The Opportunity for Addressing Racial Disparities in Farming," McKinsey & Company, November 10, 2021,
https://www.mckinsey.com/industries/agriculture/our-insights/black-farmers-in-the
-us-the-opportunity-for-addressing-racial-disparities-in-farming.

Asante-Muhammad, Dedrick, Esha Kamra, Connor Sanchez, Kathy Ramirez, and Rogelio

Tec. "Racial Wealth Snapshot: Native Americans," National Community Reinvestment Coalition, February 14, 2022, https://ncrc.org/racial-wealth-snapshot-native-americans/.

Brooks, Rodney A. "America's Racial Wealth Gap Is Enormous and Getting Worse," *Fast Company*, August 30, 2021, https://www.fastcompany.com/90670468/americas-racial -wealth-gap-is-enormous-and-getting-worse.

Browne, Robert S. "Only Six Million Acres: The Decline of Black Owned Land in the Rural South," Black Economic Research Center, June 1973, https://acresofancestry.org /wp-content/uploads/2021/08/Robert-Browne-1973-Only-Six-Million-Acres.pdf.

Chang, Mariko, and Meizhu Lui. "Lifting as We Climb: Women of Color, Wealth, and America's Future," Insight Center for Community Economic Development, Spring 2020, p. 14.

Francis, Dania V., Darrick Hamilton, Thomas W. Mitchell, Nathan A. Rosenberg, and Bryce Wilson Stucki. "Black Land Loss: 1920–1997," *AEA Papers and Proceedings*, vol. 112, 2022, pp. 38–42.

Geisler, Charles C. "Land and Poverty in the United States: Insights and Oversights," *Land Economics*, vol. 71, no. 1, 1995, pp. 16–34, https://doi.org/10.2307/3146755.

Gilbert, Jess, Spencer D. Wood, and Gwen Sharp. "Who Owns the Land? Agricultural Land Ownership by Race/Ethnicity," *Rural America*, vol. 17, no. 4, Winter 2002, pp. 55–62, https://www.ers.usda.gov/webdocs/publications/46984/19353_ra174h_1_.pdf.

Holloway, Kali. "How Thousands of Black Farmers Were Forced Off Their Land," *The Nation*, November 8, 2021, https://www.thenation.com/article/society/black-farmers -pigford-debt/.

Kuhn, Moritz, Moritz Schularick, and Ulrike I. Steins. "Income and Wealth Inequality in America, 1949–2016," Federal Reserve Bank of Minneapolis, June 7, 2018, pp. 2–6, 25–33, https://researchdatabase.minneapolisfed.org/downloads/ws859f759.

Long, Heather, and Andrew Van Dam. "Analysis: The Black-White Economic Divide Is as Wide as It Was in 1968," *Washington Post*, June 4, 2020, https://www.washingtonpost .com/business/2020/06/04/economic-divide-black-households/.

Noel, Nick, Duwain Pinder, Shelley Stewart, and Jason Wright. "The Economic Impact of Closing the Racial Wealth Gap," McKinsey & Company, August 13, 2019, https://www .mckinsey.com/industries/public-and-social-sector/our-insights/the-economic-impact -of-closing-the-racial-wealth-gap.

Perry, Andre M. *Know Your Price: Valuing Black Lives and Property in America's Black Cities* (Brookings Institution Press, 2020).

Perry, Andre M., Jonathan Rothwell, and David Harshbarger. "The Devaluation of Assets in Black Neighborhoods," Brookings Institution, November 27, 2018, https://www .brookings.edu/research/devaluation-of-assets-in-black-neighborhoods/.

Roberts, Alaina E. *I've Been Here All the While: Black Freedom on Native Land* (University of Pennsylvania Press, 2021), p. 119.

Rosenberg, Nathan, and Bryan Wilson Stucki. "How USDA Distorted Data to Conceal Decades of Discrimination Against Black Farmers," *The Counter*, June 26, 2019, https://thecounter.org/usda-black-farmers-discrimination-tom-vilsack-reparations -civil-rights/.

Song, Zijia. "U.S. Black Farmers Lost Billions in Land Value, Study Shows," Bloomberg, May 2, 2022, https://www.bloomberg.com/news/articles/2022-05-02/black-farmers-in -u-s-lost-326-billion-of-land-study-shows.

White, George H. "Defense of the Negro Race—Charges Answered. Speech of Hon. George H. White, of North Carolina, in the House of Representatives, January 29, 1901," Documenting the American South, University of North Carolina at Chapel Hill, https://docsouth.unc.edu/nc/whitegh/whitegh.html.

CHAPTER THIRTEEN

"2021 TRI Factsheet: ZIP Code—70721," TRI Explorer, Toxics Release Inventory, U.S. Environmental Protection Agency, October 2023, https://enviro.epa.gov/triexplorer /tri_factsheet.factsheet?pzip=70721&pyear=2021&pParent=TRI&pDataSet=TRIQ1.

Baurick, Tristan, Lylla Younes, and Joan Meiners. "Welcome to 'Cancer Alley,' Where Toxic Air Is About to Get Worse," ProPublica, October 30, 2019, https://www .propublica.org/article/welcome-to-cancer-alley-where-toxic-air-is-about-to-get -worse.

Edwards, Jennifer J. "Living on the Edge: African American Leisure and the Coastal Environment at Sea Breeze, North Carolina," Honors Project, University of North Carolina at Wilmington, 1998, https://digitalcollections.uncw.edu/digital/collection/honors/id/1351.

Feir, Donna, Rob Gillezeau, and Maggie E. C. Jones. "The Slaughter of the Bison and Reversal of Fortunes on the Great Plains," Yale Economic Growth Center, April 7, 2021, https:// egc.yale.edu/sites/default/files/2021-04/2021-0423%20EconHistory%20Conference /bison_short_FGJ_april_2021%20ada-ns.pdf.

Flavelle, Christopher, and Kalen Goodluck. "Dispossessed, Again: Climate Change Hits Native Americans Especially Hard," *New York Times,* June 27, 2021, https://www .nytimes.com/2021/06/27/climate/climate-Native-Americans.html.

Gerard, Philip. "The 1950s: A Shared Rhythm," *Our State,* January 29, 2019, https://www .ourstate.com/a-shared-rhythm/.

hooks, bell. "Touching the Earth," *Orion,* vol. 15, no. 4, Autumn 1996, pp. 21–23.

Jo, Hyunju, Chorong Song, and Yoshifumi Miyazaki. "Physiological Benefits of Viewing Nature: A Systematic Review of Indoor Experiments," *International Journal of Environmental Research and Public Health,* vol. 16, no. 23, November 27, 2019, doi:10.3390 /ijerph16234739.

Kahrl, Andrew W. *The Land Was Ours: How Black Beaches Became White Wealth in the Coastal South* (University of North Carolina Press, 2016), pp. 165–66, 237–38, 246–49.

Katz, William Loren. *Black Indians: A Hidden Heritage,* rev. ed. (Atheneum Books for Young Readers, 2012), pp. 207–9.

Klein, Naomi. *The Shock Doctrine: The Rise of Disaster Capitalism* (Metropolitan Books/ Henry Holt, 2007), pp. 6–14.

Klein, Naomi. *This Changes Everything: Capitalism vs. the Climate* (Simon & Schuster, 2014), pp. 161–70.

Magdoff, Fred. "A Rational Agriculture Is Incompatible with Capitalism," *Monthly Review,* vol. 66, no. 10, March 2015, https://monthlyreview.org/2015/03/01/a-rational-agriculture -is-incompatible-with-capitalism/.

Mandel, Kyla. "Ayisha Siddiqa Is Making the World Think Differently About Climate Action," *Time,* March 2, 2023, https://time.com/6259119/ayisha-siddiqa/.

Morrison, Toni. *Sula* (Knopf, 1973), pp. 2–6, 165–66.

Purnell, Derecka. *Becoming Abolitionists: Police, Protests, and the Pursuit of Freedom* (Verso, 2021), pp. 240–45.

Roberts, Alaina E. *I've Been Here All the While: Black Freedom on Native Land* (University of Pennsylvania Press, 2021), pp. 103–4, 110, 120.

Shaw, Al, and Lylla Younes. "The Most Detailed Map of Cancer-Causing Industrial Air Pollution in the U.S.," ProPublica, November 2, 2021, https://projects.propublica.org /toxmap/.

Smith, Clint. *How the Word Is Passed: A Reckoning with the History of Slavery Across America* (Little, Brown, 2021), p. 58.

Stephens, Ronald J. "Freeman Beach—Seabreeze, Wilmington, North Carolina (ca. 1885–)," BlackPast, March 9, 2014, https://www.blackpast.org/african-american-history/freeman -beach-seabreeze-Wilmington-north-carolina-ca-1885/.

Surrusco, Emilie Karrick. "Cancer Alley Rises Up," Earthjustice, May 8, 2019, https:// earthjustice.org/features/cancer-alley-rises-up.

Sze, Jocelyne S., Dylan Z. Childs, L. Roman Carrasco, and David P. Edwards. "Indigenous Lands in Protected Areas Have High Forest Integrity Across the Tropics," *Current Biology,* vol. 32, no. 22, November 21, 2022, pp. 4949–56.e3.

"USA: Environmental Racism in 'Cancer Alley' Must End—Experts." UN Office of the High Commission for Human Rights, press release, March 2, 2012, https://www.ohchr .org/en/press-releases/2021/03/usa-environmental-racism-cancer-alley-must-end -experts.

Weir, Kirsten. "Nurtured by Nature," *Monitor on Psychology,* vol. 51, no. 3, April 1, 2020, https://www.apa.org/monitor/2020/04/nurtured-nature.

CHAPTER FOURTEEN

Baker, David. Interview conducted by Brea Baker, September 26, 2021.

Baker, Jenail. Interview conducted by Brea Baker, October 2, 2021.

Baker, Karen. Interview conducted by Brea Baker, October 2, 2021.

Baker, Steven. Interview conducted by Brea Baker, October 10, 2021.

CHAPTER FIFTEEN

Bandele, Monica, et al. "Black-Indigeneity–Black Reparations, Liberation and LANDBACK," webinar hosted by the Movement for Black Lives and NDN Collective, April 6, 2022.

Brazelton, Bennett. "On the Erasure of Black Indigeneity," *Review of Education, Pedagogy, and Cultural Studies,* vol. 43, no. 5, October 2021, pp. 379–97, https://doi.org/10.1080 /10714413.2021.1968235.

Chang, Mariko, and Meizhu Lui. "Lifting as We Climb: Women of Color, Wealth, and America's Future," Insight Center for Community Economic Development, Spring 2020, p. 14.

"Dick Gregory on Nisqually River, March 1, 1966." Photograph, Museum of History and Industry, Seattle, https://digitalcollections.lib.washington.edu/digital/collection /imlsmohai/id/9822/.

"Dick Gregory Trial—12/4/16." Olympia Historical Society and Bigelow House Museum, Olympia, WA, https://olympiahistory.org/dick-gregory-trial-12416/.

Droz, Pennelys. "Stolen Lands: A Black and Indigenous History of Land Exploitation," *YES!,* November 16, 2022, https://www.yesmagazine.org/social-justice/2022/11/16 /history-land-slavery-indigenous.

Harris, Dash. "With Namor, Wakanda Forever Does What Latine Media Will Not," Refinery29, November 18, 2022, https://www.refinery29.com/en-us/2022/11/11191045/wakanda-forever-namor-indigenous-latine-representation.

Katz, William Loren. *Black Indians: A Hidden Heritage,* rev. ed. (Atheneum Books for Young Readers, 2012), pp. 169, 209–10.

Landry, Alysa. "Today in Native History: Natives Participate in Poor People's Campaign; Protest BIA," ICT News, June 20, 2017, https://ictnews.org/archive/today-native-history-natives-participate-poor-peoples-campaign-protest-bia.

Mays, Kyle. *An Afro-Indigenous History of the United States* (Beacon Press, 2021).

Miller, Diane E. "Wyandot, Shawnee, and African American Resistance to Slavery in Ohio and Kansas," dissertation, University of Nebraska, Lincoln, 2019.

Movement for Black Lives. LANDBACK Campaign Launch Webinar, October 10, 2020, https://www.facebook.com/watch/live/?extid=CL-UNK-UNK-UNK-IOS_GK0T-GK1C&mibextid=2Rb1fB&ref=watch_permalink&v=263440104943971.

NAP Staff. "Intersectional Indigenous Identities: Afro-Indigenous and Black Indigenous Peoples," Native Americans in Philanthropy, February 1, 2022, https://nativephilanthropy.org/2022/02/01/intersectional-indigenous-identities-afro-indigenous-and-black-indigenous-peoples/.

"Native Americans in the Poor People's Campaign." National Park Service, March 17, 2023, https://www.nps.gov/articles/000/native-activism-poor-peoples-campaign.htm.

Picotte, Tristan. "Dr. Martin Luther King, Jr. and Native American Rights," Partnership with Native Americans, January 15, 2019.

Scherer, Kimmy. "Martin Luther King, Jr., an Advocate for Native American Rights," *West River Eagle,* February 16, 2022, https://www.westrivereagle.com/articles/martin-luther-king-jr-an-advocate-for-native-american-rights/.

Southern Christian Leadership Conference Information Office. *Statement of Demands for Rights of the Poor Presented to Agencies of the U.S. Government by the Southern Christian Leadership Conference and Its Committee of 100,* 1968, https://www.crmvet.org/docs/6805_ppc_demands.pdf.

Starks, Amber, and Kyle Mays. "Black-Indigeneity: Historical Perspective and Relationship," webinar, LANDBACK University, December 2021.

Tizon, Alex. "The Boldt Decision/25 Years—The Fish Tale That Changed History," *Seattle Times,* February 7, 1999, https://web.archive.org/web/20140506042231/http://community.seattletimes.nwsource.com/archive/?date=19990207&slug=2943039.

U.S. Court of Appeals for the Ninth Circuit. *Plaintiff-Appellee, Quinault Tribe of Indians et al., Intervenors-Plaintiffs, v. State of Washington,* Justia, 520 F.2d 676, June 4, 1975, https://web.archive.org/web/20190101002847/https://law.justia.com/cases/federal/appellate-courts/F2/520/676/271775/.

Washington Area Spark. "Carmichael Offers Support to Native Americans: 1972," Flickr, uploaded on February 3, 2019, https://www.flickr.com/photos/washington_area_spark/46056325165/.

Wilma, David. "Native Americans and Supporters Stage Fish-In to Protest Denial of Treaty Rights on March 2, 1964," HistoryLink, March 1, 2003, https://www.historylink.org/file/5332.

Woods, Alicia (dir.). *American Red and Black: Stories of Afro-Native Identity,* Talking Fish Productions, 2006.

Woodson, C. G. "The Relations of Negroes and Indians in Massachusetts," *Journal of Negro History*, vol. 6, no. 1, January 1920, pp. 45–57.

Ziyad, Hari. "Why We Need to Stop Excluding Black Populations from Ideas of Who Is 'Indigenous,'" Black Youth Project, October 24, 2022, https://blackyouthproject.com /need-stop-excluding-black-populations-ideas-indigenous/.

CHAPTER SIXTEEN

Alexander, Gregory S. "The Complexities of Land Reparations," *Law and Social Inquiry*, vol. 39, no. 4, 2014, pp. 874–901, http://www.jstor.org/stable/24545765.

Amistad Research Center. "The Federation of Southern Cooperatives Training and Research Center (RTRC)," February 5, 2021, https://www.amistadresearchcenter.org /single-post/federation-southern-cooperatives-training-research-rtrc.

Betsey, C. L. "A Brief Biography of Robert S. Browne," *Review of Black Political Economy*, vol. 35, nos. 2/3, 2008, pp. 57–60, https://doi.org/10.1007/s12114-008-9024-0.

Black Panther Party. "Ten-Point Program" (1966), Marxists Internet Archive, https://www .marxists.org/history/usa/workers/black-panthers/1966/10/15.htm.

Brooks, J. "The Emergency Land Fund: Robert S. Browne, the Idea and the Man," *Review of Black Political Economy*, vol. 35, nos. 2/3, 2008, pp. 67–73, https://doi.org/10.1007 /s12114-008-9026-y.

Browne, Robert S. "Only Six Million Acres: The Decline of Black Owned Land in the Rural South," Black Economic Research Center, March 10, 1975, https://acresof ancestry.org/wp-content/uploads/2021/08/Robert-Browne-1973-Only-Six-Million -Acres.pdf.

Carmichael, Stokely. "From Black Power to Pan-Africanism" (speech, March 22, 1971), American RadioWorks, http://americanradioworks.publicradio.org/features /blackspeech/scarmichael-2.html.

Carmichael, Stokely, and Kwame Ture. "Pan-Africanism—Land and Power," *Black Scholar*, vol. 27, nos. 3/4, 1997, pp. 58–64, http://www.jstor.org/stable/41068750.

DeVore, Deanna. Interview conducted by Brea Baker, October 11, 2021.

"Fannie Lou Hamer Founds Freedom Farm Cooperative." SNCC Digital Gateway, https:// snccdigital.org/events/fannie-lou-hamer-founds-freedom-farm-cooperative/, accessed November 13, 2023.

Friedersdorf, Conor. "How Did Progressive Journalists Get Pigford So Wrong?," *The Atlantic*, May 7, 2013, https://www.theatlantic.com/politics/archive/2013/05/how-did -progressive-journalists-get-pigford-so-wrong/275593/.

Hale, Jon N. "The Struggle Begins Early: Head Start and the Mississippi Freedom Movement," *History of Education Quarterly*, vol. 52, no. 4, 2012, pp. 506–34, doi:10.1111 /j.1748-5959.2012.00418.x.

Henderson, Kimberly. "The Legacy of Audley 'Queen Mother' Moore and Her Battlecry for Reparations," Schomburg Center for Research in Black Culture, New York Public Library, January 10, 2023, https://www.nypl.org/blog/2023/01/10/legacy-audley-queen -mother-moore-and-her-battlecry-reparations.

"History." Federation of Southern Cooperatives Land Assistance Fund, https://www .federation.coop/news-archives, accessed November 13, 2023.

Holloway, Kali. "How Thousands of Black Farmers Were Forced Off Their Land," *The*

Nation, November 1, 2021, https://www.thenation.com/article/society/black-farmers -pigford-debt/.

Keat, Jim. "The Black Manifesto at the Riverside Church," Riverside Church, April 30, 2019, https://www.trcnyc.org/blackmanifesto/.

LaFraniere, Sharon. "U.S. Opens Spigot After Farmers Claim Discrimination," *New York Times,* April 26, 2013, https://www.nytimes.com/2013/04/26/us/farm-loan-bias-claims -often-unsupported-cost-us-millions.html.

Malcolm X. "Message to the Grass Roots," November 1963, California State University Northridge, https://www.csun.edu/~hcpas003/grassroots.html.

"Moving out of Shacks and into Tents." Tent City: Stories of Civil Rights in Fayette County, Tennessee, University of Memphis, https://www.memphis.edu/tentcity/moving -shacks-tents.php, accessed November 13, 2023.

Mullen, Kirsten. "How Audley Moore Created a Blueprint for Black Reparations," *Vanity Fair,* October 18, 2022, https://www.vanityfair.com/culture/2022/10/how-audley -moore-created-a-blueprint-for-black-reparations.

Pigford v. Glickman. 185 F.R.D. 82, 85-86 (D.D.C. 1999).

Reynolds, Bruce J. "Black Farmers in America, 1865–2000: The Pursuit of Independent Farming and the Role of Cooperatives," RBS Research Report 194, U.S. Department of Agriculture, October 2002, https://www.rd.usda.gov/files/RR194.pdf.

Rosenberg, Nathan, and Bryce Wilson Stucki. "How USDA Distorted Data to Conceal Decades of Discrimination Against Black Farmers," The Counter, June 26, 2019, https://thecounter.org/usda-black-farmers-discrimination-tom-vilsack-reparations -civil-rights/.

Saunders, Richard L. "What Happened? 'Tent City,' Tennessee," University of Tennessee at Martin, https://www.utm.edu/staff/accarls/civilrights/tent_city_history.html, accessed November 13, 2023.

"South African Issues by Angela Davis (2/2)." YouTube, posted by AfroMarxist, November 18, 2017, https://www.youtube.com/watch?v=2Mb9J5LXllk.

Towles, Ashtan, and Barry Towles. Interview conducted by Brea Baker, January 18, 2022.

Towles, Shepherd. *Tent City . . . "Home of the Brave"* (pamphlet, ca. 1960), Special Collections Division, Nashville Public Library.

Uenuma, Francine. "The Massacre of Black Sharecroppers That Led the Supreme Court to Curb the Racial Disparities of the Justice System," *Smithsonian Magazine,* August 2, 2018, https://www.smithsonianmag.com/history/death-hundreds-elaine-massacre-led -supreme-court-take-major-step-toward-equal-justice-african-americans-180969863/.

U.S. Congress. "Civil Rights at USDA: A Backgrounder on Efforts by the Obama Administration," March 25, 2021, https://www.congress.gov/event/117th-congress/house -event/LC67546/text?s=1&r=94.

Vilsack, Tom. "Secretary's Column: 'The Peoples' Department: 150 Years of USDA,'" May 11, 2012, https://www.usda.gov/media/blog/2012/05/11/secretarys-column-peoples -department-150-years-usda.

White, Monica M. *Freedom Farmers: Agricultural Resistance and the Black Freedom Movement* (University of North Carolina Press, 2018).

White, Monica M. "'A Pig and a Garden': Fannie Lou Hamer and the Freedom Farms Cooperative," *Food and Foodways,* vol. 25, no. 1, 2017, p. 20, https://www.academia.edu

/31683953/_A_pig_and_a_garden_Fannie_Lou_Hamer_and_the_Freedom_Farms
_Cooperative.

"Who Is Queen Mother Audley Moore?" National African American Reparations Commission, July 27, 2013, https://reparationscomm.org/people-you-should-know/who-is-queen-mother-moore/.

Withers, Ernest C. "'Tent City' Family, Fayette County, TN" (photograph), National Museum of African American History and Culture, https://nmaahc.si.edu/object/nmaahc_2009.16.4, accessed November 13, 2023.

CHAPTER SEVENTEEN

@JusticeForBrucesBeach Instagram account.

@WhereIsMyLand Instagram account.

"1921 Tulsa Race Massacre." *Tulsa Historical Society and Museum,* November 1, 2018, https://www.tulsahistory.org/exhibit/1921-tulsa-race-massacre/.

Alexander, Gregory S. "The Complexities of Land Reparations," *Law and Social Inquiry,* vol. 39, no. 4, 2014, pp. 874–901, http://www.jstor.org/stable/24545765.

Ardrey, Taylor. "A Black California Family Is Selling the Land Stolen from Their Ancestors Back to LA County for $20 Million," *Insider,* January 4, 2023, https://www.insider.com/black-family-bruces-beach-sold-la-county-20-million-2023-1.

Bandele, Monica, et al. "Black-Indigeneity—Black Reparations, Liberation and LANDBACK," webinar hosted by the Movement for Black Lives and NDN Collective, April 6, 2022.

Berry, Mary Frances. *My Face Is Black Is True: Calli House and the Struggle for Ex-Slave Reparations* (Knopf, 2005).

Bottomly, Therese. "I Unreservedly Apologize," *The Oregonian,* October 4, 2022, https://projects.oregonlive.com/publishing-prejudice/editor-apology.

"Bree Jones, 2021–2024 Fellow: Parity Homes." Fund for New Leadership, https://fundfornewleadership.org/fellows/bree-jones/, accessed November 13, 2023.

"Bree Jones: Parity, 2021 OSI Community Fellow." Open Society Institute—Baltimore, https://www.osibaltimore.org/fellow/bree-jones/, accessed November 13, 2023.

Brown, Deneen L. "Tulsa Plans to Dig for Suspected Mass Graves from a 1921 Race Massacre," *Washington Post,* February 4, 2020, https://www.washingtonpost.com/history/2020/02/03/tulsa-mass-graves-excavation/.

California Task Force to Study and Develop Reparation Proposals for African Americans. *Final Report,* June 29, 2023, pp. 19–24, https://oag.ca.gov/system/files/media/ab3121-interim-report-preliminary-recommendations-2022.pdf.

City of Asheville. "Community Reparations Commission," https://www.ashevillenc.gov/department/city-clerk/boards-and-commissions/reparations-commission/, accessed January 27, 2023.

Codutti, Anna. "Tulsa Race Massacre Lawsuit Moves Forward with Another Chance to Seek Reparations," *Tulsa World,* August 4, 2022, https://tulsaworld.com/news/local/racemassacre/watch-now-tulsa-race-massacre-lawsuit-moves-forward-with-another-chance-to-seek-reparations/article_d3ac7cda-1402-11ed-b8e3-bf1f2d6c029f.html.

Congressional Research Service. "Federal Land Ownership: Overview and Data," R42346, February 21, 2020, https://sgp.fas.org/crs/misc/R42346.pdf.

Cooke, Christina. "Youth Are Flipping an Abandoned North Carolina Prison into a Sustainable Farm," Civil Eats, June 15, 2020, https://civileats.com/2020/06/15/youth-are-flipping-an-abandoned-north-carolina-prison-into-a-sustainable-farm/.

Corbley, Andy. "Nonprofit Flips Abandoned Prison into Sustainable Farm with the Help of At-Risk Youth and Jobless Veterans," Good News Network, July 27, 2020, https://www.goodnewsnetwork.org/nonprofit-flips-abandoned-prison-into-sustainable-farm-with-the-help-of-at-risk-youth-and-jobless-veterans/.

Curry, Andrew. "Callie Guy House (ca. 1861–1928)," BlackPast, https://www.blackpast.org/african-american-history/callie-house-c-1861-1928/, accessed November 13, 2023.

Darity, William, A. Kirsten Mullen, and Marvin Slaughter. "The Cumulative Costs of Racism and the Bill for Black Reparations," *Journal of Economic Perspectives,* vol. 36, no. 2, 2022, pp. 99–122, https://www.jstor.org/stable/27123976.

"Environmental Liberation." Generation Green, https://www.gen-green.org/environmental liberation, accessed January 27, 2023.

"An Examination of the *Times*' Failures on Race, Our Apology and a Path Forward." Editorial, *Los Angeles Times,* September 27, 2020, https://www.latimes.com/opinion/story/2020-09-27/los-angeles-times-apology-racism.

"The Farm as Ministry: Reverend McNair on Why His Church Started a Farmer Entrepreneurship Program." RAFI-USA, June 5, 2012, https://www.rafiusa.org/blog/the-farm-as-ministry-reverend-mcnair-on-why-his-church-started-a-farmer-entrepreneurship-program/.

"GC Master Plan." GrowingChange, March 16, 2016, https://www.growingchange.org/gc-master-plan/.

Harshbarger, David, Andre M. Perry, and Jonathan Rothwell. "The Devaluation of Assets in Black Neighborhoods," Brookings Institution, November 27, 2018, https://www.brookings.edu/research/devaluation-of-assets-in-black-neighborhoods/.

Hirsh, Sophie. "How Nonprofit Generation Green Is Fighting for Environmental Liberation," Green Matters, February 24, 2021, https://www.greenmatters.com/p/environmental-liberation.

Hyman, Kierra, Margaret Sands, and Sandy Sweitzer. Zoom interview conducted by Brea Baker, September 13, 2022.

"It Takes a Community to Conserve." Triangle Land Conservancy, December 11, 2015, https://triangleland.org/about/history.

Jimenez, Omar. "Tulsa Judge Allows 1921 Race Massacre Lawsuit to Move Forward," CNN, August 4, 2022, https://www.cnn.com/2022/08/04/us/tulsa-1921-race-massacre-lawsuit/index.html.

Koop, Avery. "How Much Land Does the U.S. Military Control in Each State?," Visual Capitalist, July 27, 2022, https://www.visualcapitalist.com/how-much-land-does-the-u-s-military-control-in-each-state/.

"LANDBACK Manifesto." LandBack, https://landback.org/manifesto/, accessed January 27, 2023.

Lessie Benningfield Randle et al. v. City of Tulsa et al. Tulsa County, CV-2020-1179, September 1, 2020, https://www.documentcloud.org/documents/7199572-Tulsa-Massacre-Lawsuit.html.

Maryland General Assembly. "Legislation—Senate Bill 859," https://mgaleg.maryland.gov/mgawebsite/Legislation/Details/SB0859/?ys=2021rs, accessed January 27, 2023.

McLeod, Ethan. "General Assembly Passes Legislation to Help Confront Real Estate Appraisal Gap in Redlined Areas," *Baltimore Business Journal,* April 13, 2021, https://www.bizjournals.com/baltimore/news/2021/04/13/legislation-address-appraisal-gap-redlined-areas.html.

Miller, Ken. "Judge: Tulsa Race Massacre Victims' Descendants Can't Sue," AP News, August 4, 2022, https://apnews.com/article/lawsuits-race-and-ethnicity-tulsa-oklahoma-massacres-61e4a271a584c40483e1ba0709699159.

Moore, Audley. *Why Reparations?* (Reparations Committee, 1963), Schomburg Center for Research in Black Culture, Jean Blackwell Hutson Research and Reference Division, New York Public Library, https://digitalcollections.nypl.org/items/5a3265a0-2088-013a-67c4-0242ac110003.

Movement for Black Lives. "Reparations Now Toolkit," May 2020, https://m4bl.org/wp-content/uploads/2020/05/Reparations-Now-Toolkit-FINAL.pdf.

N'COBRA. National Coalition of Blacks for Reparations in America website, https://www.officialncobraonline.org/home-page, accessed November 13, 2023.

Parity. Website, https://www.parityhomes.com, accessed November 13, 2023.

Penniman, Leah. "To Free Ourselves, We Must Feed Ourselves." *Harper's Bazaar,* October 22, 2020, https://www.harpersbazaar.com/culture/features/a34050240/leah-penniman-food-scarcity-essay/.

Pinsky, Mark I. "Maligned in Black and White: Southern Newspapers Played a Major Role in Racial Violence. Do They Owe Their Communities an Apology?," Poynter Institute, https://www.poynter.org/maligned-in-black-white/, accessed January 27, 2023.

Purnell, Derecka. *Becoming Abolitionists: Police, Protests, and the Pursuit of Freedom* (Verso, 2021), pp. 120–22, 126.

Rashawn, Ray, and Andre M. Perry. "Why We Need Reparations for Black Americans," Brookings Institution, April 15, 2020, https://www.brookings.edu/policy2020/bigideas/why-we-need-reparations-for-black-americans/.

"Reparations Plan." National African American Reparations Commission, https://reparationscomm.org/reparations-plan/, accessed January 27, 2023.

"Resolution: Reparations." NAACP, January 1, 2019, https://naacp.org/resources/reparations.

Ron Finley Project. "About," https://ronfinley.com/pages/about, accessed January 27, 2023.

Sellars, Delphine. "Catawba Trail Farm: A Land Trust Partnership," Carolina Farm Stewards, October 2018, https://carolinafarmstewards.org/wp-content/uploads/2018/10/SAC-Panel-Presentation.pdf.

Smith, Erika D. "Bruce's Beach Was a Win for Reparations. Why It Matters That Black People Lost It," *Los Angeles Times,* January 8, 2023, https://www.latimes.com/california/story/2023-01-08/bruces-beach-reparations-matters-black-people-california.

United Nations General Assembly. "Resolution Adopted by the General Assembly on 16 December 2005," A/RES/60/147, https://www.ohchr.org/sites/default/files/2021-08/N0549642.pdf.

Urban Community AgriNomics. Website, https://ucan.today/, accessed November 13, 2023.

"We Are Deeply and Profoundly Sorry: For Decades, the *Baltimore Sun* Promoted Policies That Oppressed Black Marylanders; We Are Working to Make Amends." Editorial, *Baltimore Sun,* February 18, 2022, https://www.baltimoresun.com/opinion/editorial/bs-ed

-0220-sun-racial-reckoning-apology-online-20220218-qp32uybk5bgqrcnd732aicrouu-story.html.

Weston, Phoebe. "'This Is No Damn Hobby': The 'Gangsta Gardener' Transforming Los Angeles," *The Guardian,* April 28, 2020, https://www.theguardian.com/environment/2020/apr/28/ron-finley-gangsta-gardener-transforming-los-angeles.

Xia, Rosanna. "History Made: Bruce's Beach Has Been Returned to Descendants of Black Family," *Los Angeles Times,* July 20, 2022, https://www.latimes.com/california/story/2022-07-20/ceremony-marks-official-return-of-bruces-beach.

CHAPTER EIGHTEEN

Roberts, Neil. *Freedom as Marronage* (University of Chicago Press, 2015).

INDEX

BREA BAKER is a freedom fighter and writer (in that order) who has been working on the front lines for over a decade, first as a student activist and now as a national strategist. With a BA in Political Science from Yale University, Brea believes deeply in the need for Black story-telling and culture as a tool for change. As a freelance writer, Brea comments on race, gender, and sexuality for publications such as *ELLE, Harper's BAZAAR, Refinery29 Unbothered, Coveteur, MISSION Magazine, THEM,* and more. She also has essays published in various anthologies, including *Our History Has Always Been Contraband: In Defense of Black Studies* and Devin Allen's *No Justice, No Peace.*

For her work in coalition with other activists and organizers, Brea Baker has been recognized as a 2023 Creative Capital awardee, a 2017 *Glamour* Woman of the Year, and 2019 i-D Up and Rising. Brea has spoken globally about racial justice and coalition building toward a more equitable future, including at the United Nations' Girl Up Initiative, Duke University, Yale Law School, the University of Southern California, Pace Gallery, the Youth 2 Youth Summit in Hong Kong, and more.

Instagram: @freckledwhileblack

www.breabaker.com